Exploring the Basic Income Guarantee

Series Editor
Karl Widerquist
Georgetown University in Qatar
Doha, Qatar

Basic income is one of the most innovative, powerful, straightforward, and controversial proposals for addressing poverty and growing inequalities. A Basic Income Guarantee (BIG) is designed to be an unconditional, government-insured guarantee that all citizens will have enough income to meet their basic needs. The concept of basic, or guaranteed, income is a form of social provision and this series examines the arguments for and against it from an interdisciplinary perspective with special focus on the economic and social factors. By systematically connecting abstract philosophical debates over competing principles of BIG to the empirical analysis of concrete policy proposals, this series contributes to the fields of economics, politics, social policy, and philosophy and establishes a theoretical framework for interdisciplinary research. It will bring together international and national scholars and activists to provide a comparative look at the main efforts to date to pass unconditional BIG legislation across regions of the globe and will identify commonalities and differences across countries drawing lessons for advancing social policies in general and BIG policies in particular.

More information about this series at
http://www.palgrave.com/gp/series/14981

Elise Klein • Jennifer Mays
Tim Dunlop
Editors

Implementing a Basic Income in Australia

Pathways Forward

palgrave
macmillan

Editors
Elise Klein
John Medley Building
University of Melbourne
Parkville, VIC, Australia

Jennifer Mays
Queensland University of Technology
Brisbane, QLD, Australia

Tim Dunlop
University of Melbourne
Parkville, VIC, Australia

Exploring the Basic Income Guarantee
ISBN 978-3-030-14377-0 ISBN 978-3-030-14378-7 (eBook)
https://doi.org/10.1007/978-3-030-14378-7

Library of Congress Control Number: 2019935188

This Palgrave Macmillan imprint is published by the registered company Springer Nature Switzerland AG.
The registered company address is: Gewerbestrasse 11, 6330 Cham, Switzerland

Foreword

Back in 1999, when I first started following international developments on Basic Income (BI), not much was going on in Australia. Allan McDonald had been writing about BI in the newsletter for a group called Organisation Advocating Support Income Studies in Australia (OASIS-Australia), but when he stepped down in 2002, no one was available to take over.

But over the last several years, interest in BI in Australia has picked up greatly. Australians inside and outside of academia are producing a lot of research and literature on it, and that work is beginning to have a major impact on politics. Australia's two major parties might not yet be ready to endorse BI, but they can no longer ignore it. And in fact, the Australian Greens, a party that often holds the balance-of-power in Australia's federal Upper House, has officially adopted BI as a party policy.

Australia has become not simply one of the countries where BI is regularly discussed, but very possibly a major world centre for UBI activity. One sign is that the Basic Income Earth Network (BIEN), the only worldwide BI network, has selected Australia for the location of its 2020 conference.

Another sign became obvious to me in 2017 when Elise Klein invited me to come to Australia to speak at a BI conference. Members of Basic Income Guarantee Australia (BIGA) took the opportunity to set me up for as many talks or meetings as I could do in the time I had. That turned out to be a whirlwind of seven appearances in four days in three cities—Canberra, Sydney, and Melbourne. I spoke with members of parliament, with members of the media, with academics, and with university students. I slept on a train and on a plane, and I managed to stay awake for all or most of the two-day, BI research conference in Melbourne, where I learned a lot and had the chance to meet many of the authors of this book. I was impressed by the breadth and depth of BI work going on in Australia.

A third sign that Australia has become a major world centre for BI research can be found in this book. It includes a dozen authors from fields as diverse as Anthropology, Development, Economics, Geography, Journalism, Political Economy, Political Science, Public Health, Social Work, and Sociology. It addresses major empirical and philosophical issues of implementing BI in Australia. Although all or most of the chapters are written in a way that will be interesting to an international audience, parts of this book's focus are on issues that will be especially interesting in the Australian context, such as the specific problems and opportunities for BI in very remote areas as well as its value as a tool to counter the effects of Australian settler colonialism.

This book pays special attention to the political barriers in the way of implementation of BI in Australia and to the opportunities and prospects for political strategies to move BI forward. These include proposals to start with group-focused transfers, such as BI for young people; proposals for how community groups, professionals, and activists can effectively advocate for BI; and proposals for fitting BI into the existing welfare system.

These lessons come from the Australian context, yet the value of this book for the BI movement all over the world needs to be appreciated. It's a book about implementation—an issue that needs much more analysis by the global BI researchers and activists. Social, economic, and political strategies for BI need to be explored in different ways in every conceivable context. Comparative analysis of different strategies in different contexts is how we'll truly learn what works and what doesn't, and this book provides a valuable contribution to that effort.

This book is an excellent read and a valuable resource for researchers, students, and anyone interested in BI.

Doha, Qatar
December 8, 2018

Karl Widerquist

Contents

1 **Introduction: Implementing a Basic Income in Australia** 1
Elise Klein, Jennifer Mays, and Tim Dunlop

Part I Key Issues for Implementation 21

2 **Basic Income in Australia: Implementation Challenges** 23
Greg Marston

3 **Basic Income in the Current Climate: If Australia Can Implement Other Universal Provisions, Then Why Not a Basic Income?** 45
Jennifer Mays

4 **Feminist Perspectives on Basic Income** 69
Eva Cox

5 **Basic Income and Cultural Participation for Remote-Living Indigenous Australians** 87
Jon Altman and Francis Markham

6 **Diversion Ahead? Change Is Needed but That Doesn't Mean That Basic Income Is the Answer** 111
Dina Bowman, Shelley Mallett, and Diarmuid Cooney-O'Donoghue

Part II Avenues for Implementation 127

7 **Finding a Political Strategy for a Basic Income in Australia** 129
Tim Hollo

8 **Basic or Universal? Pathways for a Universal Basic Income** 147
John Quiggin

9 **Stepping Stones to an Australian Basic Income** 163
Ben Spies-Butcher and Troy Henderson

10 **What About Young People? Why a Basic Income for Young People Matters** 179
Jenny Kaighin

11 **Situating a Basic Income Alongside Paid Work Policies** 199
Andrew Scott

12 **Social Work, Human Services and Basic Income** 215
Phillip Ablett, Christine Morley, and Michelle Newcomb

13 **Basic Income in Canada: Lessons Learned and Challenges Ahead** 237
James P. Mulvale and Sid Frankel

14 **Concluding Remarks and an Invitation** 259
Elise Klein, Tim Dunlop, and Jennifer Mays

Index 263

Notes on Contributors

Phillip Ablett is Senior Lecturer in Sociology who coordinates the Bachelor of Social Science programme at the University of the Sunshine Coast and teaches into the social work and human service programmes. He is co-author of the book titled *Engaging with Social Work: A Critical Introduction* and conducts research on the social impact of economic inequality.

Jon Altman is Research Professor in Anthropology at the Alfred Deakin Institute for Citizenship and Globalisation at Deakin University, Melbourne, and an emeritus professor at the Australian National University in the School of Regulation and Global Governance. His research focuses on issues of social and economic justice and appropriate forms of development, especially in remote Indigenous Australia.

Dina Bowman is an economic sociologist and Principal Research Fellow in the Brotherhood of St Laurence's Research and Policy Centre, where she leads work and economic security research. She is an honorary principal fellow in the School of Social and Political Sciences at the University of Melbourne.

Diarmuid Cooney-O'Donoghue is a research officer at the Brotherhood of St Laurence Research and Policy Centre. He has an Honours Degree in Political Science and Chinese Language from Melbourne University and currently completing a PhD in Chinese Studies at Monash University.

Eva Cox AO is a sociologist, and distinguished Alumnus UNSW. She has taught research and policy making and practised them as political adviser, consultant, academic, media commentator and feminist advocate. She has been an active policy developer for children's services, welfare services and evidence-based policy making. Her 1995 ABC Boyer Lectures, A Truly Civil Society, addressed deficits in social capital. She is attached to Jumbunna Institute for Indigenous Education and Research, UTS and a regular media contributor.

Tim Dunlop is a writer, author and academic. He teaches new media at the Centre for Advancing Journalism, the University of Melbourne, Australia. He has been involved in a number of new media start-ups, and has a background in business. He has been a columnist for the Australian Broadcasting Corporation (ABC), as well for News Ltd. He writes on the future of work for The Guardian and speaks regularly in public and professional forums on the same topic. His latest book is *Why The Future Is Workless*, which includes a discussion of basic income. His forthcoming book (Sept 2018) is *The Future of Everything: Democracy, Technology and a Life In Common*.

Sid Frankel is an associate professor in the Faculty of Social Work at the University of Manitoba. He holds a BSW and MSW from the University of Manitoba and a PhD from the University of California at Berkeley. He is a member of the steering committee of Basic Income Manitoba.

Troy Henderson is a PhD candidate in the Department of Political Economy at the University of Sydney. His research topic examines Basic Income as a policy option for Australia. His articles have been published in the main international journal devoted to Basic Income (Basic Income Studies), presented at national and international conferences on the topic and is a regular media commentator on potential pathways to Basic Income in Australia.

Tim Hollo is Executive Director of the Green Institute, and CEO and founder of Green Music Australia. He was Director of Communications for the Australian Greens Leader, Christine Milne, has worked for and sat on the board of Greenpeace Australia Pacific and has performed around the world from the Sydney Opera House to Carnegie Hall.

Jenny Kaighin is Lecturer in Social Work and Human Services in the Faculty of Health Queensland University of Technology. Jenny came to academia following almost 20 years as a youth work practitioner. Jenny draws on critical social work theory and critical pedagogy to build learning environments that encourage and celebrate diversity, critical reflection, challenge and transformation.

Elise Klein is Senior Lecturer of Development Studies at the University of Melbourne. She holds a PhD from the University of Oxford and also held a post-doctoral fellowship at the Centre for Aboriginal Policy Research in the Australian National University. Klein has research projects spanning conditionality in Indigenous policy, psy-expertise in development interventions, women's economic empowerment and economic rights. She is a life member of the Basic Income Earth Network and has written extensively on issues of Basic Income and economic security. She has advised the UN High Level Panel on Women's Economic Development and has worked on the Human Rights Committee within the United Nations General Assembly.

Shelley Mallett is Professorial Fellow in Social Policy in the School of Social and Political Sciences at the University of Melbourne and Director of the Brotherhood of St Laurence's Research and Policy Centre.

Francis Markham is a Research Fellow at the Centre for Aboriginal Economic Policy Research, The Australian National University. An economic geographer, his research interests include Indigenous policy, the political economy of land in remote Australia.

Greg Marston is Professor of Social Policy and Sociology at The University of Queensland. He conducts research into social security, poverty and welfare governance. He is an Australian representative for the Basic Income Earth Network.

Jennifer Mays is an academic in the School of Public Health and Social Work, Queensland University of Technology. Jenni is recognised as an international expert on basic income and has a long history in researching, writing and advocating on basic income. She is involved in international research collaborations and symposiums around basic income to progress policy debates on the scheme. Jenni has been committed researching in areas of basic income, poverty, social policy, social justice, disability and social citizenship. She is Co-Coordinator of Basic Income Guarantee Australia (BIGA).

Christine Morley is Professor and Head of the Social Work and Human Services Discipline at Queensland University of Technology. Her teaching and research interests focus on critical social work practice and education.

James P. Mulvale is Associate Professor of Social Work and Associate Member of St. Paul's College at the University of Manitoba, Winnipeg Canada. His research focuses on basic income, social work theory and distance education in social work. He areas of teaching include Canadian social welfare history and social policy.

Michelle Newcomb is Lecturer of Human Services and Social Work at Griffith University. Her research interests include understanding the experiences of disadvantaged students, practitioner well-being and feminist research and practice.

John Quiggin is Australian Laureate Fellow in Economics at the University of Queensland. He is prominent both as an economic researcher and as a commentator on a wide range of policy topics.

Andrew Scott is Professor of Politics and Policy at Deakin University. A former adviser to senior national parliamentarians and trade unions on employment and training issues, he is the author of 5 books and 28 other publications, many of which highlight policy lessons from overseas for Australia's options now.

Ben Spies-Butcher is Lecturer in Economy and Society in the Department of Sociology at Macquarie University. Ben completed his PhD in Economics at the Macquarie University. His research focuses on the political economy of social policy. In addition to his academic publications, Ben is a regular contributor to The Conversation and is a Social Policy Whisperer for Power to Persuade. Ben is a research associate at the Retirement Policy and Research Centre at the University of Auckland, a member of the Policy Advisory Group for COTA NSW and a board member of Shelter NSW.

List of Figures

Fig. 5.1 Attendance of ceremonies in previous 12 months by Indigenous people aged 15–64 living in remote Australia, before and after the abolition of CDEP, by propensity to participate in CDEP if it existed, from the NATSISS 99
Fig. 5.2 Attendance of sports carnivals in previous 12 months by Indigenous people aged 15–64 living in remote Australia, before and after the abolition of CDEP, by propensity to participate in CDEP if it existed, from the NATSISS 100
Fig. 5.3 Production of arts and crafts in previous 12 months by Indigenous people aged 15–64 living in remote Australia, before and after the abolition of CDEP, by propensity to participate in CDEP if it existed, from the NATSISS 101
Fig. 5.4 Hunting and fishing by Indigenous people aged 15–64 living in remote Australia, before and after the abolition of CDEP, by propensity to participate in CDEP if it existed, from the NATSISS. Note that 2002 data refer to hunting or fishing in the previous 3 months, while 2014 data refer to hunting or fishing in the previous 12 months 101

List of Tables

Table 5.1	Questions about participation in cultural activities in the 2002 and 2014 NATSISS	95
Table 5.2	Labour force status of Indigenous people aged 15–64 living in remote Australia, before and after the abolition of CDEP, from the NATSISS	97
Table 5.3	Labour force status of Indigenous people aged 15–64 living in remote Australia, before and after the abolition of CDEP, by propensity to participate in CDEP if it existed, from the NATSISS	98
Table 5.4	Participation in cultural activities by Indigenous people aged 15–64 living in remote Australia, before and after the abolition of CDEP, from the NATSISS	99
Table 9.1	Proposed "affluence tested" universalism for Youth Allowance	173

1

Introduction: Implementing a Basic Income in Australia

Elise Klein, Jennifer Mays, and Tim Dunlop

A Basic Income (BI) is a simple idea: a periodic cash payment unconditionally delivered to all on an individual basis, without means-test or work requirement (BIEN, 2018). Scholars, activists and politicians are increasingly becoming aware of the radical potential a BI could have to societies around the world: from economic security, fairer wealth distribution, justice and poverty eradication through to degrowth and gender equality (Ackermann & Alstott, 2006; Altman, 2016; Atkinson, 2014; Davala, Jhbvala, Mehta, & Standing, 2015; Standing, 2014; Weeks, 2011). The idea of a BI is also gaining attention in Australia, and

E. Klein (✉)
John Medley Building, University of Melbourne, Parkville, VIC, Australia
e-mail: elise.klein@unimelb.edu.au

J. Mays
Queensland University of Technology, Brisbane, QLD, Australia
e-mail: j.mays@qut.edu.au

T. Dunlop
University of Melbourne, Parkville, VIC, Australia

E. Klein et al. (eds.), *Implementing a Basic Income in Australia*, Exploring the Basic Income Guarantee, https://doi.org/10.1007/978-3-030-14378-7_1

while there has been speculation as to how it could work in Australia, a thorough analysis of pathways forward is missing. Within the pages of this book, we present the works of intellectuals considering issues of BI implementation in Australia.

These chapters are the culmination of a two-day workshop supported by the Academy of Social Sciences at the University of Melbourne in August 2017. In attendance were academics, political organisers, economists, writers, union and welfare-provider representatives, students and other interested observers, all considering issues of implementing a BI in Australia. This workshop was convened at a time when the operationalisation of BI into trials, pilots and poverty-alleviation programmes was underway in different jurisdictions, including Namibia, India, Kenya, and even parts of Europe and North America. These trials vary in scope and length, but are largely concerned with poverty reduction, workforce participation, and, in the case of the India pilot, women's empowerment and reducing household debt. The discussion in these pages, therefore, should be seen as contribution to this worldwide investigation into the efficacy of a BI.

We use the term BI in this collection to refer to various possible models discussed by authors of the following chapters. Most prominently featured in this collection is the *Universal Basic Income* (UBI), which is paid regularly, unconditionally to everyone. Some chapters also discuss a *Negative Income Tax* where people earning below a certain amount receive an income supplement, and a *Social Dividend*, which is a regular dividend paid to residents from publicly generated wealth (the Alaska Permanent Fund is a commonly cited example of this). There is overlap between these models, especially when it comes to questions of implementation, and those issues are addressed by the contributors within.

Why a Basic Income?

Various arguments are put forward as to why a BI should be considered. As work is becoming increasingly insecure and the future of work uncertain, BI is presented as a much-needed alternative; something that goes beyond the usual understanding of the "safety net" associated with post-World War II welfare states. For those in paid work, a BI gives an unconditional economic base that improves workers' bargaining power (Gorz, 1999). A BI means if people want to withdraw or suspend their labour from exploitative or oppressive conditions, they can do so without the fear of destitution (Weeks, 2011). This is important as the GIG economy, labour precarity, and attacks on collectively mobilised labour and unions are increasing. BI gives people the freedom to say no and to get a better deal for their labour. In this way, individual security reinforces the ability of people to act collectively within the labour market. BI is thus enough to keep people's heads above water in times of increasing job and wage insecurity or to see them through a period of trying a new idea and being innovative. The idea is that individuals with formal employment would still be able to work, because there would be none of the means testing that leads to high marginal tax rates and poverty traps (Davala et al., 2015; Van Parijs, 2006). People with a BI get their subsistence wage *and* they are also able to choose to continue to work.

Some critics of BI have argued it disincentivises work. But a BI of $15,000 or $20,000 a year is unlikely to lead a mass exodus from the labour force in Australia, a conclusion supported by international trials conducted over many years. For instance, Negative Income Tax trials in North America in the 1960s and 1970s showed only a small decrease in labour market supply (Henderson, 2017). What's more, the people who delayed returning to work tended to be women re-entering the workforce after having children, or young people staying longer in education (Forget, 2011; Widerquist, 2013). The fixation on how a BI will affect labour market demand is short sighted, in part because the availability of formal and dignified employment is dramatically eroding, and there simply aren't enough secure and dignified jobs for everyone. We are also living through a period where wages are decoupled from productivity increases, and so traditional presumptions about employment being a guarantee of a sustainable income are being rendered unsafe. Under such circumstances, BI can help workers sustain themselves as technological unemployment increases or technology otherwise changes the nature of the labour market. So while some predictions of technological unemployment are exaggerated, advances in artificial intelligence and machine learning mean more jobs than ever—specifically, cognitive, white collar work—are susceptible to automation in a way never previously considered possible (Dunlop, 2016).

Importantly, a BI can also be understood as a mechanism that values the work of non-paid productive labour—a burden for the most part shouldered by women and Indigenous people, particularly Indigenous people living on country. Interestingly, an iteration of a BI proved successful for Indigenous peoples under the recently and unadvisedly axed Community Development Employment Projects (CDEP). Jon Altman (2016) documented how CDEP as a BI supported productive labour on country in remote Australia while providing economic security for populations without a formal labour market. Since the axing of CDEP, these populations have fallen further into poverty (Markham & Biddle, 2018; Markham and Altman, in this issue). A BI can be seen as a way of decommodifying labour where economic security is given regardless. This radical shift has the potential of underpinning the complete redefining of what work means, to include all forms of productive labour (Fouksman & Klein, 2017; Weeks, 2011).

A BI has also been discussed as a mechanism for promoting ecological and intergenerational justice (Marston, 2016). The ecological argument is an important one as, on a broader scale, transitioning to a low-carbon, slow-growth economy is not a small matter of a technical fix and a policy prescription to get economic incentives right within a capitalist structure. Instead it is a transformation of the whole patterns of social life in terms of work, family, transport, community, food, housing and leisure (Marston, 2016). The economic rights gained through a BI could give people the freedom to innovate towards this paradigmatic shift as economic rights are not just about the distribution of wealth but also about the distribution of time and opportunities. A BI could allow for human freedom in its fullest sense: to explore, create and connect with each other and our ecological surroundings, while not being tied to an endless drive for profit and economic growth.

BI has resonance across the political spectrum, though we should be cautious about how we interpret such apparent agreement. Neoliberal advocate Milton Friedman proposed a BI-like model that aimed to replace the welfare state with a voucher system so people could purchase services such as education and healthcare in commercial markets. But this view of BI is deeply commodifying and there is no guarantee that a subsistence wage would cover the cost of items like medical treatment and education priced by market mechanisms. Consequently, left and centrist BI advocates argue strongly that the BI should never replace, but only complement other social programmes such as healthcare, education, housing and disability support. The neoliberal model also fails to engage with notions of unfreedom inherent in capitalism—something also overlooked in the proposals coming from Silicon Valley elites and other free market proponents of what they call BI (Fouksman & Klein, 2017). As the neoliberal model prioritises the market as the primary means of redistribution, wealth concentrates in the hands of the few and thus overrides any sense of a more equitable distribution that recognises the way in which wealth has been socially generated. Instead, a BI that operates with other social programmes, and through the tax system, has the potential to be a radical redistributive mechanism—one that works to redistribute wealth, so all can enjoy economic security as a basic human right.

BI secures economic citizenship and, in doing so, creates freedom for all peoples within a society—freedom from exploitation and rising economic insecurity, and freedom to live a life people value. A BI can go beyond just a mere grant, and be a social dividend from wealth collectively created, what James Ferguson (2015) calls a "rightful share," or others—a "social dividend" (see Standing, 2017). A rightful share or social dividend understands that wealth in society is to a large extent socially generated and, as such, all residents have a right to share in that wealth. That is to say, no single person or corporation is successful without access to a broad range of factors such as our common investment in physical infrastructure, education, healthcare, the judicial system and the rule of law, systems and institutions that have developed over generations and been paid for by the people in general. Therefore, the framing of a BI in Australia should be about a human right in which BI is an inheritance, rather than a mere grant to be bestowed on residents.

Nonetheless, a BI isn't a silver bullet. It is not a panacea and needs to work in conjunction with many other important measures, and many of these are taken up by the authors of chapters in this collection.

Basic Income in Australia

Support for BI is experiencing a resurgence in Australia, in part due to the growing economic inequalities, widening poverty and changes in the labour market. The resurgence follows the 1975 Henderson Poverty Report by the Commission of Inquiry into Poverty. The report was overseen by Ronald Henderson and was ground breaking in drawing attention to the extent of poverty and the inadequacy of income levels of many Australians. To illustrate the extent of poverty, Henderson developed a comprehensive poverty measurement tool, the *Henderson Poverty Line*, underpinned by principles of universalism and adequacy. Importantly, the report also advocated for the need of a guaranteed minimum income (known today as BI), which could be derived from tax revenue (Commonwealth of Australia, 1975a).

The innovative aspect of Henderson's guaranteed minimum income proposal was that it showed how it could respond to growing poverty and inequality. The work extensively detailed economic and social modelling towards transitioning to BI (refer to Commonwealth of Australia, 1975a: 67 onwards). The report holds currency today given, among other things, the detailed description of potential stages in transitioning to a BI (see Bradbury, Saunders, & Craig, 2006). The stages refer broadly to whether a BI is introduced as a partial BI to transition to a full BI, or whether it is simply introduced in full from the outset. Noting the highly targeted nature of the existing Australian social protection system, BI was expected to address the economic inequalities within the income support system and transcend piecemeal reforms by implementing a transition to benefit all citizens (Commonwealth of Australia, 1975a, 1975b). Henderson argued for the radical transformation of the social protection and taxation system, stating that such a transformation, "involves extending social security entitlements to the whole population, and not merely to those who are in the special categories, and so introduces fundamental change" (Commonwealth of Australia, 1975a: 68). This form of universal redistribution would, he argued, redistribute money via the taxation system to those most in need, particularly for redressing poverty traps, and categorical and administrative issues (Mays, 2016). The report contrasted this universal approach to the onerous and costly nature of targeted social protection.

Notably, Henderson's work provided a conceptual framework for differentiating direct taxes, transfer incomes and pensions or benefits from market-oriented income (Commonwealth of Australia, 1975a, 1975b). Henderson's progressive approach was based on the perspective that stringent income tests for determining pension or benefits eligibility functioned as employment disincentives for people in receipt of income support. His vision for universal social protection through a guaranteed minimum income scheme led to the design of specific alternative models to implement BI, including immediate transition and staged transition (Mays, 2016). Henderson's model positioned the minimum income in terms of a right, removing the possibility that people would be categorised as deserving and undeserving of support.

Political volatility and the oil crisis shifted the impetus for Henderson's policies. The findings of the Henderson project were also not made available in the public domain under the directive of the Whitlam government. Further, following the dissolution of the Whitlam Labour government, the incoming Fraser Liberal government in 1975 rejected outright the proposal for guaranteed minimum income (Kewley, 1980: 44). In 1976, the Fraser Liberal government called for fiscal restraint and a reigning in of what they saw as burgeoning public expenditure. The Fraser government set up a conservative inquiry, led by the Social Welfare Policy Secretariat to counter Henderson's findings and commence their own official inquiry into poverty. The then Commonwealth government's official Inquiry into Poverty Measurement in 1981 was instigated to assist the government to determine an appropriate level of income support via the Social Welfare Policy Secretariat (Mays, 2016). The Social Welfare Policy Secretariat moved away from universal principles and challenged Henderson's 1975 definition of poverty by proposing a more widely held definition (Mays, 2016). Despite the fact that a change in governmental direction meant Henderson's recommendations were not adopted, they continue to be a rich source of knowledge about BI. It is the development of the Henderson Poverty Line and the continued political call for what was then the guaranteed minimum income that makes Henderson's work an invaluable source for transitioning to basic income. Drawing on Henderson's ideas, that is, the normative justifications and prescriptive conceptual framework offers a way forward today for transitioning to basic income. It also provides a starting point for social and economic modelling and moving beyond merely philosophical debates which can be counteractive by impeding progress.

To the extent that Australia's major political parties have paid BI any attention in more recent times, it has been to reject it outright. A number of participants highlighted comments by Labor figures Chris Bowen (Shadow Treasurer) and Andrew Leigh (former economics professor, Shadow Assistant Treasurer and Shadow Minister for Competition), in particular Bowen's comment that BI was "a terrible idea." In making this claim, Bowen was underlining the tendency of those on the left to see BI entirely through the frame of traditional paid work, and in so doing uncritically buy into the criticism—challenged throughout these essays—that BI undermines the willingness of people to work, or that it somehow means we have given up on the principle, in Bowen's words, "of ensuring dignity through work for Australians" (Murphy, 2017). Bowen also chose to play the populist card by highlighting that the rich would also be recipients of BI, saying, "A universal basic income would be just that, universal. Providing payments to millionaires, at a considerable cost to the taxpayer, but payments that would barely be noticed by people of means." As Dunlop (2018) has suggested, this anti-universalism approach is a dangerous tactic for the left to adopt, given that they tend to favour universalism in other policy areas such as health and education.

Somewhat ironically, Bowen's comments place him and the Labour Party on the same page as Australia's key right-wing, neoliberal think tanks. The Institute for Public Affairs (IPA), for instance, has rejected BI on the grounds that, "We should be removing welfare traps, improving skills training, cutting red tape, and reforming industrial relations to get people into work – not encouraging unemployment with massive unaffordable handouts," a comment that, like Bowen's, uncritically accepts arguments against universality and that prioritises traditional notions of paid employment (Lesh, 2018). Another neoliberal think tank, the Centre for Independent Studies (CIS), has called BI "an unbelievably bad idea" (Cowan, 2017), chiefly on the grounds of expense, but also on the grounds that estimates of job losses due to automation are wildly exaggerated. Cowan (2017: 1) argues that "there is little evidence of technological unemployment in current employment data," a claim that is reductive at best, ignoring as it does the other ways in which technology changes the structure of the economy in which jobs are embedded in the first place. In other words, the issue is not just whether "robots will take our jobs" but the way in which technology tends to concentrate wealth and put downward pressure on wages and conditions, while changing the nature of even those jobs that survive technological change (in areas as diverse as banking, architecture and transport).

The only party to openly embrace the possibilities of BI is the Australian Greens. In May 2018, leader Richard Di Natale spoke at the National Press Club and canvassed the introduction of legalised cannabis, a people's bank, as well as a fully functioning universal BI (Di Natale, 2018a). The primary justification offered for BI was the nature of work is changing, but they took this beyond the usual arguments about whether or not robots would take people's jobs and made the more nuanced (and realistic) claim that the nature of work was changing more broadly. This, in turn, he argued, meant that Australia's welfare system was therefore no longer fit for purpose, and so BI should be seen as a way of addressing growing problems with the safety net. "Our current social safety net is outdated," Di Natale (2018b) said in a press release, "and does not properly support those experiencing underemployment, insecure work and uncertain hours. A modern, flexible and responsive system would increase people's resilience, not marginalise them, and enable them to make a greater contribution to our community and our economy." At the heart of the Greens' approach was an understanding that BI could provide "the foundation of a decent, caring society."

In further evidence that the debate around BI in Australia is changing and becoming more sympathetic, Anglicare, the national umbrella organisation that includes the community services body of the agencies of diocese of the Anglican Church of Australia, released a report in October 2018 that called for the consideration of a universal BI in Australia, as well as a jobs guarantee. The report, *Jobs Availability Snapshot 2018*, assessed the current state of employment in Australia, especially for those most disadvantaged in the jobs market, stating, "These are people who may not have qualifications or experience, who are trying to re-enter the workforce after a long break, or who are living in regional or remote areas" (Anglicare, 2018: 4). And the conclusion it reaches is that "these people have been left out of the dominant narrative about jobs in Australia – a narrative that assures us we are in the midst of a jobs boom, and that the inability to find a job is an individual failure instead of a structural one" (Anglicare, 2018: 4). The nature of structural unemployment is between four and five people are competing for every advertised job vacancy in the country. Anglicare's interest in BI and a jobs guarantee, then, is that "these policies represent a new way of thinking about work and participation, and how as a society we can support everyone to contribute, recognising the value of this both for the individual and society as a whole" (Anglicare, 2018: 17). It is, in other words, driven not just by concerns about the nature of unemployment and the particular difficulties posed for various disadvantaged groups in gaining ongoing, secure employment, but in the idea of a fairer society more generally, where wealth is distributed in a way that overcomes the structural limitations of the market economy.

Beyond these specific engagements with BI, the broader discussion of the topic comes at a time when, even amongst those who oppose BI, there is a growing recognition of the problems and limitations of the current welfare system (Altman, 2007; Brown, 2015; Klein, 2016). Even key employer groups such as the Business Council of Australia (BCA) note Australia's unemployment benefit, Newstart, is too low and have called for it to be increased. In their submission to the Senate Inquiry into the Adequacy of the Allowance Payment System for Jobseekers and Others, the BCA argued the "rate of the Newstart Allowance for jobseekers no longer meets a reasonable community standard of adequacy and may now be so low as to represent a barrier to employment" (BCA, 2018).

There are also increasing concerns about the punitive nature of the welfare system; the increasing barriers or "mutual obligations" recipients must fulfil to receive even the inadequate Newstart payment, as well as growing concerns about underemployment, lack of job security and stagnant wages, even at a time when corporate profits are at record highs (Marston, Catherine, & Lois, 2014). Addressing the ACTU Congress in July 2018, Emma Dawson from the centre-left Per Capita think tank noted that "real wages have grown at an annual average of 0.4 per cent" which means that "Australians' income from labour has barely increased since 2013" (Dawson, 2018). Combine this with the fact that, "housing absorbs between a quarter and a third of working households" and that "the cost of utilities, health and education and other non-discretionary expenses are also increasing at a rate that far outpaces wage growth," it is "no wonder Australian workers are feeling squeezed" (Dawson, 2018).

The idea of a universal BI may still be controversial, even marginal, in Australian political discourse, but the idea that large-scale welfare reform is urgently needed is not. Under such circumstances, those advocating BI in Australia are likely to receive an increasingly sympathetic hearing.

Focusing on Implementation

While the philosophical issues of BI continue to be debated and discussed in Australia and elsewhere, there seems one question that keeps returning—how do you implement it? Questions of implementation are crucial and they can make or break the radical and emancipatory potential of a BI. To contribute towards an answer to this question, implementation issues around framing, political strategy, models of implementation, cost and how BI can work alongside other programmes are all discussed in this collection.

Framing Matters

In the literature, BI can be positioned as a response for many issues—from underemployment and unemployment in the labour market (due to both ongoing surplus labour issues and technological unemployment), economic insecurity, unpaid labour, economic hybridity, inequality, ecological destruction, poverty and even as a way to overcome capitalism.

The framing of the end game is also important. Is BI for everyone to have economic security, to tide people over in times of crises or as casualisation, automation and preciousness of employment increases? Is the BI about giving negotiating power back to labour? Or is it a way to completely decommodify labour and redefine what works means? Is a BI implemented because the society sees it as an economic right or a dividend that is granted as acknowledgement of a rightful share in the generation of wealth? Or is it seen as a way to transition and sustain a degrowth economy and to reduce ecological destruction? Each of these framings have been offered in various global and contextual debates on BI. We have seen in some trials that BI was implemented to increase employment. This framing is very different to other ideas of BI that see it as an alternative to employment altogether. Whilst diverse, these framings of the "problem" are not necessarily discrete and many intersect at various stages of implementation and actualisation of BI. Of course, not all are irreconcilable either, although an appreciation of what the end game is and the kind of society BI will contribute to, is important to consider. In any specific context, a BI may have various end games, yet being clear on this is important regarding implementation. Clarifying the end game will help uncover the political strategy in building support for the BI, as well as help make decisions as to how other programmes and policies will interact with the BI (e.g., the tax system), and who to involve in the implementation (e.g., Should elite capital fund private programmes, or should a BI be democratically governed?).

To Trial or Just Implement?

While trials of BI are underway around the world, they may not always be the first step of implementation. Widerquist (2017) notes the decision by BI advocates to support trials is a strategic one and he raised the possibility that this may not always be the best choice. (A staged approach to full implementation, for example, is a possible alternative to trials and pilots.) Widerquist (2017) has argued that trials cannot necessarily test the key effects of a BI, and while some evidence may accrue about health, education and work outcomes under conditions of BI amongst the trial groups, the very fact that trials involved small subsets of populations means it is impossible to measure the truly transforming effects of BI that would only appear when applied on a larger scale. Furthermore, trials can be a soft option for politicians who wanted to fob off implementation, basically using a trial as a delaying tactic. This is something we have certainly witnessed with the premature cessation of the Ottawa and Finish trials by newly elected conservative governments.

Incremental implementation, one of the options forecast by Spies-Butcher and Henderson (in this volume), is also another possibility, and Quiggin (in this volume) outlines an approach where either basic or universal is preferred in the implementation process (and the other added over time). For example, a universal focus (before basic) means implementation will begin with a small universal payment for everyone, the amount gradually increasing over time to the point where it becomes sufficient to meet basic needs. A basic (over universal) implementation starts with one group (such as young people) who are first given the full BI, and other groups are added to this over time to make it universal—an approach preferred by Quiggin and developed by Spies-Butcher and (Henderson, also in this collection). But if it is an incremental approach, this raises the question of who should be targeted first? Young people, First Nations people living remotely, artists and single mothers are groups suggested as the possible first to receive the BI.

Cost of BI

BI is expensive but not too expensive. Some of the calculations floating around about how much a BI will cost are misleading. The error here is the cost of BI is presented as the gross cost (i.e., the size of the proposed BI multiplied by the population size), rather than its true net cost (i.e., the proposed size of BI multiplied by the number of net beneficiaries, without counting the net contributors paid through redistributive tax). The BI is not a standalone measure as it interacts with the tax system to redistribute wealth. Also, the cost would be eased in over time if the BI were implemented in the staged "Basic" approach. As well, we should ask what is the cost of not going with a BI, because to not do so is to unfairly burden BI with the task of justifying itself, while not making the same demands on alternatives, particularly the status quo.

BI and Other Programmes

The diversity in BI models (such as a full universal basic income, social dividend or negative income tax) suggests the need for consideration as to how BI complements other programmes. Some BI models suggest simplifying the existing social protection system (see Standing, 2014), or introducing a transition period from partial to full BI (see Raventós, 2007; Torry, 2016), while other models tend to opt for more radical transformations of social protection, other social welfare areas and society (see De Wispelaere & Stirton, 2004). Many of these decisions are dependent on the type of scheme introduced in the first instance, together with the overarching goals and values ascribed to the model. For example, a suggested vision for the Australian context was the model of full provision for an individual, with regular payments, fortnight or monthly (Mays, 2016). If this is the design approach, then greater attention needs to be paid to the importance of BI complementing other programmes, rather than replacing them and strengthening the other public provisions across health, education, housing, employment and childcare. Responding to economic inequalities and poverty with a BI should not preclude the need for other social support services based on need if extra assistance is required (e.g., health and education, housing and disability support) (Mays, 2016). As outlined above, BI represents one approach to the redistributive strategy and does not respond to all elements of disadvantage, nor the needs of democratic society. This means, given the existing inequalities across housing, education, employment programmes, there would need to be a number of different proposals, where each programme would be restructured to strongly reflect an appropriate public good (employment, health and other community services) that runs alongside BI programmes. Such an approach would be transformative and open up the possibilities for redefining ideas of work, coalition building in social housing and generating accessible universal education.[1]

Rather than being used in place of BI, a job guarantee for all who wish to work (in whatever redefinition of work is ascribed) can work alongside, and supplement, BI (Tomlinson, Dee, & Schooneveldt, 2005). Having said this, very careful consideration of the potential that a job guarantee has to attenuate the ethos of the BI must be undertaken. One of the differences from job guarantees and work condition is that where BI has no work requirement, a job guarantee scheme's minimum demand is that applicants must be willing to do the work on offer under the

[1] See Howard and Widerquist (2012) for more on the debates.

programme (Mitchell & Watts, 2003). Where BI frees people to be more creative and innovative in their work but still have economic security, a job guarantee reinforces the very disempowering aspects of stringent work requirements, such as compelling people to be productive through any type of work rather than work as a creative expression. Under a job guarantee, the ideological message can be distorted by the suggestion that work has to be compelled. Whereas with BI, the emphasis is on income security provided as a right, which invokes quite different ethical justifications and preconditions. BI then becomes about inclusivity—the duty each of us owes to the other, rather than a compelled right. BI brings to the workplace greater bargaining power and, with it, industrial democracy because the provision provides the worker with the opportunity to opt out in the knowledge that although their income will reduce, it will remain above the poverty line (Standing, 2014).

Under a job guarantee scheme, to achieve a secure income, people are expected to engage in whatever work is available. Basic income is more inclusive to incorporate volunteer, artistic endeavours, community work and caring. Under job guarantee, people who were not willing to engage in that work or who were judged by the job guarantee managers to be unsuitable would not be assured of a secure income (Mitchell & Watts, 2003). BI advocates argue applying such stringent requirements and compulsion mechanisms to income support erodes freedom and, additionally, there is an ever-present danger some people will be unjustly excluded in any conditional scheme (Standing, 2014). For this reason, job guarantee would be seen as more of a supplementary programme to BI. There would need to be careful consideration of the way this would translate given the conflicting ethical and moral principles underpinning each programme.

The Collection

The collection is compiled in two sections. The first section outlines some of the continuing substantive and philosophical issues regarding BI. Specifically, this section explores key conceptual and theoretical concerns for implementing BI in Australia (see also Mays, Marston, &

Tomilson, 2016 for an overview of the philosophical debates in Australia). Greg Marston takes up the issue of framing to explore avenues for overcoming the political barriers to implementing a basic income through building broad social movements. In Chap. 3, Jenni Mays explores the similarities of BI to the existing Blind Pension payment in Australia and shows how learnings from this unconditional provision can help us to implement a BI. In Chap. 4, Eva Cox then addresses feminist considerations for a BI. Cox draws attention to the need to redefine work to ensure BI addresses, and not just reproduces, patriarchal relations of power, specifically regarding income inequalities and unpaid labour. Jon Altman and Francis Markham in Chap. 5 examine the prospects of a BI as a way to push back against Australian settler colonialism. Through examining positive Indigenous livelihood outcomes from the previous Community Development Employment Projects (CDEP) as a basic-income-like programme, they argue for the implementation of a true BI scheme in remote Australia. Bowman, Mallett and Cooney-O'Donoghue in Chap. 6 provide a cautionary tale of BI pilots in Australia and abroad and remind us of the need to stage implementation to complement existing social security programmes.

In the second section of the book, authors offer practical strategies and models for progressing BI in Australia. In Chap. 7, Tim Hollo outlines possibilities for political strategies to build coalitions to support the implementation of BI. In Chap. 8, John Quiggin outlines his preference for a stepping-stone approach to implementation, where starting with a particular group and including more groups over time is preferable to a straight universal implementation. Following this in Chap. 9, Ben Spies-Butcher and Troy Henderson outline a specific model to implement a BI starting with young people. Jennifer Kaighin in Chap. 10 further explores some of the ethical and political implications to implementing a BI with young people. Andrew Scott then helps us to consider how BI can work alongside other work policies in Chap. 11. The question as to how specific community sectors can contribute towards advocating for, and implementing a BI, is taken up in Chap. 12. Here, Philip Ablett and Christine Morley show the potential contribution that social workers could make through practitioner activism, professional advocacy and critical pedagogy. Finally, in Chap. 13, Sid Frankel and Jim Mulvale reflect on the Canadian experience and highlight crucial learnings for BI implementation in Australia. The book ends with an invitation for readers to keep progressing debates, advocacy activities, activism and other projects towards making BI a reality.

References

Ackermann, B., & Alstott, A. (2006). Why stakeholding? In B. Ackermann, A. Alstott, & P. Van Parijs (Eds.), *Redesigning distribution: Basic income and stakeholder grants as cornerstones for an egalitarian capitalism*. London/New York: Verso.

Altman, J. (2007). The Howard government's Northern Territory intervention: Are neo-paternalism and indigenous development compatible? *Topical Issue 16/2007*, Center for Aboriginal Economic Policy Research, the Australian National University, Canberra, ACT.

Altman, J. (2016). Basic income for remote Indigenous Australia: Prospects for a livelihoods approach in neoliberal times. In J. Mays, G. Marston, & J. Tomlinson (Eds.), *Basic income in Australia and New Zealand: Perspectives from neoliberal frontiers*. Basingstoke, UK: Palgrave Macmillan.

Anglicare. (2018). Jobs availability snapshot 2018. *Anglicare*. http://www.anglicare.asn.au/docs/default-source/default-document-library/jobs-availability-snapshot-2018.pdf?sfvrsn=2

Atkinson, A. (2014). After Piketty? *The British Journal of Sociology, 65*(4), 619–638. https://doi.org/10.1111/1468-4446.12105

BCA. (2018). *Submission to the senate education, employment and workplace relations references committee inquiry into the adequacy of the allowance payment system for jobseekers and others*. Business Council of Australia. http://www.aph.gov.au/DocumentStore.ashx?id=2418e5d0-7894-4210-bd81-432ba37ffbdb

BIEN. (2018). What is a basic income? *Basic Income Earth Network*. https://basicincome.org/basic-income//

Bradbury, B., Saunders, P., & Craig, L. (2006). *A perennial problem: Employment, joblessness and poverty*. SWPRC Discussion Paper No. 146. Sydney, NSW: The Social Policy Research Centre, UNSW.

Brown, W. (2015). *Undoing the demos: Neoliberalism's stealth revolution*. New York: Zone Books.

Commonwealth of Australia. (1975a). Australian government's commission of inquiry into poverty: Poverty in Australia Vol. 1. *Henderson Poverty Report.* Canberra, ACT: Commonwealth Government Printer.

Commonwealth of Australia. (1975b). Australian government's commission of inquiry into poverty: Poverty in Australia Vol. 2. *Henderson Poverty Report.* Canberra, ACT: Commonwealth Government Printer.

Cowan, S. (2017). Universal basic income is an unbelievably bad idea. *Centre for Independent Studies.* http://www.cis.org.au/publications/research-reports/ubi-universal-basic-income-is-an-unbelievably-bad-idea/

Davala, S., Jhbvala, R., Mehta, S. K., & Standing, G. (2015). *Basic Income: A transformative policy for India.* London/New York: Bloomsbury.

Dawson, E. (2018). Emma Dawson's address to the 2018 ACTU Congress, Percapita. https://percapita.org.au/2018/07/19/emma-dawsons-address-to-the-2018-actu-congress/

De Wispelaere, J., & Stuirton, L. J. (2004). The many faces of universal basic income. *The Political Quarterly, 75*(3), 266–274.

Di Natale, R. (2018a). *Bad faith: How government lost the people's trust and how we win it back*, National Press Club Address. https://greensmps.org.au/sites/default/files/Richard%20Di%20Natale%20-%20National%20Press%20Club%20-%20September%202018.pdf

Di Natale, R. (2018b). Legalised cannabis, People's Bank, UBI: Big ideas to upend the status quo, Press Release 20th April 2018. https://greens.org.au/magazine/legalised-cannabis-peoples-bank-ubi-big-ideas-upend-status-quo

Dunlop, T. (2016). *Why the future is workless.* Sydney, NSW: New South Books.

Dunlop, T. (2018). *The future of everything: Big, audacious ideas for a better world.* Sydney, NSW: New South Books.

Ferguson, J. (2015). *Give a man a fish: Reflections on the new politics of distribution.* Durham, NC: Duke University Press.

Forget, E. (2011). *The town with no poverty: Using health administration data to revisit outcomes of a Canadian guaranteed annual income field experiment.* Winnipeg, Canada: University of Manitoba.

Fouksman, L., & Klein, E. (2017, September 25–27). Radical transformation or a technological intervention? Critical engagements in implementing a basic income. Conference Paper, 17th BIEN World Congress 2017, Lisbon, ME.

Gorz, A. (1999). *Reclaiming work: Beyond the wage-based society.* Cambridge, UK: Polity Press.

Henderson, T. (2017). Real freedom for all revisited. *Basic Income Studies, 12*(1).

Howard, M., & Widerquist, K. (Eds.). (2012). *Alaska's permanent fund dividend: Examining its suitability as a model.* New York: Palgrave Macmillan.

Kewley, T. H. (1980). *Australian social security today: Major developments from 1900 to 1978.* Sydney, NSW: Sydney University Press.

Klein, E. (2016). Neoliberal subjectivities and the behavioural focus in income management. *Australian Journal of Social Issues, 51*(4), 1–27.

Lesh, M. (2018). A universal basic income would create a permanent underclass. *Institute of Public Affairs.* https://ipa.org.au/ipa-today/a-universal-basic-income-would-create-a-permanent-underclass

Markham, F., & Biddle, N. (2018). Income, poverty and inequality. *Centre for Aboriginal Economic Policy Research Census Paper, 2,* 1–37.

Marston, G. (2016). Greening the Australian welfare state: Can basic income play a role? In J. Mays, G. Marston, & J. Tomilson (Eds.), *Basic income in Australia and New Zealand: Perspectives from the neoliberal frontier* (pp. 157–177). London: Palgrave Macmillan.

Marston, G., Catherine, M. D., & Lois, B. (2014). *The Australian welfare state: Who benefits now?* London: Palgrave Macmillan.

Mays, J. (2016). Disability, citizenship, and basic income: Forging a new alliance for a non-disabling society. In J. Mays, G. Marston, & J. Tomlinson (Eds.), *Basic income in Australia and New Zealand: Perspectives from the neoliberal frontier.* New York: Palgrave Macmillan.

Mays, J., Marston, G., & Tomilson, J. (2016). *Basic income in Australia and New Zealand: Perspectives from the neoliberal frontier.* London: Palgrave Macmillan.

Mitchell, W. F., & Watts, M. J. (2003). Full employment. In J. E. King (Ed.), *The Elgar companion to post Keynesian economics.* Cheltenham, UK: Edward Elgar.

Murphy, K. (2017, June 9). Chris Bowen attacks universal basic income as 'payments to millionaires'. *The Guardian.* https://www.theguardian.com/australia-news/2017/jun/09/chris-bowen-attacks-universal-basic-income-as-payments-to-millionaires

Raventós, D. (2007). *Basic income: The material conditions of freedom* (J. Wark, Trans.). London: Pluto Press.

Standing, G. (2014). *A precariat charter: From denizens to citizens.* London: Bloomsbury Academic.

Standing, G. (2017). *Basic income: And how we can make it happen.* London: Pelican Books.

Torry, M. (2016). *The feasibility of citizen's income.* New York: Palgrave Macmillan.

Tomlinson, J., Dee, M., & Schooneveldt, S. (2005). From paupers to citizenship. *New Community Quarterly, 3*(3), 41–45.

Van Parijs, P. (2006). Basic income: A simple and powerful idea for the twenty-first century. In B. Ackermann, A. Alstott, & P. Van Parijs (Eds.), *Redesigning distribution: Basic income and stakeholder grants as cornerstones for an egalitarian capitalism*. London/New York: Verso.

Weeks, K. (2011). *The problem with work: Feminism, marxism, antiwork politics, and postwork imaginaries*. Durham, NC: Duke University Press.

Widerquist, K. (2013). What (if anything) can we learn from the negative income tax experiments? In K. Widerquist, Y. Noguera, J. A. Vanderborght, & J. De Wispelaere (Eds.), *Basic income: An anthology of contemporary research*. Chichester, NY: Wiley Blackwell.

Widerquist, K. (2017, September 25–27). *The political economy of basic income trials*. Conference paper, 17th BIEN World Congress 2017, Lisbon, ME.

Part I

Key Issues for Implementation

2

Basic Income in Australia: Implementation Challenges

Greg Marston

Introduction

Effective public policy development is too often the exception rather than the norm. The history of modern governance is littered with examples where good ideas and sound intentions get scuttled on the rocky shoreline of partisan parliamentary politics and local policy practice. In some cases, the policy design itself is flawed or at least poorly conceived; in other cases, bottom-up perspectives from implementing organisations have not been properly considered or communicated. In some instances, it is a matter of inadequate resourcing that means the programme has little chance of delivering on the policy goals—that is, assuming these goals have been agreed to. In short, there is a lot that can go wrong and it frequently does, which is why metaphors such as 'muddling through' or 'garbage in and garbage out' are used by public policy academics and observers when describing the modern policy process (Parsons, 1995: 16). Recent attempts

G. Marston (✉)
University of Queensland, St Lucia, QLD, Australia
e-mail: g.marston@uq.edu.au

E. Klein et al. (eds.), *Implementing a Basic Income in Australia*, Exploring the Basic Income Guarantee, https://doi.org/10.1007/978-3-030-14378-7_2

to improve policy development have promoted high-quality research to discipline the unruly politics of policy-making. Other efforts have focussed on slowing down the political process to ensure a high degree of co-design with all stakeholders, principally through greater deliberation between experts and non-experts (Neimeyer, 2013). The pace of societal change also raises its own set of implementation challenges. We are living through a period of rapid social and technological change (Agger, 2004), resulting in a great deal of uncertainty for citizens and governments. At the same time, there is no consensus on proposed policy solutions. Some researchers and commentators argue for a more radical departure from the present, suggesting we need significant changes to our economic, cultural and social institutions (Dunlop, 2016; Olin Wright, 2011).

It is in this context that the call for a basic income (BI) is being made in Australia and a host of other countries. At its simplest, a basic income is a periodic payment paid that is made to all individuals, both adults and children. There are many BI models and there are multiple trials taking place around the world, which are being used to further refine BI policy proposals. The focus in this chapter is on the ideational level and the policy actors that champion BI, rather than the technical dimensions. This chapter assesses the implementation challenges at the political and policy level, as well as the material factors that help explain the growing media and public interest in BI. In answering these questions, the starting point is that we need to be more precise about the historical and institutional conditions that facilitate the idea of a basic income percolating a little closer to the surface of a crowded public policy agenda. It is important to not only understand these developments from an analytical point of view, it is also necessary to work out which arguments for change and which policy directions have the most merit and the most chance of success in policy-framing and argumentation. Tiernan and Burke (2002: 88) argue that 'Problem, Policies and Politics' all need to align and converge if an idea has any chance of being successfully implemented. This analytical framework of alignment between the problem, policies and politics will structure the discussion.

Defining the Problem

Social problems, such as homelessness, poverty and unemployment, are subject to contestable knowledge claims about their causes and consequences. Frame analysis in policy-making theory refers to this ambiguity in the policy process and the attempts by certain policy actors to exercise power through using dominant socio-cultural discourses to frame problems (Bacchi, 2009; Marston, 2004). Policy actors may exercise power by reinforcing dominant social attitudes through their communication. A classic example is poverty—if the dominant frame is that poverty is caused by moral failing on the part of an individual, then it follows that the main role for government is to discipline the unemployed through sanctions, or nudge them towards markets to reform their moral character. These individualising ideas are reinforced by social science disciplines, particularly seen in the rise of psychology in social problem framing (Rose, 1998). A *what's the problem approach* (Bacchi, 2009) seeks to unpack the interaction between ideas and scientific knowledge in specific socio-cultural contexts. What is the problem that BI seeks to address? How are these problems framed? Which policy actors are calling for change?

There are at least four key frames that characterise the public and academic debate in Australia about whether a BI is a desirable or necessary solution: (1) technological unemployment resulting from a new wave of automation; (2) harmful effects of highly conditional income support paid at below-poverty rates; (3) rising income inequality and the need for a rightful share/social dividend to reframe the redistribution debate; and (4) a need to transform how we understand work and leisure in the twenty-first century. Which of these frames has the most supporting evidence is not a straightforward question, as some are based on future forecasting, though in the case of the social security system there is considerable evidence that the system is outdated and in need of reform (Whiteford, 2016). In the case of technological unemployment, there is some evidence of the changes already taking place and their disruptive effects on labour markets and businesses, particularly with regard to communications, finance, transport and mining; however, the most concerning impacts are forecasts about the medium-term future as machines get smarter (CEDA, 2015). It is important to acknowledge that forecasts about the degree of disruption from automation are highly contested, ranging from minimal disruption to mass unemployment over the next 20–30 years (Frey & Osborne, 2017).

The quality of jobs and the extent of insecurity in the Australian labour market are also contested, with some labour market economists indicating that the provision of secure paid employment is relatively robust (Borland, 2017), while others argue that the provision of secure jobs in the labour market is deteriorating (Carney & Stanford, 2018). Even where the evidence is not in dispute, there can be considerable resistance to change because as Lakoff (2003: 2) has argued: 'frames matter more than facts'—meaning that if the evidence does not fit the mental frame it is frequently rejected, rather than assimilated. This insight from cognitive science explains why an attachment to outdated social norms can persist even when market conditions and social systems change. Australia still has a strong attachment to an idealised version of a wage earner's welfare state, even if it is only ever been a partial victory (Marston, McDonald, & Byson, 2013). Indeed, a romanticised view of a welfare settlement obscures the harsh reality for many citizens. Highly conditional workfare and welfare-to-work policies have intensified over the past two decades in Australia at the same time as labour market opportunities have weakened for those at the bottom of the income scale. The resulting situation for low-income workers and social security recipients is a form of what Berlant (2011) calls 'cruel optimism', that is, a society remaining attached to unachievable fantasies of the 'good life' (with its promise of upward mobility, job security, political and social equality, and durable intimacy), despite evidence that liberal-capitalist societies can no longer be counted on to provide these opportunities for meaning and fulfilment. By itself a BI would not be sufficient to transcend all of these false promises, but as part of a vision for a more secure and fairer society, it at least helps to clarify what is problematic about the present.

For countries like Australia that have developed a highly targeted and highly conditional social security system, the attraction of a basic income may be more geared towards the unconditional, rather than the universal. A BI would address welfare rights advocates' concerns about the harms of strong paternalism, as well as addressing the philosophical objections that libertarians have around 'negative freedom' (Berlin, 1969) and unwarranted state interference. The goals of social security policy have shifted over the past two decades in Australia. Poverty relief has been replaced by labour force participation, in line with the Organisation for Economic Co-operation and Development (OECD) activation agenda and domestic workfare policies (Ziguras, 2014). The objective of using government policies to alleviate material poverty has always been contentious and contested in Western countries. Political opposition has often been based on a moral objection that generous state-funded income support will encourage 'idleness' among 'able bodied citizens'. Sorting the 'deserving poor' from the 'underserving poor' through eligibility tests and measures has been an ongoing feature of social administration systems since the eighteenth century (Walters, 2000). Going back as far as the English Poor laws of the 1800s, the principle of 'less eligibility' dictated that the condition of a pauper in the workhouse should be not as attractive as that of the poorest labourer outside the workhouse. The policy logic continues in the present, with the idea being that the rate at which unemployment benefits are paid should not be so high as to discourage the unemployed from accepting paid work, of whatever kind and of whatever duration. The dominance of this distinction drives a race to the bottom in terms of welfare and work conditions, and it remains one of the key ideological barriers to lifting income support payments.

The assumption of suspicion and mistrust of income support recipients is used to justify a host of intrusive and non-intrusive surveillance practices, which highlight the need to consider the distribution of both *burdens* and *benefits* when assessing whether income support policies are socially just. The onus of proof in a highly targeted social security system is on the claimant to demonstrate their need for assistance. The individualising 'blame welfare' (Handler & Hasenfeld, 2007: 1) discourse associated with market-led income support policy is a barrier to opening up a more democratic space for deliberative and inclusive policy practice. Under these circumstances, the self-sufficiency and self-reliance discourse that infuses income support policies in countries like Australia becomes a kind of comfort zone when it comes to contemplating political action against social injustice. Rosenblaum (2000) argues that part of the reason a self-sufficiency discourse thrives in present conditions is that we have a declining faith in our own political agency and '…the less confidence we have in our own democratic political agency the more we demand of others' (cited by Young, 2011: 40). Consequently, citizens come to passively regard the complex workings of society whose effects are fortunate for some individuals and unfortunate for others as solely the result of individual effort, and therefore, not a matter of justice for which all citizens should take collective responsibility (Young, 2011). A failure to problematise the performance of the labour market, particularly at the bottom end, means the income support system ends up cajoling a large number of people into a system of churning between an indifferent state bureaucracy, a marketised employment services system and short-term paid work that offers little prospect of career advancement. These trends are likely to get worse, rather than better if predictions about technological unemployment come to pass.

There is a great deal of debate at present about whether there will be widespread technological unemployment in the future, or whether a sufficient number of new jobs will be created to replace those lost to advanced AI and automation (see Chace, 2016). A related question is how these developments will interact with existing labour market trends, as there may be new winners and losers, particularly if the professions are widely affected by smart machines. The share of gains from productivity will also change with automation, as more of the rewards from productivity will go to capital rather than labour, which suggests we may need to tax labour, capital and wealth differently to address growing income inequality and deliver on the promise of sustainable prosperity. As the International Monetary Fund recently concluded in a working paper, 'automation is good for growth and bad for inequality' (Berg, Buffie, & Zanna, 2018). While there will be many opportunities for individuals and companies during this transition, there are also many risks for society that will need to be appropriately managed. These developments will change the labour market significantly by changing the skill composition of employment favouring high-skilled workers while abolishing routine jobs (Coelli & Borland, 2015). There is a gendered and age-based dimension to these transition risks, particularly as many routine tasks are concentrated in the lower end of the labour market and service industries, such as transport, hospitality and some forms of care work. Rapid technological advances in cloud services, big data, the internet of things, artificial intelligence and robotics will further change skill demands in the labour market and will have a widespread impact on the economy and employment (Committee for Economic Development of Australia, 2015).

Overall, labour markets remain weak in advanced economies and unevenly spread in terms of security and conditions. Underemployment and overemployment are both growing in Australia and other OECD countries. In Australia, the number of people wanting more hours of work and unable to get them is increasing. The number of people who are underemployed in Australia has increased from about 176,000 in the late 1970s to 1.1 million in 2017 (ABS, 2017). Australia has one of the highest percentages of part-time workers in the OECD, which is typical of countries that have a heavy reliance on a growing service sector (ABS, 2017). In light of these changes, there is an increasing concern among policy-makers about Australia's ability to create new jobs with adequate pay and conditions (Dunlop, 2016). There are 'techno-utopians' who say the new technologies will create new jobs, while others spin very pessimistic scenarios suggesting that even if the new jobs come, they are likely to skip a generation, as was the case with the introduction of steam and electricity (Ford, 2015). Overall, the labour market still has significant excess capacity available in most areas and what economic growth there is, is not making inroads into what Mitchell (2012: 1) refers to as 'the idle pools of labour'.

The uneven labour market and highly conditional social security system partly explain the growing interest in basic income in Australia. However, these structural factors have been present for at least the last 20 years. The threat of automation, and the associated uncertainty and fear, is likely to be a more prominent factor in media interest in basic income, especially as a number of Silicon Valley entrepreneurs have themselves been making an argument for BI. As such, the discourse coalition of support for a BI in Australia has become more diverse and broad based (Mays, Marston, & Tomlinson, 2016). The automation argument also brings in futurists and revives discussions that were taking place in the first half of the twentieth century around the promise of more leisure and less paid work, led by economists such as John Maynard Keynes and philosophers such as Bertrand Russell. BI might not be the best or only solution to all the challenges outlined, but it gets individuals and communities asking the right questions about justice, rights, freedom and autonomy in a 'post-work' (or at least post-labour) future. It decentres the hegemony about an ethic of paid work as the basis of social citizenship and asks whether the institutional arrangements for work and welfare are fit for purpose at the start of the twenty-first century. The next section examines the BI models that are being discussed in more detail while assessing some of the key implementation challenges.

Policy Options: From Idea to Implementation

The previous discussion has highlighted some of the key problems with how paid work is organised and how social security is administered, problems that are downplayed in discursive efforts to defend the status quo of the labour market and business as usual social policy in Australia. Addressing these challenges requires a diverse set of solutions, such as redistributing working hours, improving access to other social services, new forms of regulating emerging work arrangements in the so-called 'gig economy' and better recognition of relational labour and other forms of unremunerated work. A BI is, therefore, not a stand-alone policy option or panacea. Calls for universal services, a shorter working week and a basic income are frequently put forward as a package of reforms that can provide an economic floor for experimenting with other forms of economic and social activity (Bregman, 2016). It is for this reason the BI is called 'basic' because it is something on which a person can safely count, a material foundation on which a life can firmly rest, promoting freedom for all by providing material resources that people need to pursue their aims (van Parijs, 2007). Beyond ideals of freedom, social justice and democratic citizenship, proponents of BI argue that it also makes economic sense in terms of affordability (van Parijs, 2004) and it can be more cost-effective than 'the current wasteful array of often counter-productive, bureaucratic income security programs' (Pereira, 2014: 1). Pilot projects in Canada, India and South Africa, for example, have demonstrated that the BI supports economic growth and job creation, especially in the areas of improving the livelihoods of the poor and maintaining better risk management (Standing & Samson, 2003).

The evidence from basic income trials in developing and developed countries is generally positive, however, the politics of basic income trials raises questions and challenges for implementation. Australia, like other countries, has a history of introducing innovative pilot programmes, only to see them discontinued as a result of financial pressure and political change (Saunders & Fine, 1995). Yet, the Australian government continues to expand expensive trials for compulsory income management schemes that target Indigenous Australians and groups of social security recipients when the evaluation evidence results are mixed at best (Mendes, 2015). In Australia, greater conditionality and strong paternalism have become a case of a policy solution looking for a policy problem (Edelman, 1988). Breaking down this policy path dependency is going to be a major challenge for BI implementation, particularly as part of the promise of a basic income is that it will genuinely make a difference to people's living standards, giving ordinary people the capacity to have a degree of economic security and decommodification in meeting basic needs, and to participate in the labour market on their own terms. Given the scale of reform required, some proposals from academics in Australia (and outlined in this volume) are calling for a 'stepping stone' approach to BI, perhaps starting with one age cohort for a BI (e.g. young people or older workers), emphasising the unconditional, rather than the universal.

From an institutional perspective, advocating for a stepping stone approach makes sense, as it fits within the long-standing tradition of policy incrementalism in Australia and it would allow policy feedback loops to be put in place so the policy could be adjusted before being rolled out to other groups. However, there are also some reasons to be cautious about a stepping stone approach. There could be unintended consequences as it would set up a material and moral binary between those covered and those that are not. If we accept the moral arguments for a BI about a rightful share of the commons or creating an economic floor for all residents of a given nation, then anything less than universalism betrays the simplicity of the design. It will also compromise the principle of solidarity and cross-class buy in, which is an essential ingredient for building policy resilience (such as is the case with universal education and health care in Australia). Moreover, to have one group receiving a basic income but not another introduces a need for administration and its associated costs and it introduces a political challenge of justifying why some groups should get the payment and not others. On the other hand, a stepping stone approach addresses a major implementation challenge of keeping the costs relatively affordable while gradually extending the benefits to other groups.

In terms of affordability, an education campaign would need to accompany the introduction of a BI so that the public understood that even if the payment is universal there is a big difference between net payers and net receivers of a BI, given that a progressive income tax system would allow the government to claw back the BI from high-income earners. It would also be important to point out that the tax burden would not only need to fall on households, eco-taxes and automation taxes could also be in the mix to fund a BI in Australia. However, a mature and balanced political debate about tax reform has been difficult to sustain in Australia, particularly given powerful vested interests opposed to changing the current economic settings. The capacity of our parliamentary politics and democratic institutions to progress big ideas and recalibrate social, economic and environmental may turn out to be the greatest challenge.

The Politics of a BI

Politics is a broad domain of activity, ranging from civil society demands on the state, to the dynamic interplay between institutional actors at the global and local level and parliamentary politics involving the contest of ideas, personalities and interests. As such it is perhaps best to think about the relationship between politics and policy in liberal democracies as a form of argumentation (Fischer and Forrester, 1988) where state actors, private interests, knowledge experts and civil society groups move forward when there is sufficient agreement about the direction of travel, and then backwards when contingent agreements break down through a lack of leadership and trust, poor communication or a lack of coordination between the different levels of government and non-government actors. In the case of BI, there is some acknowledgement that there is a problem with how welfare and work have come to be organised. There is also a growing recognition that social problems, like unemployment and poverty, do not lend themselves to easy solutions as they are multifaceted and dynamic. At the level of the epistemic community of scholars, commentators, public media and think tanks there is a preparedness to examine and debate different policy options to address these problems—either in terms of either improving the rate of payment for unemployed people or implementing a partial or full basic income. However, at the level of parliamentary politics in Australia, there is very little evidence of any engagement with the concept of a BI.

A lack of political leadership on major social policy change makes it much harder to move forward when big changes are required to address labour market failures and outdated social security settings. Of course, the alternative is to do nothing and see if the crisis of technological unemployment eventuates. Australia, like other countries, could be heading for a perfect storm, where the ecological crisis caused by dominant modes of production and consumption converges with a crisis of capital accumulation (Jackson, 2009). In historical terms, big shifts in institutional arrangements for managing risk and meeting societal needs have tended to come about as a result of exogenous shocks combined with the pressure of social movements galvanised around a good idea. This combination may yet provide the catalyst for change for redirecting work and welfare policy in Australia, but the window of opportunity for a change of policy direction may close without any major action. Dissatisfaction with the present distribution of societal rewards and opportunities will continue to be a catalyst for change; however, supporters of a BI will also need to be realistic what will and will not change in society if a partial or full BI was implemented. As some scholars have pointed out, the place of a BI in any scenario about the future may well be as a saviour of capitalism, rather than a transformative force towards full decommodification, given the widespread monetisation of social life (Pitts & Dinerstein, 2017).

In any case, the debate about the impact of a BI on late capitalism is largely academic in Australia. The major political parties show little sign of diverging from the familiar script of jobs and growth and business as usual social policy. The Labor Party and the Coalition parties have both come out against the introduction of a BI, calling it wasteful and unnecessary (Bowen, 2017). The Australian Greens have been much more explicit in their support for a BI, most recently in an address by Greens' leader Richard Di Natale (2018) at the National Press Club:

> We need a universal basic income that ensures everyone has access to an adequate level of income, as well as access to universal social services, health, education and housing.

The focus on the BI in the address was positively reported in social media, while it was criticised in the mainstream press for being unnecessary and expensive (The Australian, 2018). While it is clear that media and public interest has increased over the past few years, it is also clear that at the level of mainstream party political discourse, there has been little interest in changing direction in welfare-to-work policy settings. And while some local state–based branches of the Australian Labor Party might be agitating for basic income to be discussed at the annual national conference, the leadership of the Australian Labor Party is not interested in having the debate. In fact, both the major political parties in Australia explicitly reject BI and both leaders regularly rehash the mantra of 'jobs and growth'. The major parties refuse to acknowledge the fact that the economy no longer delivers a sufficient number of full-time jobs and that a high-growth strategy is ecologically irresponsible in the twenty-first century (Jackson, 2009).

At the same time, there might be some cause for hope for advocates of a BI in Australia. The multiple experiments and BI trials being run in both developed and developing countries mean that the possibility of policy transfer is increasing (Standing, 2008), particularly in countries that, like Australia, also have high rates of long-term unemployment and a declining manufacturing sector, such as Finland. Unpredictability of income, rising living costs and fewer full-time employment opportunities will mean the public will be looking for new solutions. It is this dimension that may explain the well-attended community forums across Australia when the 'future of work' and related proposals such as shorter working hours and BI are being discussed. While no one can predict whether technological unemployment is being overestimated or underestimated, what is clear is that people have a very real sense that they are living through a time of rapid and unpredictable change and they are fearful about the consequences. Some Australian writers, such as Tim Dunlop (2016) in his book *Why The Future is Workless*, suggests that we should embrace a post-wage work future and see automation as a transformative and liberating force, as long as there is a decent economic floor (such as a BI) in place to ensure that the transition does not exacerbate widening income inequalities. It is this kind of change and a fear of greater economic insecurity and uncertainty that creates fertile conditions for more radical solutions like BI.

The discourse coalition agitating for a BI is also becoming more diverse. There are a number of policy actors such as left-of-centre think tanks, welfare peak bodies, futurists, artists and poets, academics and journalists that have added to the chorus of calls for the Federal government to consider modelling, trialling and implementing a basic income in Australia. Some trade unions have engaged in the debate. The Institute for Public Affairs wrote an opinion piece in 2015 supporting the libertarian case for a basic income along the lines of curtailing an 'over-reaching' state. However, in 2018 the Institute for Public Affairs criticised the idea as too costly and creating a permanent 'underclass' (The Institute for Public Affairs, 2018). The Centre for Independent Studies have come out opposing a basic income on the grounds that it is unaffordable (although their methods leading to this conclusion are disputed), and that there are better ways to address poverty. A collection of papers on BI and shorter working hours published by the Greens Institute in late 2016 seeks to engage with critics and keep the public discussion open (Hollo, 2016). The point about political deliberation and discussion is well taken. Part of the problem with the present debate about technological unemployment and automation, for example, is that it starts from the premise of what will technology do to us, rather than what we want to do with technology. There is a need here for social movements and the social sciences to reclaim futures talk and reinsert human agency into the equation.

Social scientists have been reluctant to enter a debate about the future, in part because blueprint utopian visions have a tendency to become their own form of domination and dogma. A number of prominent social scientists, such as Zygmunt Bauman (2011) and Erik Olin Wright (2011), have argued that utopian thinking remains useful because visions for a better life can hold a powerful mirror to existing societies as they demonstrate limitations of the present. In this sense, social futures are both performative and evaluative. This is similar to the role that utopian thinking has always played in moving societies forward, as a belief that there is nothing left to believe in makes us blind to the shortsightedness and injustice that still surround us every day (Bregman, 2016). Futurist discourses can have powerful consequences for the present, particularly if one sees the future as both constrained and open at the same time (Urry, 2016). What we know in terms of addressing past injustices and the history of the welfare state is that it is always a sight of struggle. Policy changes take shape because ordinary citizens band together to make claims on the state as they call out exclusions and injustices.

Going forward, discourse coalitions and social movements that have a broad base are likely to be more effective as it is harder to dismiss demands for change when there is more than a single vested interest making the case, which is why entrepreneurs, futurists, welfare recipients, non-profits, unions and academic-activists will need to be all represented when asking the question about how we shape a just social future. Questions about dignity, personhood and respect will need to be carefully considered as paid work has captured so much of the symbolic capital when it comes to constituting status and a meaningful life in countries like Australia. Recognition and redistribution will both need to be redefined if we are to avoid BI becoming a metaphorical 'parking lot' for the poor. Universal social services and meaningful opportunities for participation will need to be part of the solution. Social trust between citizens and between citizens and the government will need to be rekindled, as the demand for a BI is to respect what Foucault called 'moral adulthood', where citizens individually and collectively are able to determine the 'art of living' through a new politics of time that enables genuine 'temporal autonomy' (Goodin, 2010). Without adequate levels of trust, the temptation for policy-makers will be to introduce a 'participation income' to enforce a level of reciprocity between citizens and the state in a new social contract that will be broader than paid work, but which at the end of the day is still a form of 'soft paternalism'.

A BI on a national scale is a leap of faith into the unknown, but there is enough evidence from overseas trials to suggest that people will still do what they do now (such as engage in paid work), but that they will also have better health and levels of well-being and have time to pursue other activities, which in the present social order are unevenly distributed. As Gorz (1999: 39) explains:

> One of the functions of a politics of time is precisely to share out savings in working time following the principles not of economic rationality, but of justice. These savings are the work of society as a whole. The political task is to redistribute them on the scale of society as a whole so that each man and woman can benefit from them.

The liberatory promise in terms of a temporal justice must also be connected to addressing the distribution of unwaged reproductive work. The work ethic and the family ethic remain joined together by a host of historical, economic, political and cultural threads (Weeks, 2011). Weeks and other feminist scholars of work are keen to see policies in place that challenge the way that the state and capital define and constitute what counts as an acceptable family, or other intimate relationships. Returning to first principles, it is this form of freedom that will allow people the resources to make real choices as they seek to collectively 'get a life' (Weeks, 2011: 289) and refuse the political and cultural mantra to simply 'get a job'. The struggle to build something new through policies such as BI is explicitly utopian, but it is not proposing a fixed blueprint for the future, rather it is a future with a wealth of possibilities that the work and family ethic diminishes (Weeks, 2011: 233). The question posed by these writings is an old and enduring question, one that is provocative and speculative: what kind of society do we want to live in? This is a first-order question. The question of how we collectively pay for it is no less important, but to my mind at least, this is a secondary consideration. Confusing the order reduces the question of the 'good society' to an economic calculus of means, rather than ends. We need problems, policies and politics to be alignment to get real change, but we must lead with good ideas if we want the politics to follow.

To return to where we started, how we frame problems through political discourse determines solutions. If the problem is conceptualised as a labour market that is underperforming by not providing enough jobs then there can be a case made for a BI on the grounds that it would provide an economic floor and incentives for employers to improve the working conditions and wages (depending of course on the rate at which a BI was set). Or if the problem is framed on the grounds of a 'rightful share' around the access to the global commons then an argument could be made on the basis of reciprocity and BI as a new social contract between citizens and the state, one that clearly decouples income from labour. If the problem is framed as the need to recognise unremunerated work in Australia, then we would seek to implement policies that publicly value an ethic of care while being mindful to address gendered and settler constructions of paid and unpaid work. Or if we frame the problem as the need for greater ecological sustainability, then we would problematise continuous economic growth and look for eco-social policies that have better alignment between social, economic and environmental policy goals, reorienting the Australian welfare state away from its twentieth century foundations. However, to frame the problem on a larger systemic level raises a major political challenge (with regard to structural tax reform) and a cultural challenge in terms of acknowledging the limits of the paid work ethic and accepting an alternative vision of human progress, based on non-material goods (such as well-being, discretionary time and the right to realise our human capacities). A meta-framing of the policy problem requires a radical departure from a dominant political and cultural discourse that accepts that the prosperity of a developed country can still be measured by continuous economic growth and jobs, irrespective of environmental and human costs (Frayne, 2015). Moving the public debate to this level will require rediscovering the art of politics in terms of persuasion, the value of rhetoric and transformative leadership. This is no easy task, but it is a necessary one.

Conclusion

Despite the fact that a 'high road' solution to connected social, environmental and economic problems is undoubtedly much more challenging from an implementation point of view, it does provide a basis for having a public discussion about what is right and wrong about the way we continue to collectively order society, including its risks and rewards. There are always fissures and cracks in dominant policy discourses and practices. And the more attention that alternative social futures receive, the more it becomes possible to see the limitations of present arrangements. The social world is a space of competing moral values. Social change is a struggle between policy actors with different motivations and interests, and a contest of ideas and policy proposals. Politics is an inevitable and necessary part of the policy process. It is what makes policy-making messy, and which can also lead to pessimism and cynicism about the prospects for progressive social change. The history of social policy development provides cause for optimism. Social security pensions and universal healthcare were once considered dangerous ideas. Now they are part of the social and cultural fabric of Australia and politicians that seek to dismantle them are frequently forced to capitulate in the face of opposition from citizens, consumer groups and professional bodies.

It is an opportune time for Australia to contribute its voice to the global basic income debate. The right to a decent income and to a fair share of cultural, economic and social resources is central to living a 'good life'. Proposing a new redistributive strategy for the twenty-first century—one that is based on social citizenship, human rights and social justice within the ecological limits of a finite planet is necessary. The uncertain economic, social and ecological times we live in demand nothing less than big ideas and bold steps. There are significant risks and opportunities in taking radical policy steps, which is why genuine political leadership is required to navigate these troubled waters. One of the key cultural challenges going forward will be whether it is possible to decouple identity, status and belonging from income derived from paid work. There is an inevitable cultural lag for those who practice a 'post-work' politics that renders their resistance more or less invisible in the broader polity. However, to suggest there is no alternative to the present order is to submit to the idea that we are collectively incapable of envisaging a future where a sense of solidarity and purpose cannot be conceived through anything other than commodity relations (Frayne, 2015). Reclaiming work in the fullest sense is a means towards reclaiming life and an inclusive understanding of the 'good society'. The political project of reclaiming work is to recognise that work (broadly defined) provides the potential opportunity for creativity and collaboration, and to experience a satisfaction in the world. How work is currently organised and rewarded strips it of these qualities. A BI could emerge from public discussions as a central plank in the reorientation of work and the realisation of a just and democratic society, aligned with a twenty-first century conception of inclusive social citizenship.

References

Agger, B. (2004). *Speeding up fast capitalism: Cultures, jobs, families, schools, bodies*. New York: Routledge.

Australian Bureau of Statistics. (2017, December). *Labour force Australia*. Available at http://www.abs.gov.au/AUSSTATS/abs@.nsf/DetailsPage/6202.0Dec%202017?OpenDocument

Bacchi, C. (2009). *Analysing policy*. Melbourne, VIC: Pearson Education.

Bauman, Z. (2011). *Culture in a liquid modern world*. Cambridge, UK: Polity.

Berg, A., Buffie, E., & Zanna, L. (2018). *Should we fear the robot revolution: The correct answer is yes*. Available at https://www.imf.org/en/Publications/WP/Issues/2018/05/21/Should-We-Fear-the-Robot-Revolution-The-Correct-Answer-is-Yes-44923

Berlant, L. (2011). *Cruel optimism*. Durham, NC: Duke University Press.

Berlin, I. (1969). *Four essays on liberty*. Oxford, UK: Oxford University Press.

Borland, J. (2017). *Job insecurity in Australia: No rising story*. Available at https://drive.google.com/file/d/0B_H1wGTm98W3UmF3S2lVSm8zUWc/view

Bowen, C. (2017). *Chris Bowen attacks basic income as 'payments to millionaires'*. Available at https://www.theguardian.com/australia-news/2017/jun/09/chris-bowen-attacks-universal-basic-income-as-payments-to-millionaires

Bregman, R. (2016). *Utopia for realists: And how we can get there*. London: Bloomsbury Publishing.

Carney, T., & Stanford, J. (2018). *The dimensions of insecure work: A factbook*. Available at https://d3n8a8pro7vhmx.cloudfront.net/theausinstitute/pages/2807/attachments/original/1528337971/Insecure_Work_Factbook.pdf?1528337971

CEDA. (2015). *Australia's future workforce*. Available at https://www.ceda.com.au/Research-and-policy/All-CEDA-research/Research-catalogue/Australia-s-future-workforce

Chace, C. (2016). *The economic singularity: Artificial intelligence and the death of capitalism*. London: Three C Publishing.

Coelli, M., & Borland, J. (2015). *Jobs polarisation and earnings inequality in Australia*. Available at https://fbe.unimelb.edu.au/__data/assets/pdf_file/0009/1427409/1192CoelliBorland.pdf

Di Natale, R. (2018, April). *National Press Club Address*. Available at https://richard-di-natale.greensmps.org.au/

Dunlop, T. (2016). *Why the future is workless*. Sydney, NSW: NewSouth Books.

Edelman, M. (1988). *Constructing the political spectacle.* Chicago: University of Chicago Press.

Fischer, F., & Forrester, J. (Eds.). (1988). *The argumentative turn in policy analysis and planning.* London: UCL Press.

Ford, M. (2015). *Rise of the robots.* London: Oneworld Publications.

Frayne, D. (2015). *The refusal of work: The theory and practice of resistance to work.* London: Zed Books.

Frey, C., & Osborne, M. (2017). The future of employment: How susceptible are jobs to computerisation. *Technological Forecasting and Social Change, 114*, 254–280.

Goodin, R. (2010). Temporal justice. *Journal of Social Policy, 39*(1), 1–16.

Gorz, A. (1999). *Reclaiming work: Beyond the wage based society.* Cambridge, UK: Polity Press.

Handler, J., & Hasenfeld, Y. (2007). *Blame welfare, ignore poverty and inequality.* Cambridge, UK: Cambridge University Press.

Hollo, T. (2016). *Can less work be more fair: A discussion paper on universal basic income and shorter working week.* https://www.greeninstitute.org.au/wpcontent/uploads/2016/12/Less_Work_More_Fair_WEB_BM.pdf

Jackson, T. (2009). *Prosperity without growth: Economics for a finite planet.* London: Earthscan.

Lakoff, G. (2003). *Don't think of an elephant: Know your values and frame the debate.* London: Chelsea Green Publishing.

Marston, G. (2004). *Social policy and discourse analysis: Policy change in public housing.* Aldershot, UK: Ashgate Publishing.

Marston, G., McDonald, C., & Byson, L. (2013). *The Australian welfare state: Who benefits now.* Melbourne, VIC: Palgrave Macmillan.

Mays, J., Marston, G., & Tomlinson, J. (Eds.). (2016). *Basic income in Australia and New Zealand: Perspectives from the neoliberal frontier.* Basingstoke, UK: Palgrave Macmillan.

Mendes, P. (2015). *Compulsory income management: A policy solution looking for a problem.* Available at http://www.abc.net.au/religion/articles/2015/05/18/4237599.htm

Mitchell, W. (2012). *The abandonment of full employment: A national disgrace.* Available at http://bilbo.economicoutlook.net/blog/?p=21944

Neimeyer, S. (2013). Democracy and climate change: What can deliberative democracy contribute? *Australian Journal of Politics and History, 59*(3), 429–448.

Olin Wright, E. (2011). *Envisioning real utopias.* Brooklyn, NY: Verso Books.

Parsons, W. (1995). *Public policy: An introduction to the Theory and practice of policy analysis*. Cheltenham, UK: Edward Elgar Publishing.
Pereira, R. (2014). Economic security in the twenty-first century: How guaranteed annual income (GAI) confronts multiple imperatives. *Homo Economicus, 31*(1/2), 159–179.
Pitts, F., & Dinerstein, A. (2017). Postcapitalism, basic income and the end of work: A critique and alternative. *Bath Papers in International Development and Wellbeing*. Available at https://www.econstor.eu/bitstream/10419/180927/1/100921179X.pdf
Rose, N. (1998). *Inventing ourselves: Psychology, power and personhood*. Cambridge, UK: Cambridge University Press.
Rosenblaum, N. (2000). *Membership and morals: The personal uses of pluralism in America*. Princeton, NJ: Princeton University Press.
Saunders, P., & Fine, M. (1995) *Evaluation and research in social policy: Research paper no. 62*, Sydney, NSW: Social Policy Research Centre.
Standing, G. (2008). How cash transfers promote the case for basic income. *Basic Income Studies, 3*(1), 5–15.
Standing, G., & Samson, M. (Eds.). (2003). *A basic income grant for South Africa*. Lansdowne, South Africa: University of Cape Town Press.
The Australian. (2018). *Greens' income plan to cost 254 billion per year*. https://www.theaustralian.com.au/national-affairs/treasury/greens-income-plan-to-cost-extra-254bn-a-year/news-story/7e330391575e9f9787e0d0293c426127
The Institute for Public Affairs. (2018). *A universal basic income would create a permanent underclass*. https://ipa.org.au/ipa-today/a-universal-basic-income-would-create-a-permanent-underclass
Tiernan, A., & Burke, T. (2002). A load of old garbage: Applying garbage–can theory to contemporary housing policy. *Australian Journal of Public Administration, 61*(3), 86–97.
Urry, J. (2016). *What is the future*. Cambridge, UK: Polity Press.
van Parijs, P. (2004). Basic income: A simple and powerful idea for the twenty-first century. *Politics and Society, 32*(1), 7–39.
van Parijs, P. (2007). International distributive justice. In R. E. Goodin, P. Pettit, & T. W. Pogge (Eds.), *A companion to contemporary political philosophy* (Vol. 2, pp. 638–652). Oxford, UK: Blackwell.
Walters, W. (2000). *Unemployment and government: Genealogies of the social*. Cambridge, UK: Cambridge University Press.
Weeks, K. (2011). *The problem with work: Feminism, marxism, antiwork, politics and postwork imaginaries*. Durham, NC: Duke University Press.

Whiteford, P. (2016). *Welfare reform needs to be about improving wellbeing not punishing the poor.* Available at https://theconversation.com/ideas-for-australia-welfare-reform-needs-to-be-about-improving-well-being-not-punishing-the-poor-56355

Young, I. (2011). *Responsibility for justice*. Oxford, UK: Oxford University Press.

Ziguras, S. (2014). Social security: Doing more with less. In P. Smyth & A. McClelland (Eds.), *Social policy in Australia: Understanding for action* (pp. 184–199). Melbourne, VIC: Oxford University Press.

3

Basic Income in the Current Climate: If Australia Can Implement Other Universal Provisions, Then Why Not a Basic Income?

Jennifer Mays

Introduction

Global developments in basic income have reinvigorated political debates on the potential for transitioning to a universal basic income scheme in Australia. The impact of long-term austerity measures, neoliberal policies and major structural adjustments has exacerbated poverty and produced growing income and wealth inequalities (White, 2013). This chapter explores the basic income as one way forward to redress extreme poverty and inequality. It also draws on the case of the Blind Pension payment as an example of one universal and unconditional provision akin to basic income that could be extended to all people. The chapter frames the argument of exploring necessary conditions underpinning redistribution as a way of safeguarding and ensuring the sustainability of basic income. Additionally, this chapter calls for a renewed vision and architecture

J. Mays (✉)
Queensland University of Technology, Brisbane, QLD, Australia
e-mail: j.mays@qut.edu.au

E. Klein et al. (eds.), *Implementing a Basic Income in Australia*, Exploring the Basic Income Guarantee, https://doi.org/10.1007/978-3-030-14378-7_3

in the structural adjustment process encompassing egalitarianism underpinning distribution schemes. Flanagan and Stilwell (2018) referred to this restructuring in terms of a 'democratic realignment of our economic and political institutions' to produce a stronger egalitarian distribution of income and wealth (p. 8). For basic income to be introduced, some degree of structural adjustment needs to occur within the social protection structures and systems and societal levels.

Recently, there has been a change in public perceptions and attitudes in support for an alternative to the current system of welfare in the form of a basic income (Mays, 2016). The persistence of poverty, inequality and greater economic insecurity associated with labour market restructuring and automation stems from the convergence between social and economic forces, political institutions and ideologies such as neoliberalism and Piketty's (2014) of wealth and 'meritocratic extremism' (Khoury, 2015; Stiglitz, 2013; White, 2013). Thomas Piketty (2014) points to rising global inequalities and the shaping and reproducing unequal wage and capital distribution, which in turn generates an unequal concentration of wealth remaining with the top 1% of economic power elites. In Australia, a developed Western industrial country, disparities between the wealthy and people experiencing poverty are growing (White, 2013). Traditional policy responses to social protection have relied heavily on targeting and classifying those deemed 'most needy' or 'most deserving', such as people with a disability (Birnbaum, 2012, pp. 7–8). Since the introduction of the first national income support provision, the Commonwealth Invalid and Old-Age Pension in 1908, successive governments tended to fall back on traditional targeted welfare-state regime policy responses to social security measures (Mays, 2016). Welfare-state regime models (such as the notable regime advanced by Esping-Andersen, 2002) are a form of typology to help discern the type of model adopted within or across nation states. The typologies offer descriptive or explanatory insights into the nature of welfare reforms in modern political circumstances, and normative frameworks of each regime. Targeted measures tend to be adopted by advanced liberal-corporatist regimes, such as Australia, seen in the narrowing of eligibility criteria of pensions, benefits and allowances to the most needy or genuinely needy, and stringent conditions imposed on social security recipients. Targeting is the direct opposite to universalism, but it does contain normative justifications of paternalism, authoritarianism and individual rights, such as targeting those people most in need of social security as opposed to universalism which is a provision based on payment to all people, regardless of being rich or poor and grounded in social justice principles.

Although designed as a social protection measure, the level of targeting and conditionality attached to provisions over time has not led to greater improvement in the lives of those people most vulnerable. The enduring legacy of dominant targeted models of income support has perpetuated the entrenchment of ideology over time. Changes to the welfare state tended to be centred on reformist measures, as opposed to more radical redistributive changes. As in other developed Western liberal democracies, such as Canada, the recent period under neoliberalism has been characterised by stringent welfare requirements (such as mutual obligation), precarious employment, shrinking public expenditure and wage capping (Flanagan & Stilwell, 2018).

Where earlier federal governments (1945–1970s) maintained a commitment to the Australian welfare state and the distributive wage earner political economy (Flanagan & Stilwell, 2018; McKenzie, 2018), later federal governments have pursued neoliberal, free-market policies dominated by deregulation, privatisation, reduced labour costs and casualisation. In the neoliberal turn, the focus on maximising profits has eroded many of the institutional labour protections once part of the institutional framework (Flanagan & Stilwell, 2018). Not only has income and wealth inequalities proliferated under the current economic climate, but there is also greater insecurity resulting from the erosion of the minimum wage in real terms. The modern minimum wage is not set at a sufficient level to 'lift' a full-time employee out of poverty (Flanagan & Stilwell, 2018). Rather, increased privatisation and deregulation has generated downward pressure on people who can least afford the higher costs associated with essentials, costs of private housing or privatised utilities, such as electricity (Flanagan & Stilwell, 2018; Whiteford, 2011, 2015). This is seen in the 2.99 million people (13.3% of the total Australian population of 24 million) experiencing significant poverty or extreme financial hardship (Bowman, Mallett, & Cooney-O'Donoghue, 2017). Of 2.99 million people, approximately 57.3% people who live in poverty also rely on a pension or allowance as the predominant source of income

(Bowman et al., 2017). Growing evidence (Whiteford, 2011) is highlighting the gross inadequacy of social security payment levels, whereby the pensions and benefits are paid by governments at rates well below the poverty line (Whiteford, 2011).

The enduring nature of neoliberalism has had a profound impact on Australia's social protection whereby there has been an ideological and a philosophical shift away from the notion of collective benefits as a right, to individual self-reliance and market-oriented policies. At the heart of living a good life is enjoying the same rights as all other citizens, being treated fairly, and having freedom to participate socially, politically, economically and culturally in society (Torry, 2016a, 2016b). The central feature of living a good life is the right to a decent income and access to resources. The embedding of ethical justifications is critical in setting the foundation for freedom and dignity, given that the grant paid by the government to all permanent residents and provides something on which a person can function as a buffer for vulnerable groups, such as people living in poverty, children and young people, single parents and people with disabilities (Mays, Marston, & Tomlinson, 2016; Murray & Pateman, 2012; Standing, 2014).

It is acknowledged in this chapter that Australia's long history of targeting and conditionality makes it challenging to imagine any future towards basic income. The pursuit of the austerity measures, increased reliance on free-market and activation policies has significantly constrained the very social protection mechanisms and welfare safety nets necessary for supporting the most socially and economically disadvantaged groups, and for all citizens (Caputo, 2012; Murray & Pateman, 2012). The erosion of public confidence experienced in contemporary modern Australia is not a new trend. As Hanberger (2003) contends, there is an ongoing legitimising function performed by governments in relation to policy-making, yet not all government responses are adequate in reducing inequalities or entrenched social problems. Part of the problem lies with governments which, in seeking legitimate policy-making, are moving away from transformational approaches and reinforcing reformist policy. During the 1980s, Robertson (1998) pointed out that as public confidence goes down, governments tend to respond to crisis by increasing conditionality, rather than reducing conditionality or exploring universal alternatives.

Similar experiences in the erosion of public confidence carry over today. Regaining public support beyond piecemeal and conditional policy reforms requires a deeper analysis of policy's history, structural changes and possible futures with an aim to reconfigure the welfare state. This helps move beyond piecemeal reforms to envision a new way forward and reconfigure structural institutions and arrangements. By understanding these barriers, greater legitimacy can be afforded to alternatives such as basic income (Migdal, 2013; Robertson, 1998; Torry, 2016a).

Political determinations influence the distribution of resources and social security, including the structure of institutional arrangements (such as Centrelink, the administrative body charged with allocating provisions). Given the political dimension, distributive inequity in the unequal allocation of resources is closely connected to structural inequalities and disadvantage across time (Brady & Bostic, 2015). Structural disadvantage is found in dimensions of class, age, gender, culture, income distribution and institutional racism, whereby disadvantage is a consequence of oppressive, inequitable social structures and societal arrangements. Vulnerable groups (such as older women, men over 45 years of age and people with disabilities) are normatively ascribed an unequal status on the basis of unequal social relations, divergent forces, structural disadvantage and life chances (Piketty, 2014). In 2014, the Organisation for Economic Co-operation and Development (OECD) social indicators data reveal 14.4% of Australians now live in (relative) poverty. This figure sits well above the OECD average of 11.3% (OECD, 2014). At a time where poverty rates are increasing, Australia's overall welfare expenditure is shrinking well below the OECD average. Greater consequences of stigma, exclusion and disadvantage are features of unequal distributional systems. Rapidly changing socioeconomic and political conditions and government pursuit of austerity measures across advanced Western industrialised countries (the United States of America, the United Kingdom and Australia) has reinvigorated this call for a basic income (Migdal, 2013; Torry, 2016a, 2016b). As such, Australia has reached a crucial point in time to progress the implementation of an alternative basic income.

Shifting public attitudes are also driving the momentum for alternatives such as basic income. Hetherington's (2016) survey found the Australian public perception of neoliberal policies is changing. Targeted income support approaches are now seen as 'archaic' and targeting the most vulnerable people. The study also revealed that broader fiscal pressures and ideological debates particularly in the greater levels of insecure employment, low or stagnating wages and greater economic insecurity were shaping people's views. The perception of widening disparities was at the forefront of people's attitudes which suggested that the public would rather pay higher taxes for quality essential public services, but corporations and high-income earners have to pay their fair share (Hetherington, 2016). They also believed that some form of alternative to the current system is required. Similarly, Piketty (2014) recognised that the solution to ideological and wealth extremism, increased inequality and precariousness is redistribution through greater state protections and regulations, together with tighter fiscal controls (global progressive wealth tax on the extreme wealthy and super-managers). Piketty advanced the idea that the solution needed to be grounded in a universal redistributive strategy, by restructuring government structures (parliament), formal democratic institutions, statutes, legislature and civic institutions to achieve this aim. Although Piketty did not specifically refer to basic income, his defence of egalitarianism, democracy and transitioning to an alternative vision of society alludes to the implementation of a universal basic income scheme to counter the effects of neoliberalism.

A change in the existing form of Australian social protection does not happen immediately, especially the type of change required, such as modifying the general taxation revenue system. Any change requires policy debate and time. Nonetheless, the type of change required for implementing a Basic Income model is not an impossible task (Widerquist, 2013). Policy debate and consideration of the implementation challenges represents a significant progression to identifying some strategies for transitioning towards an alternative to the current system within Australia.

Basic Income: A Way Forward

The idea of a basic income aligns with the intent of egalitarian democracy and social policy, which suggests that income support is used to alleviate the effects of poverty, inequality and insecurity. In an era of a shrinking welfare state where there are greater levels of poverty, a basic income is something on which a person can safely count, a material foundation on which a life can firmly rest, promoting real freedom for all by providing the material resources that people need to pursue their aims (Mays et al., 2016). At its most basic, the universal scheme is an unconditional grant paid by government to all permanent residents at regular intervals (either monthly or fortnightly) (Birnbaum, 2012). The critical features of unconditionality and universality mean the scheme is grounded in egalitarian values and principles that reinforce social citizenship, democracy, civic virtues, rights, participation and collective solidarity. Social citizenship in this chapter is applied as an inclusive concept to denote dimensions of social inclusion and justice. While recognising the contentious nature of the term, social citizenship used here draws on the philosophical writings of basic income advocates (see Birnbaum, 2012; Raventós, 2007) to promote a more radical approach to distribution. The idea of a citizen in this chapter relates to a person who is not only formally a citizen of a nation but has also been accepted by the government to be a permanent resident. The term citizenship invokes a democratic status of being a citizen and signifies the formal status of being a citizen together with permanent residency. The ideal of citizenship then rests on the attainment of social, civil, political and human rights and social inclusion people in all aspects of in society, or everyday life (Raventós, 2007). In a similar vein to some basic income advocates, this chapter employs the concept of social citizenship as a basis for working towards an egalitarian society which promotes an inclusive income support is accessible for all. It was Thomas Paine, who during the late 1700s, argued for egalitarianism in which different pension payments, such as disability pensions, were established in terms of a right, rather than based on charitable and deserving poor ideals (Standing, 2001). Paine's thesis reminds basic income proponents of the potential for designing income support policies underpinned by normative conditions that uphold the equal, and equitable redistribution of wealth in conjunction with upholding rights and justice, particularly in terms of collective benefit. More equitable redistribution occurs through various mechanisms such as progressive taxation which are seen as central tenets of modern social policy in the aim for a good society Raventós (2007). Social citizenship rather than economic citizenship forms the foundation for universal, unconditional provision. Therefore, basic income is more than just poverty alleviation; it promotes a non-stigmatising, non-categorising payment of social protection that enhances quality of life and well-being, income security and social justice for people (Mays & Marston, 2016; Widerquist, 2013). By its very nature, a basic income necessitates a positive equality impact through transforming an oppressive economic system (Torry, 2016a, 2016b).

Basic income as a redistributive strategy is critical for countering inequalities, poverty gaps and ideological extremism. Notably, there needs to be some improvement in the lives of the most disadvantaged groups, which can be achieved through the positive equality impact (Standing, 2014). In the current political context, such a transformational change to the social protection system can function concurrently with major transformation of society to a more egalitarian one (Widerquist, 2013). This goal is to ensure a move away from unjust neoliberal corporate governance within our sociopolitical spheres to democratic governance.

If basic income is one way forward to counter the extremes of highly targeted neoliberal system, then serious consideration needs to be given to design principles, policy preparedness of the country and implementation phases. For basic income to gain greater credibility in the political space and for Australia to progress to a basic income, some critical scoping of design and implementation potentialities and challenges needs to be considered early on, for example, the type and frequency of the provision. Co-creating a common vision for the return to economic and social security, through basic income as a progressive redistributive strategy, involves designing concrete proposals to support the transition (Mays et al., 2016; Morley & Ablett, 2017). Change is achieved through a redistributive approach that is simple and transformative, rather than built in complexities such as targeting and conditionality (Mays et al., 2016) and requires more than just advancing principles, but, also social actions. As Birnbaum (2012) noted, competing normative justifications of social justice need to be considered alongside economic feasibility, strategy, power, institutional and normative continuity, and context-relevant conditions given that basic income needs to establish political and real-world feasibility, appeal and relevance, to secure a means for adoption. Birnbaum contends that normative conflicts around the best policy choice for basic income can be resolved without fully attending to the basic principles of justice. Universalism from a justice position, needs to also offer strategies for policy feasibility in social engineering and reconfiguring institutional arrangements necessary to meet the objectives and budget priorities concerns. Essentially this means balancing competing priorities. The extent of redistribution, nature and features of the national taxation system necessitates securing the support of a critical mass. This notion is in parallel with an appropriate policy lens to consider how basic income 'fits' within the larger policy context and whether it is feasible to implement. Questions about whether or not consensus can ever be achieved when it comes to tax are responded by Birnbaum (2012) who suggests majority consensus can achieve the outcome of basic income progress to implementation. Not all welfare changes have relied on a direct critical mass, such as universal Medicare scheme, however the National Disability Insurance Scheme, represents a case in point for broad consensus and critical mass that led to changes including in the tax system. Building consensus goes some way to responding to the ideological and attitudinal barriers to basic income implementation.

Transitioning to a Basic Income

Clearly, the success or failure of basic income depends upon its design features. At the heart of basic income design is the identification of ways to establish a national progressive policy research and action agenda on basic income. This point is related to policy preparedness, akin to the progressive social engineering seen in the design and subsequent implementation during the 1980s of the universal social insurance scheme—Medicare (Spies-Butcher, 2014). Securing legitimacy of the value in basic income design is paramount for ensuring the universal application of democracy to produce an egalitarian society. This means while processes in the design phase would involve democratic decision-making and participatory processes, there needs to be an initial vision crafted and owned by the majority. The vision would encapsulate social justice, rights and participatory principles. Boettke and Martin (2011) noted that developing justification and understanding the institutional environment, polity and political economy helps progress debates beyond an ideal to a grounded proposal for design. This approach paves the way for engagement in basic income scheme design, modelling and strategies for change by offering solutions to counter ideological barriers (Boettke & Martin, 2011).

Exploratory studies are needed in Australia to identify the most relevant approach for basic income provision (i.e. partial payment, full payment, age, frequency of payment) and incorporate social and economic dimensions, such as political and macro-economic context, feasibility and innovation (Murray & Pateman, 2012). This also involves examining the contemporary experience, current priorities and the conceptual framework in preparation for the social and economic modelling of basic income. Clearly, scoping these dimensions helps identify the major hurdles in design phases and in turn transitioning to a basic income. For example, some of the hurdles include the false debates about affordability (cost, distributional impact and feasibility) (Birnbaum, 2012; Standing, 2014).

Consideration of basic income design incorporates ethical, social and economic dimensions, scoping payment rates to ensure the rate at which the payment is made is sufficient to alter the relationship between labour and capital and the marketisation and commodification of daily life (Murray & Pateman, 2012; Widerquist, 2013). Complexities are found in determining the level of the monthly payment, regions or city suburbs (differences across metropolitan, major country town and rural/remote regional areas) and the design features of the model for transitioning to basic income. These considerations—for example, determining priorities in simplifying other income-related pensions, benefits and allowances, or transforming the tax system—are required to embed basic income in the Australian context (Caputo, 2012).

Design Features Inclusive of Egalitarianism

Integral to effective basic income design and implementation is the notion that social citizenship is a pre-condition for income support (see Standing, 2014) for a comprehensive discussion of social citizenship and pre-conditions. While it is acknowledged that social citizenship can be a nefarious term, in the spirit of basic income advocates who subscribe to the ethical and moral justifications of basic income, social citizenship remains an important concept. It speaks to the power of transformative change, social justice, income distribution and equity (Caputo, 2012; Murray & Pateman, 2012; Standing, 2014; Van Parijs, 1995; Vollenweider, 2008). From this stance, social citizenship (as opposed to productive and economic citizenship) is designed for the pursuit of a universal provision that is sustained over time by an egalitarian society. The foundation of a universal, unconditional and inclusive income support provision (basic income) available for all permanent citizens forms the central platform for design and implementation. Redistribution of wealth via a return to universal, collective benefit, regressive taxation and transparency helps support the moral commitment for an inclusive, socially just income support provision (Birnbaum, 2012; Caputo, 2012). Standing (2014) provides insight into redistribution through collective benefit whereby people are the beneficiaries of income distribution rather than select groups based on targeting. Birnbaum (2012), Standing (2014) and this author argue for a radical transformation of the welfare system to a more egalitarian society that benefits all people (collective benefit) not just a select few. Such an egalitarian approach runs counter to neoliberalism and dominant targeted responses. It does this by embedding into the Constitution and also legislation, policy and administrative practices, the principle of the provisions set up in terms of being a right, not as charity or deserving poor ideals (Goldsmith, 2004; Standing, 2014).

Although the Australian policy landscape is replete with targeting, and conditionality through greater social controls, there are instances where universalism has been implemented in different measures, including the Blind Pension. A detailed examination of the conditions in which the Blind Pension has been retained as a universal and unconditional provision, provides critical insights into the conditions necessary for gaining political consent to implement a basic income.

Case Study of Blind Pension and Universalism

Unlike the disability pension, the Blind Pension is available to any person who meets the medical criteria, irrespective of income and labour market participation. The Blind Pension, similar to the Aged Pension, is indexed to wages (Consumer Price Index [CPI]), so the payment remains more adequate than other benefits (Mays, 2016). The Blind Pension is a guaranteed income support, that is, a universal payment to all people who were assessed as legally blind (Mays, 2016). Functioning as an unconditional grant, the Blind Pension was perceived to operate as a natural right, thereby encouraging people who are blind to work and participate in society. It is the unique combination of government and public support, institutional arrangements and conditions that led to the introduction of the Blind Pension. Such a convergence of interrelating factors could be drawn on to move universal basic income beyond a mere ideal.

Enacted by the Fisher Commonwealth Government in 1925, the Blind Pension enshrined specific universal rights and entitlements for all people who are blind (Mays, 2016). While universal rights were applied to the Blind Pension, these rights were not similarly afforded to the then Invalid Pension (disability pension). The Blind Pension functioned to create distinctions between different disability groups and engendered notions of desirable/undesirable qualities attached to notions of 'normalcy' (Oliver, 2009). These artificial distinctions are closely connected to paradoxes in redistribution and strategies of equality. Universal social policies such as basic income seek to reduce poverty if this is the central principle applied. Universalism is related to transfer share and universal distribution to all people. Paradoxes occur when social policy principles contradict the original intent of the social policy. Brady and Bostic (2015) describe paradoxes as contradictions, seen in their statement: 'paradoxes as mismatches between the sources of social policies' effectiveness and the sources of social policies' popularity, and contradictions between the three dimensions of welfare transfers' (p. 291). For example, where basic income seeks to redress poverty, it may end up responding only to equality outcomes, if attention is not paid to the amount required to lift people above the poverty line (Brady & Bostic, 2015).

An inherent equity and uniformity paradox emerged between the Invalid Pension and Blind Pension. The equity and uniformity paradox relate to the paradoxes created when attempting to establish uniform application of particular pensions. Where the Blind Pension runs into this paradox is that it is only applied within this pension and not applied universally to disability or aged care pensions. See De Wispelaere and Stirton (2004) for a comprehensive explanation of the terms. For the

Invalid Pension, the underpinning eligibility criteria was grounded in categories of deficits tied to labour and productivity, that is, the criterion of permanent incapacity for work (Mays, 2016). In contrast, there was greater political and public support at the time for people who were blind, who were ascribed a privileged status at the expense of other vulnerable groups (De Wispelaere & Stirton, 2011, 2013). The universal Blind Pension provision assumed people who were blind were capable of working and, as a corollary, were valued, productive citizens, who actively engaged in civic life (Mays, 2016). The Blind Pension was driven by public and political leader sentiment and subsequent debates in parliament around universal income support provision. The shift came from a culmination of converging forces which functioned to garner widespread support for the introduction of the Blind Pension, such as Federation in 1901, desire to remove the so-called blind beggars from the street and increased sympathy towards people who were blind. The provision of the Blind Pension was also deemed by political leaders to be less costly over time, unlike preconceptions of the Invalid Pension, which attracted political concern over the presumed high costs associated with the provision (Mays, 2016).

The Blind Pension scheme is grounded in egalitarian values and principles that reinforce social citizenship, democracy, civic virtues, rights, participation and collective solidarity. Dimensions (universality, conditionality, adequacy, uniformity and equity) proposed by De Wispelaere and Stirton (2004) are useful for deepening the analysis of the Blind Pension. In considering, *universality* dimension, the Australian Blind Pension continues to the present day as a universal payment in the form of guaranteed, unconditional income support (Mays et al., 2016). The related dimension of *conditionality* (extent to which conditions of access are placed on payments) (Bowman et al., 2017; De Wispelaere & Stirton, 2004), is found to be absent from eligibility for the Blind Pension, that is the universal provision is not subject to stringent means-testing or other welfare-to-work requirements applied to other pensions and benefits, such as the disability pension. The only criterion for the Blind Pension is that the person needs to be assessed and legally determined to be tonally and permanently blind (Mays, 2016).

As noted above, the payment is adequate in terms of the provision of an income that meets basic needs. Further evidence of adequacy in meeting basic need is found in the contrast with other pensions and benefits such as the Newstart Allowance (now known as Jobs Allowance) and the disability or aged pensions which have been subject to sustained 'pension and benefit rate freezes' sporadically during the past four decades by different governments (for example, Howard Government, 1996–2006) (Whiteford, 2015). Degree of uniformity captures both the way the Blind Pension provision has remained unchanged since implementation (apart form rate increases) and whether there is similarity across levels of benefits (De Wispelaere & Stirton, 2004, 2011, 2013). There is a uniformity and equity paradox (Brady & Bostic, 2015) that comes into play here, given that people who were blind have long been afforded additional unconditional assistance through subsidies, privileged status and favourable attention in comparison to other groups, such as people with disabilities, people who were unemployed or older people (Mays, 2016). This uneven application of eligibility criteria points to unequal equity in distribution, whereby uniform payments have unequal consequences across differing disability experiences and classifications (Brady & Bostic, 2015). For example, there is a lack of equity present where people with disabilities have higher associated medical and other costs related to the disability experience, yet stringent welfare-to-work requirements and assessment processes means many people with disabilities will be shifted across to the lower unemployment benefits, which does not account for associated medical and transport costs (Mays, 2016). For people who are blind, the Blind Pension affords automatic access to subsidies for medical costs and transport (Miller & Hayward, 2017).

Since the introduction of the Blind Pension legislation in 1909, little attention was paid to formalising universal rights and entitlements across other pensions and benefits. Notably, the uniformity and equity paradox gain greater legitimacy in the current political climate of fiscal austerity, whereby Australia's neoliberal government continues to fund and implement the Blind Pension. However, paradoxes are also evident when the government tinkers with social security arrangements. Since 2013, minor adjustments were made to the Blind Pension, where rent assistance is subject to means-testing under this provision. Another recent adjustment is referring to the Blind Pension as the Disability Allowance, which is a discursive and policy device for creating illusions of equity. The policy challenges within Australia centre around ideological reasons, as opposed to strengthening the welfare-state safety net. The recently introduced, universal social insurance scheme, the Commonwealth National Disability Insurance Scheme (NDIS) (2013) is a case in point (Miller & Hayward, 2017). In attempting to understand design and implantation consideration that led to the introduction of the NDIS, as opposed to other alternatives, such as basic income, Miller and Hayward (2017) question the political and social conditions attached to the implementation of the NDIS and the ongoing political commitment to fund the scheme, particularly as the NDIS is considered an excessively costly new universal social insurance scheme.

The enactment of NDIS and maintenance of the Blind Pension provision comes during a period, whereby tighter targeting of other provisions (such as the Disability Support Pension and Newstart Allowance) has led to payment levels being highly inadequate and well below the poverty line, given they have not been raised in 25 years to match inflation (Bowman et al., 2017; Whiteford, 2011). While the National Disability Insurance Scheme (NDIS) concerns service provision and individual support, it is highly relevant to the debate in terms of being a universal social insurance that runs alongside the social protection system (pensions and benefits) (Miller & Hayward, 2017). The ongoing political and public support for the Blind Pension and NDIS raises questions about the potential to draw greater attention to a basic income grounded in universal rights and entitlements. Since the 1980s, various governments have called for changes to the Blind Pension legislation in terms of making the system uniform (Smyth, 2014). Yet, government proposals for reforming the Blind Pension have predominately ended in remarkable policy flip flops (i.e. when the current government makes a backflip or sudden change in policy direction, while arguing each position presented has logical consistency but in reality both may be contradictory), given the high degree of public support for the provision and the potential for 'political pain' (Smyth, 2014). The point being in this section is that when governments are truly committed to introducing universal oriented schemes, as seen with the Blind Pension and the NDIS, then these schemes become reality.

This suggest that in part there is some degree of political will and public sentiment driving the implementation of universal approaches. The case study suggests that governments based on political will can—and do—in certain circumstances, apply universal measures. If this is the case then following this logic, there is some capacity for the introduction of a universal unconditional grant to all persons, regardless of the nature of their disability experience, employment status or family status.

As mentioned earlier, distributive inequity is closely connected to concrete structural inequalities and disadvantage over time. (See Piketty, 2014 for a comprehensive analysis of the historical trends and wealth extremisms created by divergent forces that function to marginalise particular groups, but benefit other groups, such as the wealthy and corporate leaders.) Not all people have access to resources or life chances, based on health determinants, where they live, inheritance, exposure to violence in the home or experiences of unemployment or underemployment. Exclusion, stigma and disadvantage are characteristics of an unequal distribution system. Redistributive systems such as basic income are required to smooth inequality and support people during times of need or want (De Wispelaere & Stirton, 2004). The readiness with which the Australian public has recently embraced different schemes such as the NDIS and the Blind Pension, could indicate the time is right for progressing basic income onto the political agenda. Having reached a critical point in time to counter austerity measures and harness consent of the broader public for universal provisions, capturing the moment becomes a crucial strategy in progressing universal basic income (Healy & Reynolds, 2016). Given governments across the eras have extended favourable treatment of particular groups, such as people eligible for the Blind Pension, there is some legitimacy for arguing the extension of the universal provision to include *all* people.

The recent enactment of the NDIS highlights many of the lessons for consideration in the Australian basic income policy space. Many of the direct actions during the universal social insurance campaign responded not only to prevailing social attitudes but also to the changing structure of social and institutional arrangements, together with adjusting moral and cultural values (such as dignity and justice) (Miller & Hayward, 2017). Examples such as the NDIS's introduction of a national framework for basic income grounded in open, informed public debate and discussion provide models with greater means for successful implementation (Miller & Hayward, 2017). This approach moves beyond traditional dominant top down approaches to adopting solidarity and deliberative policy processes (citizens participation alongside others, technical, specialist expertise) (Birnbaum, 2012). Transforming inequitable economic systems and promoting alternative basic income visions using participatory democracy offers a way to democratise the policy landscape (Haagh, 2011). Collective representation through democratic and critical activist scholarship, in solidarity and collaboration with grassroots social movements provides one way forward in producing and reinforcing new universal policies, practices, discourses and egalitarian norms in society (De Wispelaere, 2016). Use of social citizenship rather than economic citizenship to pursue income support provision sustained by an egalitarian society is foundational to a universal, unconditional and inclusive income support provision (basic income) available for all permanent citizens.

The nature of transformation to social protection incorporates redistribution of wealth via a return to collective benefit, regressive taxation and transparency in the moral commitment for inclusive and socially just income support provision (Mays, 2016). Suggestions have been made that full basic income can be enacted alongside other schemes such as the NDIS and job guarantee scheme (Miller & Hayward, 2017). Any transition to basic income involves consolidating many existing transfer schemes (pensions, benefits and allowances) and replacing others while also changing the taxation system for equitable distribution of income (Caputo, 2012; De Wispelaere, 2016). It is clear the time has come for progressing basic income in broader political public debate, as support for basic income and universalism is growing.

Global debates on basic income have progressed beyond philosophical discussions to the design and implementation of experiments especially in parts of Europe, South America, Southern Africa and India. The outcomes of these projects demonstrate the potential of the proposal to present as an egalitarian and collective redistributive strategy (De Wispelaere, 2016; Standing, 2014). Redistributive justice has a positive effect through the removal of poverty trap effects (produced by conditionality) through the right to withdraw from employment or the labour market through necessity, without penalty or recourse (Torry, 2016b). It also means that people would not be subject to the loss of pensions or be subject to long waiting periods for crisis payments (Raventós, 2007). People would have increased bargaining power within the household and beyond (workplace), as the grant is free from imposed work requirements or stringent means-testing (Raventós, 2007). People are not subject to insecurity as it removes the potential for loss of income when there are absences from work because of illness, disability or abuse. A basic income improves dignity, and economic and social well-being, towards greater socioeconomic independence, which in turn supports positive social and psychological effects. The freedom from stigma in classification and categorisation principle afforded by basic income, according to disability or age, prevents paternal classifications and assumptions of categories according to need (Birnbaum, 2012).

Driving the initiation of concrete proposals in the transition to a basic income contributes to developing concrete proposals and building evidence to shape and influence policy debates and ultimately guide policymaking (De Wispelaere, 2016). An inclusive approach considers diverse methods of coalition building to progress social movements, generate advocacy for lobbying (government and other stakeholders) and embed basic income in law and practices. In a basic income, the absence of conditionality, behavioural conditions or classifications imposed on income support provision, allows for positive social, political, economic, cultural and psychological effects to notions of livelihoods and personhood (Torry, 2016b). This in turn helps to ensure that vulnerable groups marginalised at the lower end of income distribution (such as people with a disability, younger people) can receive some form of support that is free from a host of complex classifications grounded in moral distinctions of 'deserving' and 'underserving poor' (Birnbaum, 2012).

Conclusion

A basic income, on the basis of social citizenship principles, is the least oppressive form of income support to all people based on social citizenship and not productive citizenship or current citizenship structural barriers. Even when the idea of a universal income grant has been touted in Australian government policy debates, for example, the Blind Pension and Henderson Poverty Line (see Commonwealth of Australia, 1975a, 1975b), Australia has sporadically shown an inclination to embark on the implementation of a basic income. Thus, to redress ad hoc commitment and political will, there is the need for a concerted political commitment to change. A basic income is not perceived to be a utopian solution for all social problems, as there are complexities associated with any transition in this region (Caputo, 2012). This is not to say a utopian vision cannot be held to introduce a universal income support system. Such a utopian vision responds to the inherent tensions associated with the implementation strategies (De Wispelaere, 2016). Yet, as explored in the case of the Blind Pension, there is potential for garnering greater political support and will to initiate the change to a universal basic income and in turn, an egalitarian society. As De Wispelaere (2016) contends transitioning to a basic income requires critically analysing the strategies for and the potential barriers to implementation. At its core, the greater space for collective scholarly, activist and critical thinker voice is necessary to develop a common vision and engage in strategic planning (Haagh, 2011). This strategic approach ensures basic income is introduced and embedded as an unconditional citizenship right (Milner, 1920; Standing, 2014). In Australia there is much to be done to transition to a basic income including strategic planning to ensure it can counter the crisis of capitalism and offer a vision of a better way forward. In an era of heightened inequality, poverty together with greater economic insecurity and loss of hope, basic income proposes the opposite (Birnbaum, 2012). Basic income gives back a sense of dignity, worth and most importantly hope for the future.

The case of the Blind Pension provides an insight into the social, economic and normative conditions that led to the introduction of the universal provision. For advocates these conditions infer the need for political commitment in conjunction with realistic political action engage for generating sustainable coalitions. Rigby and Wright (2013) noted that political leaders may subscribe to the policy platforms of parties and align with middle and upper-class policy priorities at the expense of working class and people in poverty. Such an alignment can reflect preferences of those who have the least to benefit from basic income if it advances a policy platform used for political gains and to deliver policy (seen in the case of Blind Pension and NDIS), rather than secure divergent political commitment. In the case of the Blind Pension and NDIS, De Wispelaere (2016) cautions against not failing to account for the political affiliations and ideological dimensions during the design phase. He does argue for critical radical approach for sophisticated design strategies that illuminate obstacles and challenges or mismatches in normative requirements such as social justice. The Australian experience of the Blind Pension provides an analytical case study to understand political strategies underpinning the implementation of universal measures and the divergent forces that influence design considerations, including political constraints. The resulting interest garnered in the case of the Blind Pension and NDIS led to the Blind Pension and NDIS being subject to extensive parliamentary debate, mass mobilisation, and media representation and coalition building, even where some form of paternalism was involved. The universal aspect was given visibility in that it resonated with people's norms around disability social security and service delivery (De Wispelaere, 2016). But to date, even with variations of universal provisions, Australia has not introduced a full basic income for all people with a monthly payment provided to individuals. What the case study illustrates is the capacity and potential for political will in progressing to a basic income and 'real advancement' of strategies to the realisation of basic income (De Wispelaere, 2016).

This chapter not only offers a sense of hope, but also suggests concrete, strategic also function to develop a vision for the future. Over time, Australia has implemented various universal measures (Blind Pension provision). This recognition points to the potential of basic income to be introduced and nation states to advance a fairer system and redress poverty, insecure employment and minimum wages. Basic income is a redistributive strategy that helps to move to an egalitarian system promoting social justice and well-being, while also supporting both individual freedom and economic security to prosper. Basic income has a role in restructuring income support policy in the transition towards an egalitarian society, just as governments have a central role in providing an adequate level of social protection given their responsibility of resource allocation and distribution. Finally, when introduced adequately, uniformly and equitably, basic income is emancipatory and liberatory, freeing people from policy controls of conditionality and targeting.

References

Birnbaum, S. (2012). *Basic income reconsidered: Social justice, liberalism, and the demands of equality*. New York: Palgrave Macmillan.

Boettke, P. J., & Martin, A. G. (2011). Taking the 'G' out of BIG: A comparative political economy perspective on basic income. *Basic Income Studies, 6*. Available at SSRN: https://ssrn.com/abstract=1697728

Bowman, D., Mallett, S., & Cooney-O'Donoghue, D. (2017). *Basic income: Tradeoffs and bottom lines*. Fitzroy, VIC: Brotherhood of St Laurence.

Brady, D., & Bostic, A. (2015). Paradoxes of social policy: Welfare transfers, relative poverty, and redistribution preferences. *American Sociological Review, 80*(2), 268–298.

Caputo, R. (Ed.). (2012). *Basic income guarantee and politics: International experiences and perspectives on the viability of income guarantees*. Basingstoke, UK: Palgrave Macmillan.

Commonwealth of Australia. (1975a). Australian government's commission of inquiry into poverty: Poverty in Australia Vol. 1. *Henderson Poverty Report*. Canberra, Australia: AGPS.

Commonwealth of Australia. (1975b). Australian government's commission of inquiry into poverty: Poverty in Australia Vol. 2. *Henderson Poverty Report*. Canberra, Australia: AGPS.

De Wispelaere, J. (2016). The struggle for strategy: On the politics of the basic income proposal. *Politics, 36*(2), 131–141.

De Wispelaere, J., & Stirton, L. (2004). The many faces of universal basic income. *The Political Quarterly, 75*, 266–274.

De Wispelaere, J., & Stirton, L. (2011). The administrative efficiency of basic income. *Policy and Politics, 39*(1), 115–132.

De Wispelaere, J., & Stirton, L. (2013). The politics of universal basic income: Bringing bureaucracy back in? *Political Studies, 61*(4), 915–932.

Esping-Andersen, G. (2002). *Why we need a new welfare state*. Oxford, UK: Oxford University Press.

Flanagan, F., & Stilwell, F. (2018). Editorial: Causes and consequences of labour's falling income share and growing inequality. *Journal of Australian Political Economy, 81*, 5–10.

Goldsmith, S. (2004). The Alaska permanent fund dividend: An experiment in wealth distribution. In G. Standing (Ed.), *Promoting income security as a right: Europe and North America* (pp. 549–562). London: Anthem.
Haagh, L. (2011). Basic income, social democracy and control over time. *Policy and Politics, 39*(1), 43–66.
Hanberger, A. (2003). Public policy and legitimacy: A historical policy analysis of the interplay of public policy and legitimacy. *Policy Sciences, 36*, 257–278.
Healy, S., & Reynolds, B. (2016). Basic income: Radical utopia or practical solution? In B. Reynolds & S. Healy (Eds.), *Basic income radical utopia or practical solution?* (pp. 1–30). Dublin, Ireland: Social Justice Ireland.
Hetherington, D. (2016). *2016 per capita tax survey: Public attitudes towards taxation and public expenditure*. Retrieved from http://percapita.org.au/wp-content/uploads/2016/04/2016-Tax-Survey_FINAL.pdf
Khoury, P. (2015). Neoliberalism, auditing, austerity and the demise of social justice. *Social Alternatives, 34*(3), 25–33.
Mays, J. (2016). Disability, citizenship, and basic income: Forging a new alliance for a non-disabling society. In J. Mays, G. Marston, & J. Tomlinson (Eds.), *Basic income in Australia and New Zealand: Perspectives from the neoliberal frontier* (pp. 207–251). New York: Palgrave Macmillan.
Mays, J., & Marston, G. (2016). Reimagining equity and egalitarianism: The basic income debate in Australia. Special issue of *Journal of Sociology and Social Welfare* symposium on the basic income guarantee, *43*(3), Article 3, Number 3.
Mays, J., Marston, G., & Tomlinson, J. (2016). Neoliberal frontiers and economic insecurity: Is basic income a solution? In J. Mays, G. Marston, & J. Tomlinson (Eds.), *Basic income in Australia and New Zealand: Perspectives from the neoliberal frontier* (pp. 1–25). New York: Palgrave Macmillan.
McKenzie, M. (2018). The erosion of minimum wage policy in Australia and labour's shrinking share of total income. *Journal of Australian Political Economy, 81*, 52–77.
Migdal, J. S. (2013). Forward. In A. White (Ed.), *The everyday life of the state: A state-in-society approach* (pp. vii–xiv). Seattle, WA: University of Washington.
Miller, P., & Hayward, D. (2017). Social policy 'generosity' at a time of fiscal austerity: The strange case of Australia's National Disability Insurance Scheme. *Critical Social Policy, 37*(1), 128–147.
Milner, D. (1920). *Higher production by a bonus on national output: A proposal for a minimum income for all varying with national productivity*. London: George Allen & Unwin.

Morley, C., & Ablett, P. (2017). Rising wealth and income inequality: A radical social work critique and response. *Aotearoa New Zealand Social Work, 29*(2), 6–18.

Murray, M. C., & Pateman, C. (Eds.). (2012). *Basic income worldwide: Horizons of reform*. Basingstoke, UK: Palgrave Macmillan.

Organisation for Economic Co-operation and Development [OECD]. (2014). *Society at a glance: OECD social indicators* (March). OECD Publishing. Retrieved from: http://www.oecd.org/social/societyataglance.htm

Oliver, M. (2009). *Understanding disability: From theory to practice* (2nd ed.). Houndsmills, BA: Macmillan.

Piketty, T. (2014). *Capital in the twenty-first century*. Cambridge, UK: Harvard University Press.

Raventós, D. (2007). *Basic income: The material conditions of freedom* (J. Wark, Trans.). London: Pluto Press.

Rigby, E., & Wright, G. C. (2013). Political parties and representation of the poor in the American states. *American Journal of Political Science, 57*(3), 552–565.

Robertson, D. B. (1998). Introduction: Loss of confidence and policy change in the 1970s. In D. B. Robertson (Ed.), *Loss of confidence: Politics and policy in the 1970s*. University Park, PA: Pennsylvania State University Press.

Smyth, P. (2014). The historical contexts for action. In A. McClelland & P. Smyth (Eds.), *Social policy in Australia* (pp. 81–94). South Melbourne, VIC: Oxford University Press.

Spies-Butcher, B. (2014). Markets, universalism and equity: Medicare's dual role in the Australian welfare state. *The Journal of Australian Political Economy, 73*, 18–40.

Standing, G. (2001). *Beyond the new paternalism: Basic security as equality*. London: Verso.

Standing, G. (2014). *The precariat: The new dangerous class*. London: Bloomsbury.

Stiglitz, J. (2013). *The price of inequality*. New York: Penguin.

Torry, M. (2016a). Citizen's basic income: Is it feasible? In B. Reynolds & S. Healy (Eds.), *Basic income radical utopia or practical solution?* (pp. 31–47). Dublin, Ireland: Social Justice Ireland.

Torry, M. (2016b). *The feasibility of citizen's income*. New York: Palgrave Macmillan.

Van Parijs, P. (1995). *Real freedom for all: What(if anything) can justify capitalism?* Oxford, UK: Oxford University Press.

Vollenweider, C. (2008). Domestic service and gender equality: An unavoidable problem for the feminist debate on basic income. *Basic Income Studies, 8*(1), 19–41.

White, A. (2013). Introduction: A state-in-society agenda. In A. White (Ed.), *The everyday life of the state: A state-in-society approach* (pp. 3–12). Seattle, WA: University of Washington.

Whiteford, P. (2011). Income support, inequality and social risks. In P. Smyth & J. Buchanan (Eds.), *Inclusive growth in Australia.* Sydney, NSW: Allen & Unwin.

Whiteford, P. (2015). Inequality and its socioeconomic impacts. *Australian Economic Review, 48*(1), 83–92.

Widerquist, K. (2013). *Independence, propertylessness and basic income.* Basingstoke, UK: Palgrave Macmillan.

4

Feminist Perspectives on Basic Income

Eva Cox

The Back Story

Too many of the current debates on wealth, income, jobs and welfare policies are deeply embedded with gender-based assumptions. Why and how have the concept of (male) waged work taken such a hold on our political thinking? It is necessary to explore where these beliefs come from and why they remain so powerful, despite many related social changes, to be able to forge new models.

Feminist equality has been on the political agenda in most of the so-called developed states, including Australia, since the revived second wave Women's Movement. I was a part of it and we raised these equity differences politically in the 1960s, as part of the social movements seeking change in the post-war era of optimism. But defining equality was—and still is—limited by male defined assumptions about sharing material well-being. So debates about equality were dominated by claims for

E. Cox (✉)
Jumbunna Institute for Indigenous Education and Research, University of Technology Sydney, Ultimo, NSW, Australia

E. Klein et al. (eds.), *Implementing a Basic Income in Australia*, Exploring the Basic Income Guarantee, https://doi.org/10.1007/978-3-030-14378-7_4

equitable access to paid work and not much else. The assumption was the economy of production and trade was all that counted.

The gendered differences in measured contributions of unpaid tasks were clearly displayed in the 2016 Australian Census. Its data showed that women spend more than double the amount of time spent by men on unpaid tasks. When men and women start to cohabit, women's unpaid domestic work increases while men's goes down, regardless of employment status.

These assumptions and cultural mindsets run deep and started long before feminists in the 1960s started challenging it.

These limitations are rooted in the Western European Industrial Revolution's growth of mass production via the new technologies and capitalisation which divided the predominantly male factory jobs from the household. This major social shift affected communities and countries by defining these spheres as gendered. The notion of a male 'breadwinner' and responsible for funding unpaid roles added to intransigent gender pay gaps. In Australia, these were formally entrenched in 1908 in the Harvester Judgement (Commonwealth of Australia, 2012). It stipulated a basic wage to cover men and family dependents, followed by a lower wage for women workers.

These differentiations failed to recognise human interdependence. Over the millennia human society has needed more equal male and female roles to survive, as human beings have a long maturation period, social supports are essential for intergenerational well-being. Families are interdependent, plus part of wider tribes, so have been essential to human well-being. Yet the post-industrial social divides indicate this needed gender equity is not valued in 'modern' times.

The assumptions regarding paid work stem from post Reformation Weberian Protestant ethics of the virtues of hard work being as intrinsic to Western civilisation views of the sins of sloth (Weber, 1948). Weber's argument was that capitalism in Northern Europe evolved when the Protestant (particularly Calvinist) ethic influenced large numbers of people to engage in work in the secular world, developing their own enterprises and engaging in trade and the accumulation of wealth for investment. In other words, the Protestant work ethic was an important force behind the emergence of modern capitalism (Standing, 2005).

The Bolsheviks' Russian revolution promoted a (male) worker-based ideology centred on the exploitation of workers by capitalism, but also ignored the social contributions to well-being, mainly contributed by women. Thus, two very significant events generated, in different ways, the assumption that 'real work' was essentially 'paid work', usually done by men, and then devalued the relevance of community and domestic spheres. These cultural changes spread across the world as colonised nations adopted (white) male cultures of individualised greed. Older forms of local societies, that were based on small trade and subsistence farming, then disappeared in favour of big factories and waged labour as marks of progress, modernity and 'prosperity'.

While the roles of women and men, and their relative power, have always been differentiated by child bearing and rearing, the past 300-plus years have created new gender gaps. The growth of cities and states came as older more feudal power structures were replaced by industrialisation and globalised trade, which added drivers of change that reinforced gender power differences.

Even as women moved into the paid workforce over the past five decades, their inequitably shared domestic responsibilities remain an unvalued contribution to our well-being, which has been exacerbated by neoliberal 1980s market-based paradigm shifts. This mainly economic policy setting started in the late 1970s with Margaret Thatcher elected as Prime Minister in the United Kingdom. The changes to market-based policies have gradually undermined many of the post-war policies that targeted social fairness and gender equity. What was known as the welfare state (Britannica, 2018) offered social support, but was replaced by the focus on greed-driven individualised customer market-based policies.

It is the residue of these relatively recent changes that offer opportunities for serious changes as the distrust of democracy comes from the after effects of the Global Financial Crisis (RBA, n.d.).

It is worth noting, however, that there are still live examples of basic cultural valuing outside materialist market modes of economic policies. A clear local example can be seen and learned from Australia's First Nations. Despite assimilation efforts since colonisation in the late eighteenth century, Indigenous values and traditions in harmony to country continue to survive. Social structures and the collective integration of cohesive modes of living offer clear examples of integrating functional social groupings, even when at odds with current 'mainstream' models. Instead of imposing paid work-related obligations, with punitive conditions, there is much to learn by revaluing the self-determined alternatives First Nations offer for living on country and maintaining cultural responsibilities. These communities could thrive on adequate unconditional payments, but they will be meeting entrenched opposition from the mindsets discussed above.

The Current Scene

Defining what matters as the dominance of access to paid work has become the determinant of a good life, but from a feminist viewpoint, this is seriously problematic. Many factors are rising up and signalling the problems of focussing on this one area of equality. The changing nature of work due to the rise of artificial intelligence (AI) and machine learning is occurring so rapidly entire sectors are now expected to not exist for human work within decades. Former Google China president Kai-Fu Lee (2018) says, 'If we look at what AI cannot do, there are really two main things. One is creative jobs. Jobs like scientists, storytellers, artists and so on. And the other are the compassionate people who really have created a human-to-human connection, trust'.

Therefore, it is time to walk away from gender biased definitions and approaches. Good societies must reclaim, retain and reinvent more collective cultures, with fair redistribution based on needs and well-being in the undervalued feminised areas.

How a Universal BI Can Value Unpaid Social Contributions?

The revived interest in universal payments that are not related to workforce participation offers feminists the opportunity to devise new versions and definitions of such payments. A Basic Income (BI) can be a cornerstone to creating a future that re-values currently unpaid social roles and underpaid feminised jobs, by creating new ways of recognising social contributions as a collective recognition of both citizen rights and responsibilities. In doing so, the latter does not need to be defined and dependent on paid roles and/or profits.

I am not advocating a BI as a form of conditional welfare payment, but a new form of payment, a universal social dividend (USD) that distributes some common wealth.

Its objective should be to devise income support to share equitably and sustainably a community's goods and services through paid and unpaid contributions of time and skills that are not attached to gendered assumptions.

There is debate around differentiating the term 'social dividend' from basic incomes. A limited definition is that a social dividend: 'is the return on the capital assets and natural resources owned by society. The concept notably appears as a key characteristic of market socialism, where it takes the form of a dividend payment to each citizen derived from the property income generated by publicly owned enterprises, representing the individual's share of the capital and natural resources owned by society'.

The definition goes on to distinguish social dividends from a universal BI, through being connected to the actual returns on public owned entities. However, it goes on to quote the 2017 Organisation for Economic Co-operation and Development (OECD) policy brief (OECD, 2017) on basic income which recommends a social dividend as a partial alternative to BI. It sees it as a separate system from existing social protection with its function to share the benefits of technological progress and globalisation more equally.

An often-quoted example is the Alaskan payment of an oil production dividend (Goldsmith, 2011). Established in 1976, a public vote elected to preserve part of current oil production revenues for future generations. In 1982, the Alaska Permanent Fund dividend programme was created to provide an annual unconditional direct cash distribution to all Alaskan residents.

Guy Standing, a BI advocate, takes a broader view by claiming the meanings are similar and potentially interchangeable if social contributions are also counted. He says: 'a Good and Just Society must rest on some principle of social justice in which something should be equalised, whether it be income, wealth, status or opportunity to work, save, invest, and live a decent life. In this respect we claim that society should rest on a simple principle, that everybody should have basic security – to be equally free, equally protected against morbidity, and have equally good opportunity to develop their competencies and capabilities. Across a broad political spectrum, this fundamental principle is surely accepted. It defines our civilisation and our civility, the basis of our inter-generational, intra-generational and cross-national discourse' (Standing, 2005: 2).

So, as an impertinent feminist, I can see no problem in extending these assorted definitions by adding the concept of a universal payment that recognises the unpaid time contributions to social support and well-being, provided by most residents and citizens. As an equitable non-gender biased distribution of our common wealth, such a payment recognises the benefits of care and nurture and allows people to budget time for unpaid social contributions as well as economic paid ones.

The Need for Feminist Policy Leadership to Counter Male Dominated Gender Biases

Too many negative responses to the concept of a universal payment come from those who define themselves as progressive, as well the usual conservative objectors. The fact detractors cover this spectrum, with objections resting on the assumption that paid work must remain the primary desirable income stream (Hunter, 2017), reinforces the gendered biases of the debate.

Most people do not fit the model of the *homo economicus,* a self-interested individual materially driven to accumulate wealth. But the assumption that that definition fits the majority underpins neo market-based policy models. In turn, those models aggravate gender power differentiation because they fail to recognise the need for non-material contributions to social well-being and interdependence.

The separation of paid work from home and community created further divided gender roles as 'paid work' became the driver of industrial production and secured for men power roles in then rising nation states. However, the changes outlined above suggest that those currently in power are unable to move outside their comfort zones to look at serious paradigm shifts to more social agendas to redress growing distrust, inequities and environmental issues (Giridharadas, 2018).

It is clear the rising influence of market-based links to gross domestic product (GDP) contributions has overtaken social needs, so women and children have lost out in current economic policy directions.

Despite the growth of feminist movements for women's rights over the past 100 years—with many successes—the current indications are still that in terms of defining our roles, women are still the second sex, that is, male defined (Thurman, 2010). Therefore, feminists need to take the lead and promote a redefining of income to address the gender disparities. We need to lead deep proper changes.

Virginia Woolf's claim for a room of her own and £500 a year offers an early example of women's need for freedom to choose how to spend their time (Woolf, 1929). The ability for most of us to have some agency in deciding how to allocate our time would be grounds for feminist claims for some form of universal BI because it would allow more options to arrange demands and common mixes of paid and unpaid roles. Woolf's call illustrates the need for both personal controls over time and the power to decide on engagement in paid and unpaid roles, including creative ones.

One of the core demands of Second Wave feminists in the 1970s was for universal funding of children's services, to give mothers and children time away from each other as part of the changes to women's roles in families and society. At the time, the rights of mothers to have paid work were questioned and the needs of children for socialisation and learning outside home were not well recognised. Views changed and by the 1980s, Australia had planned federally funded community-based care.

As one of the contributors to these changes, the following analysis is based on my subsequent experiences of the victories as short term, as more macho priorities took over by the turn of the century.

For example, in my experience as an early advocate for child care policies I remember adding emphasis on economic, rather than social, benefits to get funding, hoping that the social side of care would survive, but this was not to be. On July 2, 2018, the Federal Coalition Government implemented changes to child care funding that removed the idea that children had a right to access children's services as part of their development as well-rounded future citizens, as well as their carers' right to relief from care time (Bedo, 2018).

This funding change removed subsidies for those children whose primary parent-carer (mainly mothers) was not contributing paid work to GDP or attempting to do so, as well as paying only for the hours of paid work or related roles. It illustrates both on the over emphasis of paid work as the best contribution to public well-being and the omission of valuing social contributions.

This example shows how potentially useful changes can be undermined. These recent changes ignored both the time spent mainly by women on care and their ability to decide how to allocate their care and earning time. Major policy changes need to address those basic assumptions that negate the positive changes driven by female intentions, being overridden by male-dominant viewpoints.

This experience is why feminism needs to promote a BI model that hopefully also changes the male-driven focus on paid work and economic goals. Feminist changes, more generally over the past three decades, have been severely limited by the dominance of market paradigms which reward individuated macho, overly masculinised economic gains.

However, times are changing. The decade long fallout of the 2007–2009 Global Financial Crisis (GFC) has shown the wider ill effects of the competitive distrust model's failure to deliver any trickle-down benefits.

The failures to ensure good jobs for all and increasing anxieties about both technology and climate damage raise other doubts on the value per se, of paid work, as the affirming status for people, as this view has many inbuilt flaws. These need to be addressed, both from feminist and wider social well-being viewpoints.

The Issues That an USD/BI Could Address

Fixing the Gender Pay Gap for Work of Equal Value

This has been a core demand of the feminist agenda since the Basic Wage decision of 1908 set up lower pay for women. In 1972, the incoming Australian Labor Party (ALP) Federal Government under Gough Whitlam took the case to the Commonwealth Conciliation and Arbitration Commission (now the Australian Industrial Relations Commission), which approved it (National Museum of Australia, n.d.). Yet the pay gap persists, with women still earning on average, up to 20% less per hour, over many years with a pay gap favouring men in most industries (Workplace Gender Equality Agency, 2018). The systemic devaluing of paid work which is service-to-people based continues to have a concentration of women in the lower paid jobs.

The Valorisation of Long Full-Time Working Hours

One suspects the focus on the presumed virtues of longer working hours may have support from men wanting to continue the perceived male privilege of being too busy to share care and avoid the need to go home early enough to contribute to cooking dinners. Otherwise, it is hard to fathom why the evidence above is consistently ignored. The last serious debate on cutting full-time defined hours in Australia was in the 1970s, with actual average full-time hours growing after that 35 hour week decision.

There is a widespread perception that a part-time work commitment is incompatible with being a serious worker or career oriented. This explains the failure of many women, and a few men, seeking or being awarded deserved promotions, as most women need shorter and more flexible hours while juggling family responsibilities. As 46% of women are employed part time, and others seeking time off for care needs, this also goes a long way to explaining the continuing gender pay gap.

According to a report by the Australian Human Rights Commission (2014), discrimination on the basis of pregnancy and parental responsibilities is pervasive and includes job loss or reduction of hours, missed promotions, inappropriate low expectations of competence, and antagonism to taking parental leave and flexible working conditions on return. Note, the report shows that men who take on primary parenting responsibilities suffer similar disadvantages in many cases.

The potential effects of a universal BI offer a useful starting point to address so many serious problems deriving from the rigidities of dependence on the current over validation of long paid working hours. The concept has the capacity to address a range of other related problems, so it offers possible examples of radical good policy change, depending on its design.

Making the Case for a Universal BI

The following sections look at issues that need to be considered in any campaign for changes to our income provision and support policies. Reframing a payment as a social dividend—that is, a recognition that societies' well-being depends on most people's unpaid jobs—would redefine the valuing of paid over unpaid work so these are not gendered hierarchies. Budgeting time rather than money would allow people to have second thoughts about many of the tasks that can and do make their lives more possible and enjoyable. In the English language at least, this would mean the term 'women's work', which devalues many essential tasks, could be abolished.

Recognising the Unpaid Work Contributions

These often-feminised roles include parents, carers, neighbours, community members, or others in socially useful roles who offer time and/or skills unpaid, for example, volunteering, sports training, singing in choirs, organising events, and so on. None of these activities are counted in GDP because they are not traded for cash or its equivalent.

Campaigners for an unconditional income argue this payment would not constitute money for nothing, since more than 50% of work is currently unpaid forms of care work (Bregman, 2018). This work is typically carried out by women and often compels economic dependency on men, thus creating systemic discrimination and creating conditions conducive to dependency and the gender pay gap.

PricewaterhouseCoopers' (PWC) Understanding the Unpaid Economy report (Thorpe, Tyson, & Neilsen, 2017) estimated that the Australian economy would be one third bigger if unpaid work was included in the national accounts. Unpaid childcare, if added to the formal economy, would be the biggest single 'industry' in Australia. It says: 'Quantifying and valuing the time spent on unpaid childcare implies that it is a $345 billion sector (in 2011 terms), almost three times the financial and insurance services industry, the largest industry in the formal economy'.

Upvaluing unpaid work is fundamental to creating social and financial equity. Policies, such as some form of universal payment, are needed because any other form of valuing such complex contributions would be overly bureaucratic and judgemental.

Creating More Flexible and Shorter Paid Working Hours

One of the main factors that determines the gender gap is the difference between male and female paid hours. The concepts of full-time and part-time work are really out of date. Even in full-time work women are more likely to work shorter hours because of unpaid responsibilities.

Globalisation, 24/7 trading, technological advancements and broader issues about the future of paid work, suggests the need for flexibility in revaluing and setting shorter and flexible working hours. Another factor is the increasing indicator that shorter working hours offer benefits in both productivity and life satisfaction (Lufkin, 2018).

Author and journalist Rutger Bregman (2018) says:

> Excessive work and pressure are status symbols. If we worked less we'd make fewer errors, address inequality and have a better life. Had one asked John Maynard Keynes what the biggest challenge of the twenty-first century would be, he wouldn't have had to think twice. Leisure.

> … Countless studies have shown that people who work less are more satisfied with their lives. In a recent poll conducted among working women, German researchers quantified the 'perfect day'. The largest share of minutes (106) would go toward 'intimate relationships'. Down at the bottom of the list were work (36) and commuting (33). (Bregman, 2018)

The evidence that part-time workers often deliver higher per hour productivity has been available for a long time but has rarely been acted on by those seeking workplace change. The reasons, in gender terms, seem to be a consequence of the out of date but still widely held views of the 'sanctity' and virtues of paid work per se (Ashford & Kallis, 2013).

Fixing Seriously Flawed Malfunctioning Social Security Payments System

The beliefs underlying the debates on welfare and economic policies valorise paid work and limit our access to 'unearned' public income. Australia's attempt to be 'the working man's paradise' (John Curtin Prime Ministerial Library, 2002) last century led to a welfare system that was heavily means tested, conditional and focused on avoiding 'bludgers' to reduce costs and tax levels. Traditional models of tightly defined welfare payments are neither adequate or fair, nor can the current structures deal with the possibility of reduced paid work and demand for labour.

Federal government forms of financial support are expensive, controlling and ineffective. The major focus of the social security system is on pressuring people to find paid work and/or justifying their incapacity to do so. This characterises the failure to earn income as a personal defect that needs to be fixed.

Major reform (Arthur, n.d.) is required to counter the shame and stigma damages done to most recipients, particularly those unfairly affected by structural barriers. Currently, the system for working age recipients does not allow for other unpaid activities, except limited, conditional payments for approved forms of care of very young children or those requiring extensive personal care. These are available but with the primary ongoing assumptions that the National Disability Insurance

Scheme (NDIS) or child care will increase carer and recipient access to paid work. Only some activities are deemed to have economic value and are failing to shift the system to less punitive systems (Cox, 2017).

Designing the Options for a Universal Social Dividend

There is a serious need to view BI through a feminist lens and included feminist options to ensure gender inequity issues of the current over emphasis on paid work as some intrinsic virtue are addressed.

A universal BI also needs to be renamed to a USD. This would redefine such income as produced by valuing wide-ranging unpaid contributions to collective social well-being and counter some of the materialist gender inequities of economic models.

Paying all citizens and long-term residents a basic income to cover essentials, for example at pension levels, would give both employed and not employed people more ability to choose how they could allocate their time. Gendered beliefs and habits may continue to divide unpaid work and paid work roles, but the financial possibilities of men reducing paid hours and gaining more status and pleasure from unpaid roles will offer the potential to reduce the differences. It would substantially increase the income of those on part welfare payments (Ingles & Plunkett, 2016).

The USD concept, in its pure form, should be an entitlement to a universal basic level of income, not means-tested, but taxed. Those with high incomes and continuing well-paid work would retain little or none of the payment. But those with lower or no other income would gain the capacity to choose what mix of paid and unpaid work would meet their own needs and that of their family and community.

Given the future of paid work is not clear, a USD could offer a secure base to build on, and ensure that continued underpaid and unpaid roles were also supplemented. It would assist workers' security if they are in the gig economy (Featherstone, 2018), and/or give people the choice to reject unacceptable or inappropriate work, or to negotiate better pay offers.

Importantly, in many ways, it would also fill the gender pay gaps left by the unpaid and underpaid feminised activities that disrupt paid work time, as well as ability to choose more creative pursuits.

As a wealthy country, redefining the payment as a USD would mean the payment would be presented as people's share of the benefits of our resources. It would be evidence for recipients/voters that their government did respect and reward their contributions in many ways. It would validate contributions to the common good, made by citizens, and so would also act to counter some of the current distrust of democracy and those in power. Such a form of social contract would indicate that those in power support dignity and security for all.

A USD would allow society to move away from assuming that wages/earned incomes are the only valid forms of income. If there was a redistribution of paid work and if everyone received a basic income that covered core costs, this could deliver freedom and greater choices to all. These changes would allow governments more space to plan for less paid work, shorter working hours and more environmental work and social volunteers.

The evidence from various trials overseas does not support the assumption, often stated, that the removing of pressure to find paid work would result in sloth. The data from Canada's Mincome trial in Manitoba in the 1970s and others shows that this type of income does not necessarily reduce contributions of paid time but often creates wider involvement in paid and unpaid work (Forget, 2011).

From a feminist point of view, it would serve to recognise our unpaid social contributions, and underpay rates. Instead of the market model focus on traded goods and traded time to achieve individual material gains, we would be paid public support for our unpaid work. Such a payment would allay anxieties about a lack of paid work undermining social cohesion by creating divisive debates on who would suffer from income redistribution.

Both men and women could explore how to make much less gender-based decisions about allocating time and money, were the basic question of how to pay for essentials not such a major issue. It would supplement those reducing income by taking on fewer paid hours and assist those without access to paid work by ensuring they had some income entitlements to depend on.

Conclusion

Feminist groups are still too focused on paid work, so generally have not yet addressed the idea of alternatives such as a universal basic payment. Official policy responses from neoliberal, affected policy makers assume the solution to female income inadequacies is to make women act like men in their choice of jobs, time commitments and replace by purchase the social services needed.

Feminism needs to recognise that advocacy for redefining sources of financial equity should create more civil societies when contributions are accepted on gender balanced terms. Only then can women claim their legitimate shares of power and control, and stop being the second sex, that is being defined by masculinised values.

References

Arthur, D. (n.d.). Welfare – Where to reform? Parliamentary library briefing book. *Parliament of Australia*. https://www.aph.gov.au/About_Parliament/Parliamentary_Departments/Parliamentary_Library/pubs/BriefingBook45p/WelfareReform

Ashford, N. A., & Kallis, G. (2013, April 30). A four-day workweek: A policy for improving employment and environmental conditions in Europe. *The European Financial Review*. http://www.europeanfinancialreview.com/?p=902

Australian Human Rights Commission. (2014, October 31). *Supporting working parents: Pregnancy and return to work national review*. https://www.humanrights.gov.au/our-work/sex-discrimination/projects/supporting-working-parents-pregnancy-and-return-work-national

Bedo, S. (2018, May 31). *Push to get families registered for government's new childcare subsidy: What it means for you*. News.com.au. https://www.news.com.au/lifestyle/parenting/push-to-get-families-registered-for-governments-new-childcare-subsidy-what-it-means-for-you/news-story/4365b42ad6ec237b7d733b4f3ef7ac19

Bregman, R. (2018, April 18). The solution to (nearly) everything: Working less. *The Guardian*. https://www.theguardian.com/commentisfree/2016/apr/18/solution-everything-working-less-work-pressure

Britannica. (2018). *Welfare State, Encyclopaedia Britannica*. https://www.britannica.com/topic/welfare-state

Commonwealth of Australia. (2012). *Sir Richard Kirby Archives, harvester case summary*. http://ww3.e-airc.gov.au/archives/harvester

Cox, E. (2017, September 5). Welfare needs a radical restructuring. *Pro Bono Australia*. https://probonoaustralia.com.au/news/2017/09/welfare-needs-radical-restructuring/

Featherstone, T. (2018, September 6). Where is the gig economy taking us? *The Sydney Morning Herald*. https://www.smh.com.au/business/small-business/where-is-the-gig-economy-taking-us-20180904-p501p1.html

Forget, E. (2011, October 1). *The town with no poverty: The health effects of a Canadian guaranteed annual income field experiment*. https://www.utpjournals.press/doi/abs/10.3138/cpp.37.3.283

Giridharadas, A. (2018, August 24). Beware rich people who say they want to change the world. *The New York Times*. https://www.nytimes.com/2018/08/24/opinion/sunday/wealth-philanthropy-fake-change.html?rref=collection%2Fbyline%2Fanand-giridharadas&action=click&contentCollection=undefined&region=stream&module=stream_unit&version=latest&contentPlacement=3&pgtype=collect

Goldsmith, S. (2011). *The Alaska Permanent Fund dividend: A case study in the direct distribution of resource rent*. https://scholarworks.alaska.edu/handle/11122/4161

Hunter, B. (2017, September 8). The top three arguments against a universal basic income. *Foundation for Economic Education*. https://fee.org/articles/the-top-three-arguments-against-a-universal-basic-income/

Ingles, D., & Plunkett, D. (2016, August). *Tax and transfer policy institute policy brief: Effective marginal tax rates*. Tax and Transfer Policy Institute, Crawford School of Public Policy, The Australian National University. https://taxpolicy.crawford.anu.edu.au/files/uploads/taxstudies_crawford_anu_edu_au/2016-08/ingles_plunkett_policy_brief_1_2016_last.pdf

Lee, K. (2018, September 17). If they don't want to lose their jobs to a machine, doctors will need to become compassionate 'human connectors'. *Recode Decode*. https://www.recode.net/2018/9/17/17867990/kai-fu-lee-ai-superpowers-book-artificial-intelligence-jobs-doctors-kara-swisher-decode-podcast

Lufkin, B. (2018, August 29). Just how short could we make the working week? *BBC Capital*. http://www.bbc.com/capital/story/20180828-just-how-short-could-we-make-the-workweek

National Museum of Australia. (n.d.). *Defining moments: Equal pay for women*. http://www.nma.gov.au/defining-moments/resources/equal-pay-for-women

OECD. (2017, May). *Basic income as a policy option: Can it add up?* http://www.oecd.org/employment/emp/Basic-Income-Policy-Option-2017.pdf

Reserve Bank of Australia. (n.d.). *The global financial crisis* [PDF]. https://www.rba.gov.au/education/resources/explainers/

Shaping the Nation: John Curtin and Australia. (2002). *John Curtin Prime Ministerial Library*. http://john.curtin.edu.au/shapingthenation/htm/theme1.htm

Standing, G. (2005). About time: Basic income security as a right. In I. Parker (Ed.), *Promoting income security as a right: Europe and North America* (pp. 1–40). London: Anthem Press.

Thorpe, J., Tyson, R., & Neilsen, N. (2017, March). *Understanding the unpaid economy*. https://www.pwc.com.au/australia-in-transition/publications/understanding-the-unpaid-economy-mar17.pdf

Thurman, J. (2010, May 27). Introduction to Simone de Beauvoir's 'The Second Sex'. *The New York Times*. https://www.nytimes.com/2010/05/30/books/excerpt-introduction-second-sex.html

Weber, M. (1948). *Essays in sociology*. London, UK: Routledge.

Woolf, V. (1929). *A room of one's own*. London, UK: Hogarth Press.

Workplace Gender Equality Agency. (2018). https://www.wgea.gov.au/

5

Basic Income and Cultural Participation for Remote-Living Indigenous Australians

Jon Altman and Francis Markham

Settler Colonialism and Surplus Populations

It is symptomatic of Australia's colonial history and post-colonising[1] present that unemployment, and consequently cash poverty, is at dire levels among Indigenous peoples. In 2016, just 46.6 per cent of Indigenous people of working age were employed, compared with 71.8 per cent of non-Indigenous Australians (Venn & Biddle, 2018); in that

[1] Here we use the term post-colonising after Moreton-Robinson (2015), where the term refers to the active and continuing nature of non-Indigenous colonial occupation of Australia, as distinct from post-colonial contemporary multiculturalism.

J. Altman (✉)
Australian National University, Canberra, ACT, Australia

Deakin University, Geelong, VIC, Australia
e-mail: jon.altman@deakin.edu.au

F. Markham
Australian National University, Canberra, ACT, Australia
e-mail: francis.markham@anu.edu.au

E. Klein et al. (eds.), *Implementing a Basic Income in Australia*, Exploring the Basic Income Guarantee, https://doi.org/10.1007/978-3-030-14378-7_5

same year an estimated 31.4 per cent of Indigenous people were living in households below the poverty line (Markham & Biddle, 2018a). The economic impoverishment of Indigenous people is particularly acute in what is generally referred to in policy and public discourse as 'remote Australia', that sparsely populated part of the continent where just 1.5 per cent of the non-Indigenous population lives, in contrast to 18.7 per cent of Indigenous peoples (Markham & Biddle, 2018b).[2] Indigenous poverty is growing in prevalence in very remote Australia, with poverty rates reaching 53.4 per cent in 2016. Working-age Indigenous employment rates in that same region were just 30.1 per cent in the same year. Consequently, Indigenous people rely on the Australian state for income support and are highly vulnerable to policy fluctuations, sometimes called 'reform' and always presented by the politically powerful as beneficial. Vulnerability to state coercion is greatest in the remotest parts of the country.

The present-day economic deprivation of Indigenous peoples can be attributed in large measure to the colonisation process (Walter & Andersen, 2013). The spread of the frontier across the Australian continent was intended to supplant Indigenous peoples and their diverse economies, largely replacing Indigenous livelihoods with colonial capitalism (Altman & Biddle, 2014; Hunter, 2014). The invasion of Indigenous territory was driven by settlers' desire to control land and its resources, a territoriality that Patrick Wolfe (2006) has argued necessitates the elimination of Indigenous societies, at times by genocidal means, at times by other means. In the process of usurping Indigenous land, sustainable and largely self-sufficient Indigenous economies were everywhere destroyed. In Coulthard's (2014) Marxian account, the separation of Indigenous peoples from control over their means of social reproduction—land—rendered them a dispossessed class, positioned by colonial occupation in opposition to settler society. Indigenous people who survived the triple onslaught of disease, settler violence and the destruction of livelihoods

[2] Clearly what is termed 'remote' from the perspective of the settler society is not remote for Indigenous people who have occupied these regions for millennia. Relying in this chapter on official statistics, we adopt the Australian Bureau of Statistics' definition of remoteness, a classification that is best considered an index of inaccessibility to population centres and consequently services (Holmes, 2009).

were—from the perspective of the capitalist state—transformed into a surplus population whose labour was peripheral to the economy. While Indigenous people were often dependent on the settler economy to survive, the reverse was rarely true. Indigenous labour was seldom of structural importance to the settler economy except perhaps in the pastoral industry prior to mechanisation (Fijn, Keen, Lloyd, & Pickering, 2012; Keen, 2010).

However, colonisation was historically and geographically uneven. While the settler project of value extraction began in south-eastern Australia in the late eighteenth century, in remote regions the colonial frontier did not arrive until the late nineteenth to mid-twentieth centuries. Successive settler-colonial state policy interventions aimed at 'protection' (to the 1950s) and assimilation (officially in the period 1961–1972) resulted in the centralisation of Indigenous people in missions and government settlements with no economic base. The sparsity of the settler population in remote Australia reflects the unsuitability of the land for intensive commercial agriculture owing to climatic, environmental and other factors. In market-economic terms, the land in remote Australia was and remains of little value as a factor of production, with the notable exemptions of scattered mining enclaves and sprawling pastoral runs.

The marginal economic value of remote lands explains the relative incompleteness of the settler-colonial project of expropriation and elimination in remote parts of Australia. Furthermore, the marginal economic value of remote lands explains the contemporary colonial ambivalence to remote-living Indigenous people, where on the one hand the state has facilitated the return of vast areas of land (Altman & Markham, 2015), and on the other continues to perpetuate eliminationist policies (Altman, 2018a). A vast 'territory of difference', to borrow Arturo Escobar's (2008) evocative term, now exists across about 40 per cent of Australia's landmass. In this region, less than 20 per cent of the population are settlers and almost all land is controlled with variable rights of exclusion and control by Indigenous land owners (Altman & Markham, 2015).

The economy of this 'territory of difference' is overdetermined by its history. Its primary residents are Indigenous peoples, whose self-sufficiency was destroyed by colonial invasion, and who now inhabit land that is seldom of value in the capitalist market economy.

Consequently, demand for waged labour in these places is chronically deficient. Fewer than one-in-three Indigenous people in very remote Australia are in formal employment, and 70 per cent of those unemployed report a lack of local jobs as the most important barrier preventing them from finding paid work (Altman & Markham, 2018). Half of the jobs that do exist are in the state-funded provision of education, health and social care and public administration, with a further 10 per cent of jobs in the Indigenous not-for-profit sector.[3] Put simply, in the remotest parts of Australia, the market provides paid employment to only 12 per cent of Indigenous people of working age, with the majority forming a surplus population whose labour is of no apparent value for capital accumulation. Instead, remote-living Indigenous people operate by necessity and by choice in a 'hybrid economy', that includes both state and market sectors but also a customary or non-market sector with similarities to pre-colonial hunting and gathering for livelihood (Altman, 2009). Although the closure of the market is far from complete even in the metropolitan Global North (Gibson-Graham, 1996), in very remote Australia the mainstream labour market comprehensively fails to provide a livelihood for the vast majority of its Indigenous inhabitants.

The Community Development Employment Projects Scheme as Basic Income

It was this context of barely existing labour markets and few prospects for market-linked economic development the long-running Community Development Employment Projects scheme (henceforth CDEP) was introduced in 1977. CDEP was innovatively designed to allow the provision of block grants from the Commonwealth government to local Indigenous organisations such as councils or incorporated bodies to create part-time jobs for Indigenous people. But where there were no work

[3] In the 2016 Census, 49.8 per cent of employed Indigenous people living Very Remote areas were employed in ANZIC Divisions 'O', 'P' and 'Q', a classification which excludes a further 11.7 per cent working in the largely state-funded Indigenous sector, classified as 'S9559' or 'Other Interest Group Services'.

opportunities, especially when people lived at small outstation or homeland communities, CDEP was paid as a basic income with no work requirements beyond those negotiated with community leaders (Altman, 2016). CDEP was principally funded by the national social security benefit entitlements of participants. Significantly, those participating in the scheme were paid award wages and were classified as employed. The scheme was extremely successful according to a number of official metrics. At its peak in 2003, it provided one-third of the jobs occupied by Indigenous people nationally (Jordan & Altman, 2016). Despite these successes, CDEP was effectively abolished from 1 July 2013 with the establishment of the work-for-the-dole-linked Remote Jobs and Communities Program, with a few remnant 'grandfathered' participants continuing till 30 June 2015.[4] This abolition coincided with a shift in government policy that critiqued any form of self-determination and saw Indigenous policy takes a neoliberal paternalist turn (see Jordan, 2016). In its place, successive governments in the last decade have implemented punitive workfare style schemes that have attempted to train and discipline Indigenous people to enter labour markets that have few or no jobs to offer.

This chapter affords no opportunity to properly outline the history and character of CDEP (but see Altman, 2016; Altman & Sanders, 1991; Jordan, 2016; Morphy & Sanders, 2004; Sanders, 1988, 2012). Instead, we reiterate an argument made elsewhere (Altman, 2016; Altman & Klein, 2018) that in its institutional design, CDEP had certain characteristics that made it similar to both basic income and job guarantee schemes. CDEP had five distinguishing features: it was community controlled; participation was voluntary; it was not workfare; it was flexible, allowing for culturally productive and valued forms of labour falling outside the formal economy; and it emphasised, community development allowing Indigenous organisations the autonomy to pursue forms of 'development' that aligned with local aspirations and priorities focus (Altman & Klein, 2018). CDEP was not designed as a basic income scheme, but over its life it was refigured to operate in this way. Indeed, CDEP became the nearest institutional arrangement to basic income seen in Australia to date.

[4] A statistically negligible 2220 people remained grandfathered on CDEP by 16 March 2015 (Hunter, 2016).

Statistical studies of the impacts of CDEP during this period have typically compared standard economic indicators of scheme participants with non-participants at a single point in time. These studies have found that those participating in CDEP had higher average incomes than the unemployed or those not in the labour force (Altman & Gray, 2000; Altman, Gray, & Levitus, 2005; Sanders, 1997) and reduced financial stress (Hunter, 2009). Other findings include an increased likelihood for CDEP participants to have undertaken vocation education than the unemployed or those not in the labour force (Altman et al., 2005; Hunter, 2009) and a decreased incidence of social harms such as violence victimisation, arrest and substance abuse (Hunter, 2009).

One previous study examined customary and cultural (non-market) activities undertaken by CDEP participants (Altman et al., 2005). It found that more CDEP participants engaged in such activities than either the unemployed or those in mainstream employment. CDEP is likely to have directly and indirectly supported Indigenous cultural life in several ways. Most directly, CDEP participants may have been tasked with customary activities such as land management or cultural production as part of their CDEP duties. Indirectly, the CDEP may have subsidised cultural activities through the provision of cash incomes that were greater than those available to the unemployed. These incomes may have been expended on vehicles and fuel essential today for engagement in customary and cultural activities. Furthermore, CDEP strengthened the Indigenous sector more broadly, especially those organisations which administered the scheme. This increased organisational capacity is likely to have also increased the ability of organisations to support cultural participation (Altman, 2016). That such an effect might exist is hardly surprising given that one of the primary aims of basic income schemes is to increase the capacity of people to pursue their individual and collective goals beyond those mandated by the labour market (Parijs, 2017).

However, it is difficult to attribute the correlations between CDEP participation and customary and cultural activities identified by Altman et al. (2005) just to CDEP. Because of the cross-sectional nature of this research, it is possible that some of the differences between the outcomes for CDEP participants compared to non-participants are the result of underlying differences between these groups of individuals that are unrelated to CDEP. It is always important not to confuse statistical correlation with causality. As an example, substance abuse might be lower among CDEP participants than the unemployed because substance abuse precludes participation rather than because CDEP participation reduces the prevalence of substance abuse (Hunter, 2009). Similar critiques might be made of other correlations between customary and cultural activities and CDEP. The findings for other outcomes appear to be more robust, due to the likely monodirectionality of plausible causal effects. For example, the links between CDEP and income are much more likely to be causal given that CDEP participation was directly remunerated with award wages.

In our view, the abolition of CDEP and its replacement with a punitive workfare regime are regrettable for a number of reasons including that it deepens the poverty experienced by Indigenous people who are unemployed (Altman & Markham, 2018; Jordan, 2016). But this abolition does afford a rare opportunity to investigate how the scheme that we might take as a proxy for basic income affected participants. This is what social scientists sometimes refer to as a 'natural experiment', an unintended possibility to check on the effects of a scheme because of the availability of before-and-after information. No quantitative studies of the impact of the abolition of CDEP have been published, with the single exception being Venn and Biddle's (2018) preliminary analysis of census data. Examining the marked decline in Indigenous employment outcomes in remote areas between 2011 and 2016 Venn and Biddle speculatively attribute most, but not all, job losses to the abolition of CDEP.

In this chapter we examine the impact of the withdrawal of the CDEP, in order to learn more about the likely impact of a future basic-income-like programme. We investigate the relationship between access to a basic-income-like scheme and cultural flourishing. Specifically, we analyse the impact of the abolition of CDEP on three indicators of cultural activity in the National Aboriginal and Torres Strait Islander Social Survey (NATSISS) of 2002 and 2014. A simple before-and-after description of the prevalence of these three indicators is supplemented by an analysis based on a propensity score matching approach used to classify Indigenous persons according to their likelihood of participating in CDEP on the basis of their socio-demographic characteristics. Changes in the prevalence of cultural participation are then disaggregated by the propensity to participate in a CDEP-like programme.

Methods

The NATSISS is a nationally representative sample survey of the Indigenous population living in private dwellings, conducted by the Australian Bureau of Statistics (ABS). It asks Aboriginal or Torres Strait Islander household members question about their socio-economic circumstances, aspects of Indigenous cultures and their health and well-being. It is conducted in every six years, allowing for the comparison of snapshots of the Indigenous population at different points in time. We chose the 2002 NATSISS and the 2014 NATSISS intentionally, as in the former CDEP was at its peak and in the latter, it had been abolished across most of remote Australia. The 2014 NATSISS interviewed 11,178 individuals from 6611 households, with an in-scope household response rate of 80 per cent. Interviews were conducted between September 2014 and June 2015. The 2002 NATSISS interviewed 9359 Indigenous persons in 5887 households between August 2002 and April 2003, with a household response rate of 79 per cent. Further information on survey design is available from the ABS (2005, 2016).

Our analysis focuses on remote areas of Australia, where CDEP was most prevalent. Only the responses of Indigenous people of working age (i.e. aged 15–64 years) were considered. In the 2002 NATSISS, 3886 respondents met these inclusion criteria, with 2317 eligible survey respondents in the 2014 NATSISS.

Both the 2002 and 2014 NATSISS interviews asked respondents about their participation in 'cultural' activities: whether they had attended ceremonies and sports carnivals, produced art or craft, or hunted or fished. All questions referred to participation in these cultural activities within the previous 12 months, except that in the 2002 NATSISS the question on hunting and fishing referred to participation within the previous 3 months.[5] Although the questions differed slightly between surveys, wording was similar enough to make the results directly comparable, with the exception of the important livelihood question about hunting and fishing (see Table 5.1).

[5] Altman, Buchanan and Biddle (2006, p. 149) were critical of the 2002 NATSISS for potentially ignoring the economic significance of 'cultural' work like hunting and gathering and art and crafts, a critique that was ignored in subsequent 2008 and 2014 surveys.

Table 5.1 Questions about participation in cultural activities in the 2002 and 2014 NATSISS

	2002	2014
Attended ceremonies	In the last 12 months, have you gone to any Aboriginal or Torres Strait Islander ceremonies?	In the last 12 months, have you gone to or been involved in any of these Aboriginal or Torres Strait Islander cultural activities or ceremonies: Ceremonies?
Attended sports carnivals	In the last 12 months, have you gone to any Aboriginal or Torres Strait Islander sports carnivals?	In the last 12 months, have you gone to or been involved in any of these Aboriginal or Torres Strait Islander cultural activities or ceremonies: Sports carnivals?
Produced art or craft	In the last year, did you make any Aboriginal or Torres Strait Islander arts or crafts? (including activities done as part of your job)	Have you done any of the following activities in the past year: Made Aboriginal or Torres Strait Islander arts or crafts?
Hunted or fished	In the last three months, have you done anything else with other people such as going fishing or hunting in a group?	Have you done any of the following activities in the past year: Hunted? Fished?

We expect that cultural participation in ceremonies, sporting carnivals and customary food gathering would be higher during the existence of a basic-income-like programme for several reasons. Relative to those in regular employment, the CDEP generally afforded participants a greater degree of flexibility to attend to cultural events, facilitating cultural participation. Relative to the non-employed for whom workplace flexibility is not an issue, the CDEP provided resources which are likely to have assisted with the financial costs of cultural participation, such as petrol and car maintenance. The case of art and craft production is somewhat different. In many notable instances, the production of arts and crafts was undertaken as a CDEP activity, with participants receiving an income from an art centre for such production (Altman, 2005). In other places, CDEP participants may have worked in a support role in art centres, facilitating increased cultural production by others.

Responses to questions about cultural participation were tabulated and compared to show trends in cultural participation between 2002–2003 and 2014–2015. However, it is difficult to attribute trends detected using this approach to the abolition of CDEP. Cultural participation may have changed between 2002 and 2015 for reasons unrelated to the CDEP. For example, art and craft production may have declined due to the crash of the Indigenous art market in the aftermath of the Global Financial Crisis of 2007–2008 (Day, 2014; Office of the Registrar of Indigenous Corporations, 2012).

Consequently, a propensity score matching approach was taken to examine changes in cultural participation. Ideally, we would like to compare cultural participation between CDEP participants and non-participants in 2002 and 2014. However, directly identifying CDEP participants in the 2014 NATSISS is not possible, as the scheme no longer existed at that time. If suitable longitudinal data existed, we might track the changes to cultural participation after the abolition of CDEP among CDEP participants and compare that to changes in cultural participation among CDEP non-participants. Yet, no such data are available. Consequently, we use propensity score matching to build a model of the likelihood that individuals would participate in CDEP in 2002,[6] and apply that model to predict CDEP participation propensity in both the 2002 and 2014 data.

Based on this model, we classify respondents in 2002 and 2014 in terms of their likelihood to participate in CDEP if it existed. Specifically, model-based predictions of propensity to participate in CDEP were calculated, and individuals' propensity was grouped into quintiles, from least likely to participate in CDEP (Quintile 1) to most likely to participate in CDEP (Quintile 5). Using these propensity scores, we can com-

[6] Specifically, the propensity of working-age remote-living Indigenous persons to participate in the CDEP in the 2002 NATSSIS was modelled using logistic regression. Our model predicted CDEP participation of individuals on the basis of their age, sex, state or territory of residence, whether English was the main language spoken at home; whether the persons identifies with a specific Indigenous tribe, clan, language group, regional group or mission; self-assessed health status; whether the person had a profound disability; whether the person lived in a house that was owned or being purchased, rented privately or in social housing; whether the person ever attended high school and whether the person had attained a post-school qualification at Certificate III level or higher. Interaction terms and quadratic terms were used where appropriate. All predictor variables in the model were significantly associated with CDEP participation. McFadden pseudo-R^2 for the model was 0.12.

pare changes in cultural participation between likely CDEP participants and unlikely CDEP participants in a consistent way between 2002 and 2014, albeit with limited precision. All analyses were conducted using individual-level population weights calculated by the ABS.

Results

As shown in previous research (e.g. Venn & Biddle, 2018), the abolition of CDEP coincided with a decrease in employment among the Indigenous working-age population (see Table 5.2). While employment outside CDEP rose by 16.9 per cent, employment in total fell by 17.3 per cent. The fall in employment resulted in both a rise in unemployment (an increase of 7.9 per cent) and the proportion of the population outside the labour force (an increase of 9.5 per cent).

These changes in remote employment are disaggregated by propensity to participate in CDEP in Table 5.3. It shows that the model predicted CDEP participation in 2002 with moderate accuracy. In consequence, the abolition of the CDEP affected the group most likely to participate in it the hardest. Unemployment among those most likely to participate in CDEP rose by 13.7 percentage points, compared to 5.6 percentage points among those least likely to participate in CDEP. Labour force participation fell dramatically among those most likely to participate in the CDEP (25.0 percentage points), compared to a modest decrease among those unlikely to participate in the CDEP (2.7 percentage points).

Table 5.2 Labour force status of Indigenous people aged 15–64 living in remote Australia, before and after the abolition of CDEP, from the NATSISS

	2002 (%)	2014 (%)
Employed in CDEP scheme	34.2	–
Employed outside CDEP	20.2	37.1
Unemployed[a]	6.2	14.1
Not in labour force	39.4	48.9

Notes: [a] The percentage unemployed is much smaller than the familiar 'unemployment rate', as the latter does not include those not in the labour force in the denominator. The unemployment rate was 10.2 per cent in 2002 and 27.5 per cent in 2014

Table 5.3 Labour force status of Indigenous people aged 15–64 living in remote Australia, before and after the abolition of CDEP, by propensity to participate in CDEP if it existed, from the NATSISS

		Employed in CDEP scheme (%)	Employed outside CDEP (%)	Employed, total (%)	Unemployed[a] (%)	Not in the labour force (%)
2002	Quintile 1 (least likely to participate in CDEP)	10.5	38.1	48.6	4.7	46.7
	Quintile 2	20.4	25.0	45.4	5.9	48.7
	Quintile 3	32.0	15.1	47.1	4.9	47.0
	Quintile 4	46.3	11.0	57.3	7.0	35.7
	Quintile 5 (most likely to participate in CDEP)	59.2	12.2	71.4	7.4	21.1
2014	Quintile 1 (least likely to participate in CDEP)	–	45.7	45.7	10.3	44.0
	Quintile 2	–	38.1	38.1	10.2	52.7
	Quintile 3	–	32.9	32.9	13.2	53.9
	Quintile 4	–	32.9	32.9	16.9	50.2
	Quintile 5 (most likely to participate in CDEP)	–	32.8	32.8	21.1	46.1

Notes: [a] The percentage unemployed is much smaller than the familiar 'unemployment rate', as the latter does not include those not in the labour force in the denominator

Table 5.4 shows that the period 2002–2014 saw a substantial drop in participation in cultural activities among remote-living Indigenous people surveyed by the NATSISS. Specifically, 12-month participation in ceremonies and sports carnivals dropped by 12.2 and 13.4 per cent respectively. Participation in art and craft production only declined

Table 5.4 Participation in cultural activities by Indigenous people aged 15–64 living in remote Australia, before and after the abolition of CDEP, from the NATSISS

	2002 (%)	2014 (%)
Attended ceremonies	44.9	32.7
Attended sports carnivals	54.2	40.8
Produced art or craft	18.7	17.5
Hunted or fished[a]	52.0	79.2

Notes: [a] The 2002 and 2014 participation rates for hunting or fishing are not directly comparable, as the 2002 NATSISS asked about 3-month participation, where the 2014 NATSISS asked about 12-month participation

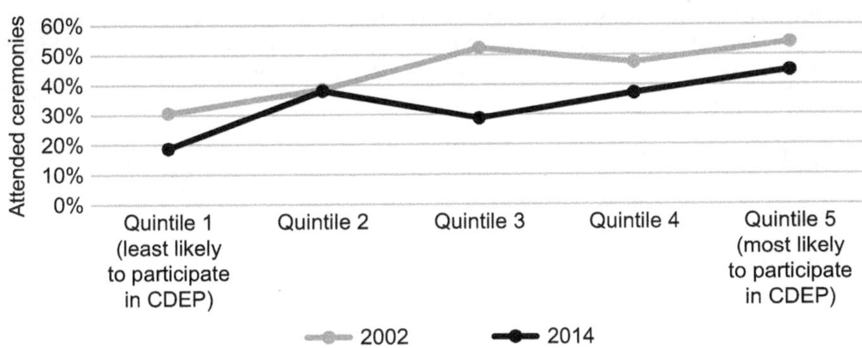

Fig. 5.1 Attendance of ceremonies in previous 12 months by Indigenous people aged 15–64 living in remote Australia, before and after the abolition of CDEP, by propensity to participate in CDEP if it existed, from the NATSISS

slightly over this period, despite the downturn in the Indigenous art market. The apparent increase in hunting and fishing is deceptive, as the 2002 and 2014 NATSISS questionnaires measured participation over different time periods.

The distribution of these changed participation rates by propensity to participate in CDEP is plotted in Figs. 5.1, 5.2, 5.3, and 5.4. Figure 5.1 shows little reduction in ceremony attendance by propensity to participate in the CDEP, with a fairly consistent drop of around 10 percentage points across propensity quintiles.

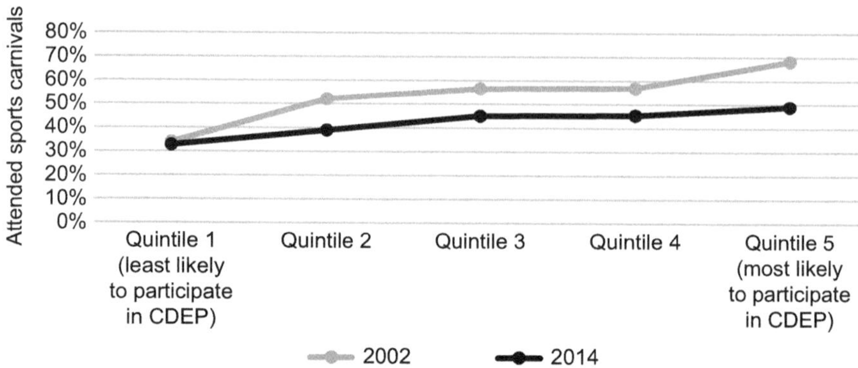

Fig. 5.2 Attendance of sports carnivals in previous 12 months by Indigenous people aged 15–64 living in remote Australia, before and after the abolition of CDEP, by propensity to participate in CDEP if it existed, from the NATSISS

Figure 5.2, however, shows that the reduction in the propensity to attend sports carnivals that is strongly patterned by propensity to participate in the CDEP. For those least likely to participate in the CDEP, there was little reduction in the sports carnival attendance (1.2 percentage points). For those in Quintiles 2, 3 and 4, however, the reduction in attendance was more substantial (13.2, 11.6 and 11.5 percentage points respectively). Finally, for those most likely to participate in CDEP, the reduction in participation was most dramatic, falling 19.2 percentage points.

In the case of arts and craft production, no clear trend emerged when examined by CDEP participation. Figure 5.3 shows that while production increased for Quintile 2 between 2002 and 2014, it decreased for Quintile 3.

Finally, in the case of hunting and fishing, interpretation is compromised by the changing time periods interrogated in the questions between the 2002 and 2014, meaning that participation rates cannot be directly compared. However, the slopes of the two lines in Fig. 5.4 can be compared. In 2002, those most likely to participate in CDEP were more likely to hunt or fish in the previous three months than those who were unlikely to participate in the CDEP. Specifically, 19.2 per cent of those in Quintile 1 hunted or fished in the previous three months in 2002, compared to 69.7 per cent in Quintile 5. By 2014, that gradient had decreased significantly, with 65.2 per cent of those in Quintile 1 hunting or fishing

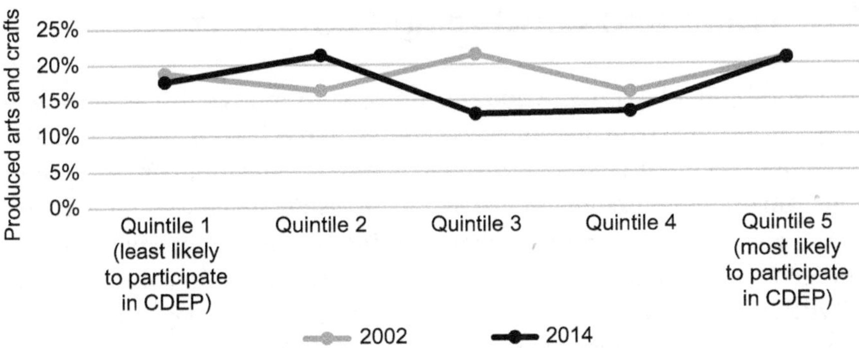

Fig. 5.3 Production of arts and crafts in previous 12 months by Indigenous people aged 15–64 living in remote Australia, before and after the abolition of CDEP, by propensity to participate in CDEP if it existed, from the NATSISS

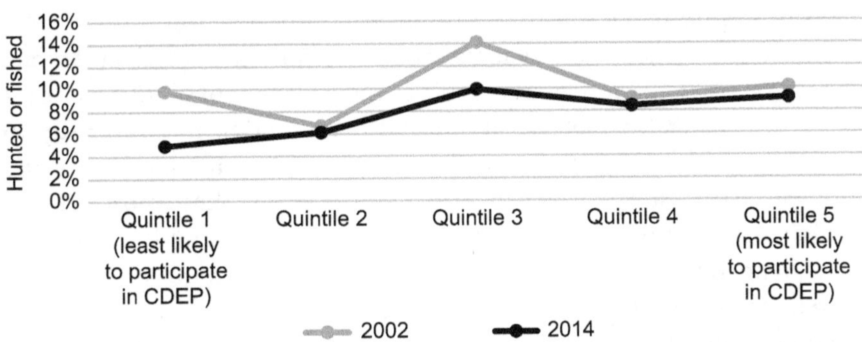

Fig. 5.4 Hunting and fishing by Indigenous people aged 15–64 living in remote Australia, before and after the abolition of CDEP, by propensity to participate in CDEP if it existed, from the NATSISS. Note that 2002 data refer to hunting or fishing in the previous 3 months, while 2014 data refer to hunting or fishing in the previous 12 months

in the previous 12 months, compared with 85.1 per cent of those in Quintile 5. While some of this pattern may be the result of those in Quintile 5 having a greater frequency of hunting and fishing, it is also consistent with a reduction in the prevalence of hunting and fishing between 2002 and 2014 among those most likely to participate in CDEP.

Discussion and Concluding Comments

The abolition of CDEP, a long-running Commonwealth government programme with basic income characteristics, has had extremely negative consequences for the employment of remote-living Indigenous people. This lamentable outcome is entirely unsurprising, given that CDEP provided employment for more than a third of the remote working-age Indigenous population in 2002. However, by examining the effects of CDEP abolition, we can learn something about the likely results if a basic income programme were introduced in remote Australia.

The abolition of CDEP coincided with a substantial drop in reported participation in cultural activities, especially attendance at ceremonies (12.2 percentage points) and attendance at sports carnivals (13.4 percentage points). The prevalence of the reported production of arts and crafts was more stable when the scheme was abolished.

Because it is unclear to what extent these reported changes in the rate of cultural participation are the result of the abolition of CDEP, we compared the change in the rate of cultural participation by propensity to participate in CDEP. Clear patterns emerged in participation in sporting carnivals, with a steep decline in participation among those most likely to participate in CDEP and almost no decline among those least likely to participate in CDEP. Such a pattern indicates that the abolition of CDEP played an important role in reducing cultural participation in this domain. Conversely, there was little evidence that changes in the rate of participation in ceremonies or arts and craft production were associated with the abolition of CDEP. It seems that other factors caused the decline in the prevalence of ceremonial attendance. Finally, the case of hunting and fishing is more difficult to interpret due to changes to the survey questionnaire. The evidence is consistent with declining patterns of food gathering and the abolition of CDEP, but it is unclear if customary food harvesting did decline over this period. The results for hunting and fishing are far from conclusive because of inconsistencies in the questions asked between the 2002 and 2014 surveys; the empirical results may be attributable to CDEP participants engaging in hunting and fishing activities more frequently than non-participants.

One caveat around these findings is that the propensity matching approach used does not precisely classify survey respondents by CDEP-participation propensity. One consequence of this is that the effects found in this study are likely to be underestimated by as much as 80 per cent. Future research using this approach might benefit from methods found in the intention-to-treat literature to adjust estimated effects to the correct magnitude (Angrist & Pischke, 2014).

CDEP was an innovative programme designed in large measure in recognition of the absence of sufficient jobs in remote Australia that has resulted from the uneven geography of settler colonisation. The abolition of CDEP has seen a substantial increase in unemployment in remote Australia and has resulted in many Indigenous people withdrawing from the labour force. This withdrawal provides a likely explanation for rising poverty rates in remote Australia (Markham & Biddle, 2018a).

In the absence of CDEP, new approaches are needed both to alleviate poverty and to facilitate the cultural flourishing of remote-living Indigenous people. All people have a right to remain on the land that they own, especially Indigenous people living remotely who have particularly strong ontological links to their ancestral lands. The exercise of such a right to live on their lands (or to leave if they so wish) requires economic redistribution, potential via state support of Indigenous forms of livelihood where labour market and commercial opportunity might be absent. State support might come directly through payments to alleviate cash poverty and indirectly through the support of sustainable livelihoods.

One way for this to occur is via the introduction of a scheme to provide a minimum guaranteed income alongside supplementary opportunities for individual or collective enterprise. This is how CDEP operated when it worked well (see, for example, the case studies in Jordan, 2016; Morphy & Sanders, 2004). This chapter demonstrates that the benefits of the introduction of a basic income scheme would not be limited to poverty alleviation but would also lie in the realm of cultural participation. To the extent that a basic income scheme would reverse the economic, social and cultural harms caused by the abolition of CDEP, any basic income programme would be expected to increase cultural participation. Such increased participation is likely to include country food self-provisioning, which not only maintains Indigenous cultural vitality, but could also play an important economic role in poverty alleviation. Policy that alleviates the material deprivation of Indigenous people will also lead to their cultural flourishing.

The implementation of an Indigenous-specific basic income scheme nationally is likely to encounter a range of practical difficulties. First, political resistance from elements of non-Indigenous society would be expected, with accusations of 'reverse racism' likely. Such objections are unjust—Australia has never paid reparations to Indigenous peoples for their dispossession and mistreatment, except in the case of manifestly inadequate stolen wages redress schemes (Kinnane, Harrison, & Reinecke, 2015). A great debt of reparations for stolen and degraded land (Altman, 2018b), violence and other numerous forms of expropriation is owed by the state to Australia's Indigenous peoples. In this context, a national Indigenous basic income might be construed as offering those whose material interests have been harmed by colonialisation a rightful share of Australia's wealth (Ferguson, 2015). Second and more problematically, the introduction of a national, Indigenous-only basic income scheme of any serious magnitude would face the difficulty of determining eligibility. A single criterion of self-identification would be too imprecise to be useful, while the three-criteria definition of Indigeneity that includes recognition by other Aboriginal and Torres Strait Islander peoples may be overly exclusionary and lead to political conflict (Carlson, 2016).

While remaining in favour of reparations nationally as a separate policy goal, we argue that an initial basic income scheme limited to those remote areas with dysfunctional to non-existent labour markets is more readily achievable and politically palatable. Such a proposal—which would explicitly not be a form of redress—would have several advantages over a national Indigenous basic income scheme. First, it would be more affordable, as it would cover well under 20 per cent of the Indigenous population. Basic income costs would be offset by a substantial degree by the relatively high rates of welfare receipt in remote areas, and would enable the abolition of a futile and punitive workfare scheme which costs over $10,000 per participant per year simply to administer (The Auditor General, 2017). Second, because eligibility for a scheme would be assessed on the basis of geographical labour markets rather than ethnic origin, difficulties in determining the Indigeneity of citizens would be eliminated, even though we would anticipate that the vast majority of recipients would be Indigenous. For this reason, this scheme would be less likely to encounter political resistance, either from Indigenous peoples themselves or from populist opponents.

We remain in favour of a universal basic income scheme for Australia as a whole. However, such a scheme need not be implemented in a single phase. A remote basic income scheme might be considered as the first step towards a truly universal scheme. Our geographic targeting might easily precede or complement the demographic targeting suggested by Spies-Butcher and Henderson (this volume) as the first priority for implementing basic income in Australia.

The parlous state of remote labour markets makes the introduction of a basic income scheme in remote Australia a matter of policy urgency given the inappropriateness of the current approach based on the unrealistic expectation that people will find standard forms of mainstream work in situations where no or few opportunities exist. The analysis in this chapter supports the broader proposition that the introduction of a basic income scheme could lead to self-determined human flourishing (Parijs, 2017). Rather than experiencing the discipline (and associated punishment) imposed by the wage-labour relationship in situations where there are few jobs, individuals could be liberated to pursue the activities of greatest importance to them, activities that will generate economic, social and cultural benefits not just to individuals but also to their families and communities.

References

Altman, J. C. (2005). *Brokering Aboriginal art: A critical perspective on marketing, institutions, and the state* (Kenneth Myer Lecture in Arts & Entertainment Management). Geelong, VIC: Deakin University.

Altman, J. C. (2009). The hybrid economy and anthropological engagements with policy discourse: A brief reflection. *The Australian Journal of Anthropology, 20*(3), 318–329. https://doi.org/10.1111/j.1757-6547.2009.00039.x

Altman, J. C. (2016). Basic income for remote Indigenous Australians: Prospects for a livelihoods approach in neoliberal times. In J. Mays, G. Marston, &

J. Tomlinson (Eds.), *Basic income in Australia and New Zealand: Perspectives from the neoliberal frontier* (pp. 179–205). Houndmills, UK/New York: Palgrave Macmillan.

Altman, J. C. (2018a). Raphael Lemkin in remote Australia: The logic of cultural genocide and homelands. *Oceania, 88*(3), 336–359.

Altman, J. C. (2018b, May). Threatened Aboriginal country and the right to proper redress. *Land Rights News – Northern Edition*, 19–21.

Altman, J. C., & Biddle, N. (2014). Refiguring Indigenous economies: A 21st-century perspective. In S. Ville & G. Withers (Eds.), *The Cambridge economic history of Australia* (pp. 530–554). Melbourne, VIC: Cambridge University Press. https://doi.org/10.1017/CHO9781107445222.008

Altman, J. C., Buchanan, G., & Biddle, N. (2006). The real 'real' economy in remote Australia. In Assessing the evidence on Indigenous socioeconomic outcomes: A focus on the 2002 NATSISS (pp. 139–152). Canberra, ACT: ANU Press.

Altman, J. C., & Gray, M. (2000). *The effects of the CDEP scheme on the economic status of Indigenous Australians: Some analyses using the 1996 Census.* Discussion paper no. 195 (p. 36). Canberra, ACT: Centre for Aboriginal Economic Policy Research, ANU.

Altman, J. C., Gray, M., & Levitus, R. (2005). *Policy issues for the Community Development Employment Projects scheme in rural and remote Australia.* Discussion paper no. 271. Canberra, ACT: Centre for Aboriginal Economic Policy Research, ANU.

Altman, J. C., & Klein, E. (2018). Lessons from a basic income programme for Indigenous Australians. *Oxford Development Studies, 46*(1), 132–146. https://doi.org/10.1080/13600818.2017.1329413

Altman, J. C., & Markham, F. (2015). Burgeoning Indigenous land ownership: Diverse values and strategic potentialities. In S. Brennan, M. Davis, B. Edgeworth, & L. Terrill (Eds.), *Native title from Mabo to Akiba: A vehicle for change and empowerment* (pp. 126–142). Sydney, NSW: Federation Press.

Altman, J. C., & Markham, F. (2018). *Submission to the senate select committee inquiry into the future of work and workers.* Submission no. 34 (p. 10). Canberra, ACT: Parliament of Australia. Retrieved from http://hdl.handle.net/1885/148244

Altman, J. C., & Sanders, W. (1991). The CDEP scheme: Administrative and policy issues. *Australian Journal of Public Administration, 50*(4), 515–525. https://doi.org/10.1111/j.1467-8500.1991.tb02323.x

Angrist, J. D., & Pischke, J.-S. (2014). *Mastering' metrics: The path from cause to effect* (with French flaps edition). Princeton, NJ/Oxford, UK: Princeton University Press.

Australian Bureau of Statistics. (2005). *National Aboriginal and Torres Strait Islander Social Survey: Expanded confidentialised unit record file, technical paper, 2002.* Cat. no. 4720.0. Canberra, ACT: Australian Bureau of Statistics. Retrieved from http://www.abs.gov.au/AUSSTATS/abs@.nsf/allprimarymainfeatures/35785040B0899214CA2576D50016BB4C?opendocument

Australian Bureau of Statistics. (2016). *National Aboriginal and Torres Strait Islander Social Survey: User guide, 2014–15.* Cat. no. 4720.0. Canberra, ACT: Australian Bureau of Statistics. Retrieved from http://www.abs.gov.au/AUSSTATS/abs@.nsf/allprimarymainfeatures/880A750EFFDE2611CA2570BF007B1CD4?opendocument

Carlson, B. (2016). *The politics of identity: Who counts as aboriginal today?* Canberra, ACT: Aboriginal Studies Press.

Coulthard, G. S. (2014). *Red skin, white masks: Rejecting the colonial politics of recognition.* Minneapolis, MN: University of Minnesota Press.

Day, D. (2014). The art market down under: A case study of Australian aboriginal art market regulation and U.S art market implication note. *Cardozo Journal of International and Comparative Law, 23*, 133–164.

Escobar, A. (2008). *Territories of difference: Place, movements, life, redes.* Durham, NC: Duke University Press Books.

Ferguson, J. (2015). *Give a man a fish: Reflections on the new politics of distribution.* Durham, NC/London: Duke University Press.

Fijn, N., Keen, I., Lloyd, C., & Pickering, M. (Eds.). (2012). *Indigenous participation in Australian economies II.* Canberra, ACT: ANU Press.

Gibson-Graham, J. K. (1996). *The end of capitalism (as we knew it): A feminist critique of political economy.* Cambridge, MA: Blackwell Publishers.

Holmes, J. (2009). Rethinking remoteness. *Geographical Research, 47*(3), 331–333. https://doi.org/10.1111/j.1745-5871.2009.00603.x

Hunter, B. (2009). A half-hearted defence of the CDEP scheme. *Family Matters, 81*, 43–54.

Hunter, B. (2014). The Aboriginal legacy. In S. Ville & G. Withers (Eds.), *The Cambridge economic history of Australia* (pp. 73–96). Melbourne, VIC: Cambridge University Press. https://doi.org/10.1017/CHO9781107445222.008

Hunter, B. (2016). Some statistical context for analysis of CDEP. In K. Jordan (Ed.), *Better than welfare? Work and livelihoods for Indigenous Australians after CDEP* (pp. 51–83). Canberra, ACT: ANU Press.

Jordan, K. (2016). *Better than welfare? Work and livelihoods for Indigenous Australians after CDEP*. Canberra, ACT: ANU Press. Retrieved from https://press.anu.edu.au/publications/series/centre-aboriginal-economic-policy-research-caepr/better-welfare

Jordan, K., & Altman, J. C. (2016). From welfare to work, or work to welfare? In K. Jordan (Ed.), *Better than welfare? Work and livelihoods for Indigenous Australians after CDEP* (pp. 1–29). Canberra, ACT: ANU Press.

Keen, I. (Ed.). (2010). *Indigenous participation in Australian economies*. Canberra, ACT: ANU Press.

Kinnane, S., Harrison, J., & Reinecke, I. (2015). Finger money: The black and white of stolen wages. *Griffith Review, 47*, 49–70.

Markham, F., & Biddle, N. (2018a). *Income, poverty and inequality*. 2016 census paper no. 2. Canberra, ACT: Centre for Aboriginal Economic Policy Research, ANU. Retrieved from http://caepr.cass.anu.edu.au/research/publications/income-poverty-and-inequality

Markham, F., & Biddle, N. (2018b). Recent changes to the Indigenous population geography of Australia: Evidence from the 2016 census. *Australian Population Studies, 2*(1), 1–13.

Moreton-Robinson, A. (2015). *The white possessive: Property, power, and indigenous sovereignty*. Minneapolis, MN: University of Minnesota Press. Retrieved from https://www.upress.umn.edu/book-division/books/the-white-possessive

Morphy, F., & Sanders, W. (2004). *The Indigenous welfare economy and the CDEP scheme*. Canberra, ACT: ANU Press. Retrieved from https://press.anu.edu.au/publications/series/centre-aboriginal-economic-policy-research-caepr/indigenous-welfare-economy-and

Office of the Registrar of Indigenous Corporations. (2012). *At the heart of art: A snapshot of Aboriginal and Torres Strait Islander corporations in the visual arts sector*. Canberra, ACT: Office of the Registrar of Indigenous Corporations. Retrieved from http://www.oric.gov.au/publications/other-report/heart-art

Parijs, P. V. (2017). *Basic income: A radical proposal for a free society and a sane economy* (1st ed.). Cambridge, MA: Harvard University Press.

Sanders, W. (1988). The CDEP scheme: Bureaucratic politics, remote community politics and the development of an aboriginal 'workfare' program in times of rising unemployment. *Politics, 23*(1), 32–47. https://doi.org/10.1080/00323268808402044

Sanders, W. (1997). *Opportunities and problems astride the welfare/work divide: The CDEP scheme in Australian social policy*. Discussion paper no. 141. Canberra, ACT: Centre for Aboriginal Economic Policy Research, ANU.

Sanders, W. (2012). Coombs' bastard child: The troubled life of CDEP. *Australian Journal of Public Administration, 71*(4), 371–391. https://doi.org/10.1111/1467-8500.12000

The Auditor General. (2017). *Design and implementation of the Community Development Programme: Department of the Prime Minister and Cabinet, Department of Employment and Department of Human Services.* ANAO report no. 14, 2017–18. Canberra, ACT: Australian National Audit Office. Retrieved from https://www.anao.gov.au/work/performance-audit/design-and-implementation-community-development-programme

Venn, D., & Biddle, N. (2018). *Employment outcomes.* 2016 census paper no. 5 (p. 30). Canberra, ACT: Centre for Aboriginal Economic Policy Research, ANU. Retrieved from http://caepr.cass.anu.edu.au/research/publications/employment-outcomes

Walter, M., & Andersen, C. (2013). *Indigenous statistics: A quantitative research methodology*. Walnut Creek, CA: Left Coast Press.

Wolfe, P. (2006). Settler colonialism and the elimination of the native. *Journal of Genocide Research, 8*(4), 387–409.

6

Diversion Ahead? Change Is Needed but That Doesn't Mean That Basic Income Is the Answer

Dina Bowman, Shelley Mallett, and Diarmuid Cooney-O'Donoghue

Introduction

Renewed interest in basic income (BI) policies reflect concerns about the unequal impacts of technological, environmental, political, social, economic and demographic change (Balliester & Elsheikhi, 2018). The Australian labour market is changing, with shifts from manufacturing to service jobs (Wilkins & Wooden, 2014), more part-time than full-

D. Bowman (✉)
The Brotherhood of St Laurence, Fitzroy, VIC, Australia

University of Melbourne, Melbourne, VIC, Australia
e-mail: dbowman@bsl.org.au

S. Mallett
University of Melbourne, Melbourne, VIC, Australia
e-mail: s.mallett@unimelb.edu.au

D. Cooney-O'Donoghue
The Brotherhood of St Laurence, Fitzroy, VIC, Australia
e-mail: Diarmuid.Cooney.Odonoghue@bsl.org.au

E. Klein et al. (eds.), *Implementing a Basic Income in Australia*, Exploring the Basic Income Guarantee, https://doi.org/10.1007/978-3-030-14378-7_6

time jobs and growth in casual and short-term contract employment (Cassidy & Parsons, 2017). Underemployment has now overtaken unemployment (ABS, 2018) and wages are stagnating (Bishop & Cassidy, 2017), undermining the economic security of workers. At 13%, the nation's income poverty rate is above the Organisation for Economic Co-operation and Development (OECD) average of 11% (OECD, 2016). In 2014, 2.99 million or 13.3% of the population in Australia lived in poverty—and over half (57.3%) of them relied on social security as their main source of income (ACOSS & SPRC UNSW, 2016).

Australia's social security system is one of the most targeted and conditional system in the OECD (Whiteford, 2016). In this context, basic income can appear to provide a way of cutting through and providing an alternative means of responding to current and future challenges. Yet debate continues about the impacts of basic income on the policies and programmes that provide social protection (Arthur, 2016; Friedman, 1982; Murray, 2006), work and work incentives (Lewis, Pressman, & Widerquist, 2005; Painter & Thoung, 2015; Rubery, Grimshaw, Keizer, & Johnson, 2018; Srnicek & Williams, 2015; Standing, 2013), gender and care (Bergmann, 2008; McLean, 2016; Robeyns, 2001; Schulz, 2017; Zelleke, 2008), and our ability to adapt to an uncertain future (Crocker, 2014; Marston, 2016; Standing, 2013).

The Basic Income Earth Network (BIEN) defines basic income as being a universal and unconditional periodic, cash payment, which is paid to the individual. However, several terms are used in social policy literature to refer to different approaches to ensuring income (re)distribution and a guaranteed basic level of income. These terms include universal basic income (Van Parijs, 1991), a basic income guarantee (Lewis et al., 2005), guaranteed minimum income (Commission of Inquiry into Poverty, 1975), guaranteed annual income (Hum & Simpson, 1993a), citizens' income (Atkinson, 2016), negative income tax (Friedman, 1982) and a demogrant (Le Grand, 2003). These terms reflect approaches that differ in ambition, scope and focus. In this chapter, we use the term 'basic income' (BI) as a general term to include the full range of approaches.

Making Sense of Basic Income

Basic income proposals range from those that are universal and utopian (Van Parijs, 2013) to the partial and pragmatic (see Finland and Canada trials below). Advocates of more ambitious versions of basic income claim that they could contribute to a more equitable society, providing unconditional, universal income (Standing, 2013, 2017). These types of proposals are often criticised as being idealistic and unaffordable (Chalmers & Quigley, 2017), though these critiques are challenged by supporters of basic income. More pragmatic proposals tend to trade-off income adequacy for affordability: typically, they suggest phased approaches (see Quiggin; Henderson and Spies-Butcher), partial income supplements and targeted or conditional payments (see Canadian and Finnish trials).

But even advocates recognise that basic income is 'not a panacea' (Standing, 2017). While proposals can be utopian, policies include trade-offs, informed by political judgements about social, cultural and economic considerations. As Ravallion (2018) observes, 'A longstanding concern with rights-based approaches is that any policy can be justified, with no basis for setting trade-offs'. With this is in mind, De Wispelaere and Stirton's (2004) 'many faces of basic income' framework is useful in assessing different basic income policy approaches and the trade-offs they entail. They identify seven dimensions: universality, individuality, conditionality, uniformity, frequency, duration, and adequacy.

Universality refers to scope of the basic income coverage. The term suggests that universal policies apply to the whole population; however, in practice 'universal' benefits tend to be restricted to groups, such as those of 'working age' or 'pension age'. Individuality describes the focus of basic income policies on individuals rather than households. This individual focus reduces concerns about equity between household types and about intra-household power relations and distribution.

Conditionality denotes the extent to which conditions to access or maintain eligibility are placed on payments. While the BIEN (2018) describes a basic income as being unconditional, some proposals include an element of conditionality. For example, Atkinson's (2015) proposed participation income was conditional on participation in socially beneficial activities such as caring roles, education or volunteering. Under his proposal, those who are idle, apart from those who are incapacitated, would not receive participation income. In this sense, his proposal is conditional. Uniformity refers to the extent to which similar levels of benefit are available to different individuals. As Hum (1981) points out, the welfare system is complex *because* it works with people in diverse circumstances and with differing needs. De Wispelaere and Stirton (2004) argue that distinguishing uniformity from conditionality is important as it allows room to advocate uniform payments for certain groups, such as pensioners or children. This approach recognises the differing needs of different cohorts. They argue that this provides the opportunity to implement basic income 'via the back door' (p. 269) (see Henderson and Spies-Butcher).

Frequency/duration relates to how often payments are made. For example, payments may be one-off, weekly, fortnightly or monthly and there may also be time limits on how long the payments can be received. Modality concerns the form of income transfer—whether cash or in kind or in public or private goods.

Adequacy refers to a level of income that is considered adequate. De Wispelaere and Stirton (2004) point out that a universal income need not be basic, and could be more or less generous (see Quiggin in this volume). While BIEN (2018) takes an expansive view of adequacy, the assessment of adequacy is often understood in terms of poverty (e.g., the Henderson Poverty Line). As Ruth Lister (2004) points out, the concept, definitions and measurements of poverty are contested and confused. The foundational assumptions about how to assess poverty and income adequacy remain contested, as do basic income policies.

To these seven dimensions, we add affordability. This is largely a political consideration and depends on budget priorities. Affordability is a key aspect of criticisms of basic income proposals. By adding this dimension, we seek to make the political decisions about expenditure more visible, especially where affordability concerns trade-off considerations of income adequacy. Concerns about affordability often mean that basic income proposals are phased or partial. While some advocates argue that basic income could balance out the costs associated with increased retirement incomes due to demographic change (Grudnoff, 2015), other scholars have highlighted overall cost as and issue (Whiteford, 2017a; Ingles, Phillips, & Stewart, 2019).

We also add equity as a dimension that is often overlooked. Because needs differ, uniform payments may have unequal consequences. Whiteford (2017b) argues that in fiscally restrained times targeting social security to those on the lowest incomes is more important than a universal basic income set at a low rate. However, uniform payments can be equitable, if there are equitable tax arrangements, which is why it is important to consider proposals within a broader policy context (see Marston this volume). Ingles et al. (2019) further argue that a basic income would require changes to the tax system and might lead to worse outcomes for people on low incomes.

These nine dimensions are useful in assessing the aims and trade-offs of proposals and trails.

Learning from the Limitations of Past Trials

While very limited, the earlier proposals and trials of the 1960s and 1970 shed light on the key elements of basic income approaches that need to be considered in the design, implementation and evaluation of subsequent proposals in the twenty-first century. They underline the integral role of poverty measures in determining the rate of basic income payments. They also point to the challenges of social policy experiments where, as Hum and Simpson (1993a) point out, academic research and political motivations both converge and conflict.

In the United States and Canada, five experimental trials of basic income were conducted between 1968 and 1980 (Widerquist, 2005). The four US experiments were part of the 'war on poverty' instigated by President Lyndon Johnson in 1964 and funded by the federal Office of Economic Opportunity and Department of Health, Education and Welfare.

The Canadian trial was influenced by the US trials and concern about how to rationalise the social security system and alleviate poverty. It was funded jointly by the Canadian federal and Manitoba state governments (Forget, 2011).

None of the trials were designed to test universal approaches to basic income. Rather, each experiment aimed to test the impact of a basic income on work incentives and hours worked, to examine the costs and assess the impact on measures of general well-being (Hum & Simpson, 1993a, 1993b; Widerquist, 2005). Subsequent analyses have examined the impact of basic income on health, family formation and fertility, and 'human and other capital accumulation' (Forget, 2011, p. 4).

Each trial was established as a social science experiment, with a treatment group and a control group (who remained on the existing social security system) (Widerquist, 2005). Hum and Simpson (1993a) provide an overview of the political and academic drivers of these experiments, which were at times conflicting and affected the design and implementation of the experiments.

All five trials targeted households of different types, rather than individuals, and the samples were selected from specific populations in each location. Widerquist (2005) notes that few childless households were represented in the studies.

No conditions were placed on the payments made in any of the trials. All provided cash payments, which were tailored to different household types. Except for the Mincome trial in Canada where payments were monthly, no information about payment frequency in the trials is available. Across the trials, the period for which participants received payments varied from two to nine years.

The guaranteed income varied for each study; in four cases, the guaranteed income was a percentage of the poverty line (varying widely from 50% to 150%). The Manitoba study, by contrast, tested guarantee levels in dollar amounts rather than relative to the poverty line. Different marginal tax rates were used to examine impacts.

Numerous articles have been published about these trials (see Widerquist, 2005 for an overview) offering critiques of the scope of the basic income policies, the implementation, the scale and methodological limitations of the evaluations and their capacity to yield interpretable results. For example, these critiques highlight the non-random selection of participants (Hum & Simpson, 1993b), as well as variations in basic income and marginal tax rates, which reduce the statistical reliability of the results (Widerquist, 2005).

Evidence from the experiments is inconclusive regarding the costs and impacts on work incentives. Funding for the Canadian study was withdrawn before detailed analysis could be done. But the data was made available to researchers for subsequent analyses, which focused on outcomes including health (Forget, 2011). Because of the small sample sizes in the US trials, researchers often average the results of the four basic income experiments across the United States, limiting the ability to isolate specific findings. As Widerquist (2005) notes, the variable basic income levels, marginal tax rates, regions, short time frames, size and characteristics of the selected population make it difficult to infer clear implications for broader scale policy. For instance, it would be difficult to estimate how much a basic income would cost at a national level based on the smaller regions of the trials (Hum, 1981). The variety of different basic income guarantee levels and marginal tax rates also makes it hard to extrapolate the effects of work incentives to the national level.

The inconclusive results of these experiments led Widerquist (2005) to comment that 'It would be very easy to spin the results' positively or negatively depending on political perspective, and suggest that these experiments prove nothing more than 'that a basic guaranteed income is financially feasible at the cost of certain side effects that people with differing political beliefs may take to be desirable or disastrous' (pp. 68–9).

Basic Income Initiatives in Australia

The National Inquiry into Poverty (1968–1975) is the most extensive examination of the composition and extent of poverty and inequality in Australia to date (Social Welfare Policy Secretariat, 1981). The inquiry drew attention to poverty in Australia in the 1960s and 1970s (Trembath, 2008a) through its efforts to measure poverty and identify the role of the social security system in mitigating its effects. The inquiry was led by Professor Ronald Henderson, the founding director of the Institute of Applied Economic and Social Research at the University of Melbourne. The Brotherhood of St Laurence, a community-based, not-for-profit organisation, also played a significant role, publicly advocating and mobilising support for this work and its findings (Trembath, 2008b).

The Henderson poverty line and a guaranteed minimum income were two key recommendations of the Commission of Inquiry into Poverty

(1975). This guaranteed minimum income can be classified as a two-tiered basic income, with cash payments provided at a level below the poverty line for those able to work and one at the poverty level for those who could not. Such classification would have required assessment to determine who was able to work, so there is an element of conditionality. Adequacy was central to the Henderson poverty line, which sought to identify the point below which different household types would experience poverty, and the proposal for a guaranteed minimum income. The aim was to protect those unable to work from poverty and ensure that those able to work could top up their payment with labour market participation (Australian Government Commission of Inquiry into Poverty, 1975).

In 1972, the Brotherhood of St Laurence, a Melbourne based NGO, took up the idea of a guaranteed minimum income articulated in the Poverty Inquiry. Seeking new approaches to empower poor people, it proposed a trial of guaranteed minimum income as part of its Family Action Centre project (1972–1975). This trial aimed to examine the best method to provide adequate financial resources to low-income families.

The Family Centre Project focused on 60 low-income families, most of whom used Brotherhood of St Laurence's services. The participants included some sole parents, couples with children, some who were employed, and they had varied housing.

Weekly unconditional cash payments were provided directly to the female head of the house over a period of three years. Consistent with the fundamental objective to provide adequate income, payments were based on the Henderson poverty line and adjusted according to income from other sources, the number of dependants in each household, and housing costs (for detail about how this the payment was calculated (see Liffman & Salmon, 1975, pp. 29–43). In 1975, the income supplements ceased (Gilley, 1990).

Like the trials in the United States and Canada, the Brotherhood of St Laurence trial had methodological and analytical limitations. Participants were not randomly selected, and there was no comparison group (Benn, 1977). The short duration of the project also made it difficult to determine the longer term effects or costs and affordability because the participants knew they would receive payments for limited time. Yet there were suggestive findings. Participants reported increased financial security and reduced financial stress; and women reported greater financial autonomy, and a more effective use of income for the family. There was no measurement or evidence related to the impact on work incentives (Gilley, 1990).

After the Whitlam government was dismissed in 1975, the Guaranteed Minimum Income (GMI) proposal was shelved nationally, and in the United States and Canada trials were scrapped with changing government priorities and changing political motivations.

The recent trials face similar challenges, below we consider two trials that are underway.

Ontario, Canada 2017–2018

The three-year Ontario trial is based on a proposal by Segal (2016) to test a basic income by replacing unemployment and disability payments with a form of a negative income tax or refundable tax credit. The proposal sought to give more freedom to welfare recipients to make life decisions, and test how different policy combinations can reduce poverty, while not discouraging people from labour force participation. However, in 2018, amid protests, the Conservative Ontario government announced that it would end the trial created by the previous Liberal government citing concerns about affordability (Kassam, 2018).

The trial entailed a sample of individuals aged 18–65 living in poverty. It was proposed that areas with a high concentration of individuals living in poverty would also be included as 'saturation sites' to investigate the community-level impacts of a basic income. A saturation site could provide evidence to demonstrate impacts of universal basic income on problems associated with poverty (such as health and poor housing). Sites in southern and northern Ontario locations were suggested, as well as a site chosen and planned in close collaboration with First Nations communities. According to Segal (2016), the trial was not intended to test replacing the whole welfare system with a single payment.

The trial entailed an increase in base payments for the poorest citizens, with unconditional monthly cash payments to individuals for a minimum of three years at different treatment levels of Basic Income (starting at 75% of Canada's Low-Income Measure (LIM)) and different tax rates on income earned on top of the basic income. This was intended to test and identify how different parameters and combination of parameters can reduce poverty, while not discouraging people from improving their incomes through labour force participation.

The tax credit would lift income support from 45% to 75% of the LIM. This means that recipients could claim a minimum of approximately CAD1320 per month, non-taxable. To increase work incentives, they could keep partial additional income earned from participation in the labour market. People with disabilities could receive an additional monthly sum of at least CAD500.

There have been protests in response to the scrapping of the trial with claims from anti-poverty activists that the payments enabled people to buy better food and afford their rent and heating (Kassam, 2018). This highlights the inadequacy of income support and minimum wages in Canada and points to the difficulty of garnering broad political support for long-term trials or broader implementation (Riley, 2018).

Finland 2017–2018

On 1 January 2017, Finland began a two-year, partial basic income trial. This came at a time of growth in insecure work, relatively high unemployment, and some concern about possible disincentive effects of the unemployment insurance payments, which are set at 55% of replacement wage (Esser, Ferrarini, Nelson, Palme, & Sjöberg, 2013; Kela Social Insurance Institution, 2017a; Statistics Finland, 2017). The trial has two related objectives: to simplify social security by streamlining benefits and reducing bureaucracy and to reduce the poverty trap by increasing work incentives, allowing people to receive both unemployment insurance and private income, acting as a way to supplement wages, especially for those in insecure and intermittent employment (Kela Social Insurance Institution, 2017b).

The trial was restricted to 2000 selected unemployed individuals aged 25–58 who were receiving unemployment benefits. Payment was made to individuals rather than families. There was no means testing of private income or tapering of benefits for participants, unlike other non-trial social security recipients who can only earn €300 per month before their benefits are reduced.

A single uniform cash payment of €560 was provided to individuals monthly over the period of the trial. This payment is not designed to provide an adequate income in Finland, where the average monthly income per person is around €3400 (OECD Stat, 2017). A uniform cash payment set at such a low level appears to provide a large incentive to find paid employment. With no means test of their earned income, low income recipients will be able to maximise income.

Affordability was a key concern in the design of this trial. The basic income was seen as supplementary rather than replacement income. Some commentators have expressed concern that findings from this trial could be used to increase conditionality in Finland (Foster, 2018). Analysis will begin at the conclusion of the trial, yet there is concern that politics will overtake this process, as findings are expected to be published at around the time of the Finnish general election (Lehto, 2018). The Finnish government plans to continue with trials of different social security policies such as Universal Credit after the basic income trial (The Economist, 2018). While there has been some excitement regarding the trial (Lehto, 2018), ultimately it was not successful politically and, indeed, may have opened the way for potentially more regressive policies.

Reclaiming Social Security

The idea of a basic income to alleviate poverty, enable economic security and respond to technological change and environmental challenges is undoubtedly attractive. Yet discussion of basic income tends to be either be 'free-floating' (Dent, 2017, p. 6), and disconnected from political and other concerns or linked to specific contexts within trials.

Policy change needs to be understood in context—historically, socially, politically, economically and culturally. What worked in the past or works in Finland is unlikely to work in the same way in Australia. Careful consideration of the detail of any proposal is required, within the context of broader issues and the intersecting domains and policies.

It is evident that social security needs to be reclaimed and reimagined, but as Henderson (Commission of Inquiry into Poverty, 1975, p. vi) pointed out, 'it would be unwise to make suggestions without a lively appreciation of the strengths of the existing provisions'. The adapted framework that we propose enables an assessment of proposals and identification of trade-offs. We also need to consider the interrelationships between basic income and other polices which can affect the capacity of basic income proposals to achieve their objectives. For example, Ingles et al. (2019) note that major reforms to the tax and transfer system may leave some low-income groups worse off.

Past and present trials have shown inconclusive benefits arising from basic income. All the experiments that we have considered have foundered on political and budgetary concerns. Despite some political interest in basic income in Australia, major political parties show little interest (Leigh, 2017) and there is little prospect of basic income being considered in the short-term. Basic income proposals can act as beacons for change, but because they often lack detail they risk distracting attention from the challenges and opportunities for social security reform. The adapted framework we propose enables detailed assessments of the dimensions of proposals for change. By identifying these dimensions and associated trade-offs, basic income proposals could contribute to rather than distract from reform of social security so that it is better able to respond to current and future challenges.

References

ACOSS & SPRC UNSW. (2016). *Poverty in Australia 2016. Poverty and inequality in Australia*. Sydney, NSW: ACOSS.

Arthur, D. (2016). *Basic income: A radical idea enters the mainstream*. Research paper series, 2016–17. Canberra, ACT: Parliamentary Library, Department of Parliamentary Services.

Atkinson, A. B. (2015). *Inequality: What can be done?* London: Harvard University Press.

Atkinson, A. B. (2016). How to spread the wealth. *Foreign Affairs, 95*(1), 29–33.

Australian Bureau of Statistics. (2018). *Trend underemployment falls to 8.3%, labour force, Australia, Feb 2018*. Canberra, ACT: Australian Government.

Retrieved from http://www.abs.gov.au/ausstats/abs@.nsf/lookup/6202.0Media%20Release1Feb%202018

Australian Government Commission of Inquiry into Poverty. (1975). *Income support: A guaranteed income scheme, poverty in Australia V1*. Canberra, ACT: Australian Government Publishing Service.

Balliester, T., & Elsheikhi, A. (2018). *The future of work: A literature review*. Working paper no. 29. Geneva, Switzerland: International Labour Office.

Basic Income Earth Network. (2018). *About basic income*. Retrieved from https://basicincome.org/basic-income/

Benn, C. (1977). *Participation by the poor.* Master of arts thesis. Melbourne, VIC: Departments of Political Science and Social Studies, University of Melbourne.

Bergmann, B. (2008). Basic income grants or the welfare state: Which better promotes gender equality? *Basic Income Studies, 3*(3), 1–7.

Bishop, J., & Cassidy, N. (2017). Insights into low wage growth in Australia. *Reserve Bank Bulletin*. March Quarter 2017. Canberra, ACT: Reserve Bank of Australia.

Cassidy, N., & Parsons, S. (2017). The rising share of part-time employment. *Reserve Bank Bulletin*. September Quarter 2017. Canberra, ACT: Reserve Bank of Australia.

Chalmers, J., & Quigley, M. (2017). *Changing jobs: The fair go in the new machine age*. Carlton, VIC: Redback.

Crocker, G. (2014). *The economic necessity of basic income*. Retrieved from http://www.centreforwelfarereform.org/library/by-date/the-economic-necessity-of-basic-income.html

De Wispelaere, J., & Stirton, L. (2004). The many faces of universal basic income. *The Political Quarterly, 75*(3), 266–274.

Dent, A. (2017). *From utopia to implementation: How basic income has progressed from radical idea to legitimate policy solution*. MSC public policy thesis, University of Bristol. Retrieved from https://basicincome.org/news/2018/03/ann/

Esser, I., Ferrarini, T., Nelson, K., Palme, J., & Sjöberg, O. (2013). *Unemployment benefits in EU member states*. Stockholm, Sweden: Swedish Institute for Social Research.

Forget, E. L. (2011). The town with no poverty: The health effects of a Canadian guaranteed annual income field experiment. *Canadian Public Policy, 37*(3), 283–305.

Foster, G. (2018). Finland's basic income trial exposes timeless welfare reform dilemma. *ABC News*. https://www.abc.net.au/news/2018-05-01/finland-universal-basic-income-welfare-reform/9709798

Friedman, M. (1982). *Capitalism and freedom*. Chicago: University of Chicago Press.
Gilley, T. (1990). *Empowering poor people: A consumer view of the Family Centre Project*. Fiztroy, VIC: Brotherhood of St Laurence.
Grudnoff, M. (2015). *A super waste of money: Redesigning super tax concessions*. Canberra, ACT: The Australia Institute. Retrieved from http://www.tai.org.au/content/super-waste-money-redesigning-super-tax-concessions
Hum, D. (1981). Canada's administrative experience with negative income taxation. *Canadian Taxation: A Journal of Tax Policy, 1*, 2–16.
Hum, D., & Simpson, W. (1993a). Economic response to a guaranteed annual income: Experience from Canada and the United States. *Journal of Labor Economics, 11*(1), 263–294.
Hum, D., & Simpson, W. (1993b). Whatever happened to Canada's guaranteed income project? *Canadian Public Administration, 36*(3), 442–450.
Ingles, D., Phillips, B., & Stewart, M. (2019). From guaranteed minimum income to BI: What would it look like today? In P. Saunders (Ed.), *Revisiting Henderson* (pp. 377–399). Carlton, VIC: Melbourne University Press.
Kassam, A. (2018, August 1). Ontario's new conservative government to end basic income experiment. *The Guardian*. https://www.theguardian.com/world/2018/aug/01/ontarios-new-conservative-government-to-end-basic-income-experiment
Kela Social Insurance Institution. (2017a). *Experimental study on a universal basic income*. Helsinki, FI: Kela. Retrieved from http://www.kela.fi/web/en/experimental-study-on-a-universal-basic-income
Kela Social Insurance Institution. (2017b). *Objectives and implementation of the Basic Income Experiment*. Retrieved from https://www.kela.fi/web/en/basic-income-objectives-and-implementation
Le Grand, J. (2003). *A demogrant motivation, agency, and public policy: Of knights and knaves, pawns and queens*. Abingdon, UK: Oxford University Press.
Lehto, O. (2018). An earthquake in Finland. In A. Downes & S. Lansley (Eds.), *It's basic income: The global debate* (pp. 165–170). Bristol, UK: Policy Press.
Leigh, A. (2017). *Speech- how can we reduce inequality*. Canberra, ACT: Crawford School of Public Policy, Australian National University. Retrieved from http://www.andrewleigh.com/speech_how_can_we_reduce_inequality_anu_crawford_school_of_public_policy
Lewis, M., Pressman, S., & Widerquist, K. (2005). The basic income guarantee and social economics. *Review of Social Economy, 63*(4), 587–593.
Liffman, M., & Salmon, J. (1975). *The family centre project: A second overview*. Fitzroy, VIC: Brotherhood of St Laurence.

Lister, R. (2004). *Poverty*. Cambridge, UK: Polity Press.
Marston, G. (2016). Greening the Australian welfare state: Can basic income play a role? In J. Mays, G. Marston, & J. Tomlinson (Eds.), *Basic income in Australia and New Zealand: Perspectives from the neoliberal frontier* (pp. 157–178). New York: Palgrave Macmillan.
McLean, C. (2016). … and justice for all? Basic income and the principles of gender equity. *Juncture, 22*(4), 284–288.
Murray, C. (2006). *In our hands: A plan to replace the welfare state*. Washington, DC: American Enterprise Institute.
OECD. (2016). *Society at a glance 2016: A spotlight on youth – How does Australia compare?* Paris: OECD. Retrieved from https://www.oecd.org/australia/sag2016-australia.pdf
OECD Stat. (2017). *Average annual wages*. Paris: OECD. Retrieved from https://stats.oecd.org/Index.aspx?DataSetCode=AV_AN_WAGE
Painter, A., & Thoung, C. (2015). *Creative citizen, creative state: The principled and pragmatic case for a universal basic income*. London: The RSA.
Ravallion, M. (2018). *Guaranteed employment or guaranteed income?* Washington, DC: Center for Global Development.
Riley, M. (2018). Dozens in Lindsay rally to protest cancellation of basic income program. *The Star*. https://www.thestar.com/news/canada/2018/08/07/dozens-in-lindsay-rally-to-protest-cancellation-of-basic-income-program.html
Robeyns, I. (2001). Will basic income do justice to women? *Analyse and Kritik, 23*(1), 88–105.
Rubery, J., Grimshaw, D., Keizer, A., & Johnson, M. (2018). Challenges and contradictions in the 'normalising' of precarious work. *Work, Employment and Society, 32*(3), 509–527.
Schulz, P. (2017). Universal basic income in a feminist perspective and gender analysis. *Global social policy, 17*(1), 89–92.
Segal, H. (2016). *Finding a better way: A basic income pilot project for Ontario*. Toronto, ON: Massey College, University of Toronto.
Social Welfare Policy Secretariat. (1981). *Report on poverty measurement*. Canberra, ACT: Department of Social Security.
Srnicek, N., & Williams, A. (2015). *Inventing the future: Postcapitalism and a world without work*. New York: Verso Books.
Standing, G. (2013). Why a basic income is necessary for a right to work. *Basic Income Studies, 7*(2), 19–40.
Standing, G. (2017). *Davos 2017 – A basic income for all: Dream or delusion? Panel discussion*. Davos, Switzerland: World Economic Forum.

Statistics Finland. (2017). *Labour market*. Retrieved from http://www.stat.fi/til/tym_en.html

The Economist. (2018, April 26). The lapsing of Finland's universal basic income trial. *The Economist*. Retrieved from https://www.economist.com/finance-and-economics/2018/04/26/the-lapsing-of-finlands-universal-basic-income-trial

Trembath, R. (2008a). The 1960s and the rediscovery of poverty. In C. Holden & R. Trembath (Eds.), *Divine discontent: The Brotherhood of St Laurence – A history* (pp. 129–160). North Melbourne, VIC: Australian Scholarly Publishing.

Trembath, R. (2008b). A decade of empowerment. In C. Holden & R. Trembath (Eds.), *Divine discontent: The Brotherhood of St Laurence – A history* (pp. 161–208). North Melbourne, VIC: Australian Scholarly Publishing.

Van Parijs, P. (1991). Why surfers should be fed: the liberal case for an unconditional basic income. *Philosophy and Public Affairs, 20*(2), 101–131.

Van Parijs, P. (2013). The universal basic income: Why utopian thinking matters, and how sociologists can contribute to it. *Politics and Society, 41*(2), 171–182.

Whiteford, P. (2016, April 21). Ideas for Australia: Welfare reform needs to be about improving well-being, not punishing the poor. *The Conversation*. Retrieved from https://theconversation.com/ideas-for-australia-welfare-reform-needs-to-be-about-improving-well-being-not-punishing-the-poor-56355

Whiteford, P. (2017a). Cited in Janda M. Rise of the machines: Is a universal basic income the answer for mass unemployment? *ABC News*. https://www.abc.net.au/news/2017-07-04/universal-basic-income-money-for-nothing/8676834

Whiteford, P. (2017b). *Social security and welfare spending in Australia: Assessing long-term trends*. Canberra, ACT: Tax and Transfer Policy Institute, Crawford School of Public Policy, Australian National University.

Widerquist, K. (2005). A failure to communicate: What (if anything) can we learn from the negative income tax experiments? *The Journal of Socio-Economics, 34*(1), 49–81.

Wilkins, R., & Wooden, M. (2014). Two decades of change: The Australian labour market, 1993–2013. *Australian Economic Review, 47*(4), 417–431.

Zelleke, A. (2008). Institutionalizing the universal caretaker through a basic income? *Basic Income Studies, 3*(3), 1–9.

Part II

Avenues for Implementation

7

Finding a Political Strategy for a Basic Income in Australia

Tim Hollo

In order to implement a Basic Income (BI) in Australia, it will be necessary to first understand the existing political context and, over time, develop a political strategy to achieve it. The key elements of such a strategy include (the interlinked processes of) shifting the political discourse in favour of the reform, and building political power behind it—drawing together ever-increasing coalitions of support, building the public demand and confronting those opposed.

In Australia in 2018, it would be fair to say that both the dominant political discourse and the weight of power are against BI. Our major political parties, dominant civil society players, and mainstream media are bound up in narratives that either deliberately denigrate those receiving welfare or fetishise paid labour, both of which oppose the principles of universalist, unconditional respect that underpin a BI. Although there is broad interest in the idea amongst the public at large, the majority of those who hold and influence power are either opposed or uninterested.

T. Hollo (✉)
The Green Institute, Turner, ACT, Australia
e-mail: tim.hollo@greeninstitute.org.au

E. Klein et al. (eds.), *Implementing a Basic Income in Australia*, Exploring the Basic Income Guarantee, https://doi.org/10.1007/978-3-030-14378-7_7

This chapter reviews the current political context for Basic Income in Australia in 2018, and proposes approaches which could begin to move the discourse down the path towards implementation. The author is Executive Director of the Green Institute, an independent think tank associated with the Australian Greens, and is both a participant in and an observer of Australian politics, as well as an advocate for BI.

Australian politics, and the bulk of the Australian political discourse, has a tendency in recent years towards conservatism and risk aversion (e.g. Megalogenis, 2010). Floating big ideas is risky; they tend to get shot down quickly, leaving people having to explain perceived failures. In this context, forging a political path to a BI could be a difficult road.

On the other hand, there are already large numbers of people intrigued by the idea, wanting to look into it more, or already supportive, across the political spectrum. In addition, many of the old narratives of politics, both in Australia and around the world, are evaporating as the neoliberal consensus crumbles. Universal basic income (UBI) could become, in the foreseeable future, an idea whose time has come. And that, after all, is how big change happens in politics. It rarely, if ever, happens by winning arguments, or "convincing" opponents to switch sides.

Big change happens when campaigners successfully shift the cultural context and, by doing so, turn an idea from inconceivable to inevitable. The Eight-Hour Day, free tertiary education, Medicare, the end of the White Australia policy—all happened because the old politics couldn't stand up in the new political culture driven by social changes and lengthy public campaigns. Consider, in more recent memory, how former Prime Minister John Howard, after 11 years in power, was forced into proposing an emissions trading scheme before the 2007 election, when he clearly didn't (and still doesn't) respect the climate science. Consider the apology to the Stolen Generations. Consider the introduction of marriage equality. These were all ideas whose time had come, pushed through against internal and external opposition, because the political discourse had been actively shifted in their favour and power-holders who were opposed could no longer hold them back.

Where Does Australia's Political Discourse Currently Sit on BI?

While, outside politics, people are looking for alternatives, in politics itself right now, the dominant stories are of "lifters vs leaners"—the stigmatisation and punishment of the poor and unemployed—and of the "dignity of hard work"—the fetishisation of paid employment above all other modes of participation and contribution. These ideas, their provenance and their prevalence, will be discussed by the following discussion of where the parties stand.

The governing Liberal Party and their coalition National Party, at the time of writing this chapter, have, as far as this research has been able to find, made no explicit mention of the idea of Basic Income at all.[1] Certainly, current Prime Minister (and former Treasurer) Scott Morrison, Human Services Minister Michael Keenan and Social Services Minister Paul Fletcher have all been silent on the issue, as have Nationals Leader and Deputy Prime Minister Michael McCormack and his predecessor, Barnaby Joyce.

However, it's not as though it isn't clear where they stand on the underlying question. This is the party that has consistently targeted "dole cheats" with a deeply punitive approach, and split society into "lifters and leaners" and "taxed and taxed-nots". Morrison's stated approach (when he was Treasurer) was "if they're not taking those jobs [stacking shelves and picking fruit], then they shouldn't be getting the dole" (Benson, 2016). Former Human Services Minister, Alan Tudge, who in 2016 propounded that "in our desire to be a generous and caring society we may have reached a point where we have taken our good intentions too far, and are now causing harm" (Tudge, 2016) made headlines by seeking to redefine poverty as a level of "absolute deprivation" (Taylor, 2017). Tudge's successor in the ministry, Michael Keenan, has taken a softer rhetorical approach, but has nevertheless continued the government's ongoing policies to reduce the number of people receiving benefits, "defending the

[1] NB: at time of writing, the governing Liberal Party has been once again wracked by internal divisions, replacing the Prime Minister and triggering a substantial ministerial reshuffle. Consequently, previous ministers are quoted, as new ministers have not yet spoken publicly on their issues.

integrity and sustainability of our welfare system and ensuring government lives within its means" (Keenan, 2018). Kelly O'Dwyer, former Minister for Jobs and Industrial Relations and now Minister for Women, said in her maiden speech, "Basic fairness and compassion mean a strong social safety net is essential. But I want as few people as possible to rely on it" (O'Dwyer, 2010). All these statements reflect a rejection of the universalism and egalitarianism that are necessary to underpin a BI, as well as a punitive, controlling approach towards vulnerable people, which is the inverse of a BI.

This is the party that scrapped the Community Development Employment Program that Altman and Klein (2017) identify as being effectively a BI-type model for Indigenous Australians in remote communities. This is also the party that initially introduced Work for the Dole, that wants to drug test people on unemployment benefits, and is introducing a demerit point system for those receiving benefits. This punitive, exclusionary approach, treating support as a privilege to be earned, is the polar opposite of a universalist approach that sees it as society's responsibility to keep everyone out of poverty just as we see it as our responsibility to provide public education and health to all.

However, there is within the broad church of the Liberal Party a libertarian element, seeking the most minimal possible government intervention in the economy and therefore possibly open to a move from highly complex welfare structures to a simpler BI approach. In particular, there are two MPs in the Federal Coalition Party room who are former employees of the Institute of Public Affairs (IPA, a libertarian think tank): Tim Wilson and James Paterson. While I can find no explicit reference to either of them making public statements about BI, the IPA has backed the idea, with Senior Researcher Mikayla Novak writing about it in positive terms (Novak, 2016).

This is, however, the only small chink of possibility in a party for whom stigmatisation of the poor and unemployed is totemic. To get the Coalition to move, it will be necessary to shift Australian politics into a position where they cannot afford to reject the idea, just as with emissions trading in 2007 and marriage equality in 2017. Rather than attempt to convince the Liberal Party, advocates need to win the fight against them. It would be a mistake to believe this reform has to be bipartisan or cross-partisan—a mistake which has doomed climate action. Indeed, negotiating the introduction of a BI with the Coalition would likely lead to deeply problematic outcomes. Advocates need to build power and implement it, against the Coalition's opposition if necessary.

What of the alternative Federal Government, the Australian Labor Party (ALP)? On this front, there is somewhat greater potential. While currently the centre of gravity within Labor still lies firmly opposed to BI on what could be characterised as outdated conceptual grounds, there are already individuals and forces working within the party to make change, as the following section sets out.

If the cultural politics opposing BI on the part of the conservatives is one of stigmatisation of the poor and unemployed (a tendency which, it should be noted, the Labor Party has been prey to, as well), the equivalent cultural opposition for the bulk of Labor is the fetishisation of paid labour.

The labour movement was born of campaigns to reduce work, with the eight-hour day and holiday and sick leave all about helping working people not have their lives driven, determined and defined by their work. At some point as Labo(u)r parties slowly but surely embraced the neoliberal agenda, the focus on the "dignity of working people" was replaced by a focus on the "dignity of work". There is an important distinction here that has been lost in current analysis of the Labor party.

It is fascinating the extent to which a norm privileging paid work over any other form of social or economic contribution has become embedded in Labor politics. Former Prime Minister Julia Gillard made the value of working hard a special focus of her personality as leader, raising it consistently in parliamentary debate, in interviews and in speeches. In her speech to the ALP campaign launch in the 2013 election campaign, for example, Ms. Gillard said, "I have believed all of my life in the power of hard work, in the importance of work, in defining a life in the importance of work" (Gillard, 2010). Similarly, Shadow Treasurer Chris Bowen has spoken of Labor's goal of "ensuring dignity through work for Australians" (Murphy, 2017) in explicitly rejecting the idea of a BI and shutting down those from the grassroots and left of his own party wanting to talk about it.

This is an understandable but problematic perspective from the labour movement, which is couched in an over-riding belief in labour as the only legitimate space for social organisation, and an outdated conception of work which internalised the "protestant work ethic" imposed on workers by early industrial capitalists. From this perspective, BI is seen as a threat to organised labour, because it is read as challenging the primacy of paid work in our society.

A slightly more nuanced but still misplaced aspect of the Labor opposition to BI is that idea that it will lead to a loss of agency for people. This is part of the fetishisation of work as it assumes that agency can only come from paid labour. In fact, all the evidence from BI-related trials both in the 1970s in the US and more recently, as well as from places with more generous and less punitive welfare arrangements than our own, is that it increases people's agency, making them feel more in control of their own lives. And of course it does. That's the point. It's all about enabling people to make their own choices in life.

The other objection to BI from Labor circles is one which is easier to overcome because it runs counter to the universalist philosophy of the party behind Medicare, the aged pension and public education: that it isn't fair to give money to millionaires. No Labor politician would suggest that millionaires shouldn't be allowed to send their children to public schools or use public hospitals, and this should be the same for BI. The great philosopher of the welfare state, Richard Titmuss, is famous for defending universalism by saying "a policy for the poor is a poor policy" (in Bregman, 2017, 43) because it drives a wedge through society, excluding "the poor" from equivalent participation. Bowen, on the other hand, talks in glowing terms, for example, of "our highly targeted welfare system", which "means that we get greater bang for our poverty alleviation buck" (Murphy, 2017). He and his Shadow Assistant Treasurer, former ANU economics professor Andrew Leigh (Leigh, 2017) claim in this context that a BI would drive greater inequality because of its scale and untargeted nature. This is an argument from neoliberal austerity politics that is already losing ground rapidly in the centre left in Australia and around the world.

On the other hand, there are moves afoot within Labor left's grassroots to promote the idea of a BI. In particular, Godfrey Moase (Moase, 2013), Assistant General Branch Secretary of the National Union of Workers in Melbourne, and Luke Whitington, the deputy chair of the NSW Labor

Left's economic policy committee, who is also an adviser to Senator Doug Cameron (Daily Telegraph, 2017), have been campaigning internally and moving motions on the issue. They present it as a response to rising inequality and inadequate welfare, a path to greater social solidarity, and, importantly, a way to support workers to make choices with greater confidence and power.

These activists with Labor in Australia are given important intellectual backing and leadership globally by British journalist and UK Labour activist, Paul Mason, whose book *Post-Capitalism* articulates the practical and theoretical justification for a BI (Mason, 2015). Mason argues that we are approaching an era of abundance in which we can drastically reduce the amount we need to work, and that BI is a central tool to support people and redistribute wealth in this context. Following Mason's lead, UK Labour leader, Jeremy Corbyn, and his Shadow Chancellor, John McDonnell, have signalled an intention to bring BI into their manifesto for the next election (Cowburn, 2018). Given the extent to which social democratic parties around the world are currently watching the British experience, the impact of Mason and Corbyn's leadership shouldn't be understated. Australian Labor, while currently opposed to a BI, could conceivably flip rapidly, with the right shift in discourse and external support.

Next we have the Greens,[2] Australia's third political force. The Greens have expressed interest in and support for BI, up to and including leader Richard Di Natale calling for a public conversation on the idea at the National Press Club in 2017 (Di Natale, 2017), following the Green Institute's initial research paper on it (Hollo et al., 2016). The principle that everyone should be entitled to a Guaranteed Adequate Income has long been in the party platform; however, there will be more work needed to get the party to embrace BI as an agreed way to implement Guaranteed Adequate Income and move from interest towards active support.

While the Greens are philosophically deeply committed to universalism, some in the party, particularly those who come more directly from the socialist and union traditions, are more attracted to Job Guarantee

[2] Disclosure: the author is a member of the Greens, Executive Director of the Greens' think tank, The Green Institute, and a Greens candidate for election.

style approaches. Amongst this group there is suspicion of BI as a neoliberal approach because of its association with Milton Friedman, although the Green Institute's efforts to better explain the history and philosophy of the idea and link it to both pre- and post-capitalist thinking are clearing up these misconceptions. Most importantly, the party has a strong, and justified, opposition to any conception of BI which would see it as part of a libertarian, small government approach, removing or reducing vital support for most vulnerable communities, or even using it as an excuse to weaken commitment to universal public health and education.

The Greens' interest in BI is grounded in an appreciation of the broad range of contemporary challenges in the work space: both underemployment and overemployment, unequal distribution of work, rampant casualisation and insecurity, and the spectre of rapid and broadscale automation. They have consistently and vociferously opposed the moves by Liberal/National and Labor governments to restrict access to welfare, and to stigmatise and denigrate those on welfare. They have even officially called for a Living Wage for artists, announced by Industrial Relations spokesperson and Acting Co-Deputy Leader Adam Bandt before the 2016 election (Cuthbertson, 2016).

The Greens have a more sophisticated and contemporary understanding than Labor's conception of the "dignity of work", grounded in the party's different political base in what Guy Rundle calls the "knowledge culture classes" (Rundle, 2015). Social Services spokesperson and the other Acting Co-Deputy Leader, Senator Rachel Siewert, for example, talks of the dignity of participation and contribution. One of the great attractions of BI for the Greens is the way in which it can begin the vital process of valuing the contribution of unpaid work, from caring to creativity, from community participation to volunteering of all kinds.

With support, the Greens can and likely will become the key advocates for a BI in Australian party politics.

The final feature of our political landscape is the independents and micro parties making up the crossbench. None of the Senate crossbench has made any comment about BI. While one could not expect the far-right Senators of Pauline Hanson's One Nation, David Leyonhjelm's Liberal Democrats or the Katter Party to consider the issue with any seriousness, given they compete with the Liberal/National Coalition's stigmatisation of the unemployed, the Centre Alliance (the remainders of Nick Xenophon's populist libertarian political project) may well find it attractive. In the Lower House, centre left independent, Andrew Wilkie, notes on his website that he "supports the implementation of a universal basic income as a mechanism for fair and equitable wealth. Such a system would better address the rising cost of living and remove the separate system for the disadvantaged, which is often stigmatising and currently set well below the poverty line" (Wilkie, n.d.). It is certainly worth engaging with Wilkie and the Centre Alliance over time to build understanding and interest.

Within Federal Parliamentary politics, that is where we currently sit. If we are seeking to build a political path towards a BI, our challenge is not to "convince" our opponents with logical arguments. Our challenge is to shift the frames of our political discourse, from fetishisation of paid work and stigmatisation of the poor and unemployed to the dignity of participation and making life better for everybody, and mobilise coalitions and constituencies as we do so. In that way, we can build support and power, change the cultural context and move BI from inconceivable to inevitable.

A crucial element of building political power behind an idea is, of course, mobilising public support. Anecdotally, numerous people are interested in the idea. Whenever I mention UBI, people are fascinated, and glad that someone is working on it. But there is currently no clear constituency or sector of society barracking for it. Indeed, some potential allies are currently actively opposed. It will be vital, for effective organising and mobilising, to bring existing constituencies and sectors into active support.

In the category of potential allies who are currently opposed sit, perhaps most pivotally, the unions. The bulk of the union movement in Australia is currently deeply sceptical of BI, based primarily on the same philosophy as the ALP, seeing paid labour as the only legitimate site for social organisation. Embracing BI is dismissed as "giving up on work"—a phrase I've had put to me directly by senior union leaders. As a long time union member and supporter of the movement, my belief is that it is vital for its survival and continued relevance in the twenty-first century for it to move beyond this conception and embrace a far broader conception of work.

More practically, there is also legitimate fear amongst unionists that BI could increase the use of free internships and similarly abusive practices. While this is a risk in a deregulated industrial marketplace, it simply means we need to ensure that implementation of BI is carried out in conjunction with stronger regulation, not continued deregulation. It is also a fear which fails to take account of the countervailing shift in bargaining power between employers and employees that a BI would drive: while employers could conceivably seek to abuse the existence of a living wage to demand that employees work for lower wages or worse conditions, employees with a guaranteed real safety net would no longer have to fear leaving their job if they felt abused, shifting power substantially in their favour. Indeed, BI has been characterised as a "universal strike fund" (Santens, 2018). This is a factor that the bulk of the union movement, certainly in Australia, has not yet appreciated, although internationally major unions such as SEIU, UNISON, GMB, TUC and others public support BI.

A strategy to build support in the Australian union movement is a vital task in forging a political path to a BI. This should involve working with those, such as Godfrey Moase, who are already supportive, and bringing to Australia representatives of international unions who back the idea. It could also involve lobbying specific unions with specific approaches: for example, the National Union of Students may be interested in the idea of a Youth Basic Income as a stepping stone towards BI. The National Tertiary Education Union may be open to the idea as a mechanism for supporting an increasingly casualised workforce.

Importantly, while in recent years the union movement has quite rightly focussed on improving conditions for workers, there is also a long and proud history of the union movement fighting for shorter working hours, for the right to less work. The earliest victories for unions anywhere in the world included the Australian stonemasons winning an eight-hour day in 1856 (Moase, in Hollo et al., 2016), as well as achieving weekends and public holidays, paid sick leave, and more.

Far from "giving up on work", fighting for a BI can be seen as simply the next logical step for the labour movement, embracing a broader understanding of work, and fighting for the right to work less and live more. I believe it will be critical for the success of any political path to implementing a BI in Australia to progressively bring unions on board, reframing the political discourse to make it clear why they should do so.

Social service groups such as the Councils of Social Services, Anglicare, St Vincent de Paul Society, and others are also, at this point, quite sceptical of BI. None to my knowledge have publicly promoted the idea, although some individuals involved have told me they are warming to it. From personal conversations, the suspicion is based on a fear of losing the broad social compact which they have spent many decades fighting for and which they see embodied in the complex mesh of interwoven policies currently in existence. There are two lessons from this. Firstly, advocates have thus far failed to present BI as a new, and far broader, embodiment of the social compact than is currently in place, which is precisely what it should be. Secondly, it suggests that some in the social services sector have, alongside those in the ALP such as Chris Bowen and Andrew Leigh, internalised neoliberal assumptions that targeted support is better than universalist approaches, and that truly deep change is impossible. It may be that the slow shift already being perceived is due both to the rapid decay of those neoliberal assumptions and also the increasing realisation that the distributed, targeted approach is being so drastically whittled away that a step change may be necessary. There is a big opportunity here to get groups with enormous memberships and great social credibility on board.

Churches and other faith groups are also a prime candidate for powerfully supporting moves to a BI. As driving forces in movements from civil rights and Indigenous self-determination to fossil fuel divestment and refugee support action, faith groups play a critical role in shaping moral discourse and bringing millions of people with them. In this context, they will be vital to shifting our politics from punitive, exclusionary welfare policy to a universalist approach which seeks to make life better for all people, and leaving nobody behind. I am not aware of any faith groups actively pursuing the issue currently, but I believe the major barriers will be prioritisation and time, rather than any intrinsic opposition.

Feminist leaders will be an important part of any political path to a BI. Eva Cox, for example, already promotes understanding of the gender politics inherent in a shift to BI. As she and others characterise it, a BI can begin to shift the way society values work which has historically been "male", giving value to unpaid work which has historically been "female". Kathi Weeks argues, from a feminist perspective, that paid labour should not be assumed to be a social good (Weeks, 2011). In addition, others such as Petra Bueskens have written about how a BI can give women greater freedom to leave abusive relationships or to more easily combine parenting and work (Bueskens, in Hollo et al., 2017).

For Indigenous groups, BI is at this stage very low on the priority list. While some individuals see it as a form of reparations, if given to First Nations people first and early, and others support it as a way of recognising non-market contributions (e.g. Goreng Goreng in Hollo et al., 2017), the prime focus for most Indigenous people and groups is understandably elsewhere. There is an opportunity, if key Indigenous leaders choose to take it on, to make BI a plank of their fight for sovereignty, but this must, of course, be their choice. What we can do is frame the BI conversation in ways which match their world views, show them how it can be useful and important for them, and offer it in a spirit of genuine conciliation.

The business community poses an interesting challenge. There are already individuals such as venture capitalist Mark Carnegie playing a role similar to that which Elon Musk and Mark Zuckerberg have been playing in the USA, stimulating discussion around a BI from a business perspective. It is important to note the tensions between business/libertarian approaches to BI and left/universalist approaches. Broadly, Australian business leaders tend to be firmly in the camp of denigrating workers, suppressing wages and seeking ever greater power over employees. There is a risk that working with this group could backfire, leading to a BI paired with further deregulation and undermined social support. A better approach would be to seek out more individuals like Mark Carnegie to lead a new drive from outside existing business lobby groups, sidelining those lobby groups in the conversation, and creating external pressure that slowly forces acceptance. Although a troubling strategy, it is also possible to present BI to business leaders as a risk management exercise, in the same way that the introduction of the welfare state came in response to growing social unrest and fear of revolution.

The media form an important, and diverse, constituency of their own, not just reporting on the issue. At a systemic level, there is the interplay between the right-wing press, cheering on the Liberal/National stigmatising of vulnerable people, and often baying for more blood, and the "sensible centre" of Fairfax and the ABC news reporting, firmly in the Bowen/Leigh neoliberal camp, treating BI as unrealistic, expensive and untargeted. On the edges sits the Guardian, showing real interest in ideas, and, of course, being connected to sister publications around the world where experiments are already taking place. That last factor—international experiments—is one which creates some potential for reporting in Australia. Australia's ongoing cultural cringe—the assumption that something happening elsewhere in the world is likely to be more important or higher quality that the same thing happening at home—drives interest in ideas from overseas far more than anything domestic, and advocates can take advantage of this by promoting international experts and experiences in the Australian context.

A greater potential, though, comes from shifting the focus from the systemic media level to that of journalists themselves. With every media corporation shedding journalists at a great rate, they are on the front line of the disruption of work, and there is active discussion amongst media practitioners of ways to fund public interest journalism. With legitimate doubts about government funding for journalism directly (other than public broadcasting), there is real potential for a BI as a means to help journalists to take the plunge in setting up independently. If advocates can convince a handful of influential journalists of this, it will help the cause gain traction more swiftly and broadly. In addition, working with journalists—highly trained professionals ending up jobless through no fault of their own—helps reframe the political discourse of work away from lifters and leaners and towards a universalist attitude of all of us pulling together.

The same critical reframing applies to communities directly affected by industrial change—automation, trade and technological shift—leading to the closure of manufacturing plants, coal mines and power stations. With these changes only likely to increase, ever more skilled jobs will disappear, and the implication that the workers themselves are responsible is offensive and untrue. Further, the idea that these jobs can or will all be replaced by other new industries with similar skill sets is reasonably treated with disdain by the workers themselves. A BI provides the possibility of moving into that uncertain future with confidence and security. If some of these communities could be convinced of this, they would be powerfully influential on the union movement, helping create greater momentum towards political change.

Other civil society groups, for example, environmental NGOs, community associations, the health sector and farmers' federations, have mostly not even considered BI yet. Partly this is because they are all kept structurally too busy to look outside their existing frameworks. Partly it is because BI has not yet reached a high enough profile to be on their radar—something BI advocates can and should address, of course. It is my view that BI can provide an exciting and important plank in platforms for several constituency groups among these. As set out in contributions to the Green Institute's recent collection, *Views of a UBI* (Hollo et al., 2017), farmers, carers, university students, single mothers, artists, and others stand to gain substantially and structurally from BI.

It is worth singling out the online progressive group GetUp!, which plays an important role in Australian civil society. Currently, GetUp! is influenced powerfully by the Bernie Sanders campaign's embrace of Job Guarantee, and, while supporting a Guaranteed Adequate Income, opposes prioritising BI. However, the Mason and Corbyn UBI approach may be just as influential, if the right circumstances can be organised.

As an artist myself, I would finally single out that constituency as a highly relevant one. Artists have always been on the edges of the market economy, and find ourselves very much on the frontlines of technologically driven change. It is harder than ever to make a decent income from the arts. Several countries, such as Belgium, Denmark and France, have some form of living wage for artists, and this precedent has already triggered open conversations across the arts about working introduce one here (see, e.g. David Pledger in Hollo et al., 2017). As mentioned earlier, this is in fact already announced policy by the Greens. Beyond its importance in supporting arts and artists, it is worth considering artists' role as cultural influencers in our society. Artists can become powerful advocates for BI, and help us tell the stories of a different society that will be vital to making this change happen.

It is also worth noting that, beyond organising with existing constituencies, a broad public campaign to involve people in redesigning and rethinking our approach to work and social support is vital. BI is, among other things, a tool for transforming the relationship between citizen and state, a fundamentally democratising tool, about ensuring that we, as a society, put the welfare of all of us at the heart of our project (Hollo et al., 2016). As such, a broad participatory and deliberative democratic process of designing a BI would be a perfect path. This is most likely to be achieved if we are successfully shifting the political discourse and bringing on board a series of existing constituency groups. But rather than leaving it to those groups to deliver, BI advocates should work through them to bring their members into an active role.

In this way, by shifting the discourse from fetishisation of paid work and stigmatisation of the poor and unemployed to universalism and the dignity of participation, by building union support, bringing some churches and social services groups on board, securing the active support of farmers federations, artists, Indigenous peoples' groups, and journalists, we can inch towards a tipping point where BI switches swiftly from inconceivable to inevitable.

Importantly, successfully doing this can put BI advocates in the right place at the right time. Because, very often in politics, whoever has a workable solution on the table when the crisis hits is the one who wins.

Between global economic shifts, social changes, and ecological destruction increasing the impacts of both, crisis is coming. We need to be ready.

References

Altman, J., & Klein, E. (2017). Lessons from a basic income programme for Indigenous Australians. *Oxford Development Studies, 46*(1), 132–146.

Benson, S. (2016, December 11). Welfare con job: Thousands of Aussies reject job offers to stay on benefits. *Daily Telegraph*. http://www.dailytelegraph.com.au/news/nsw/welfare-con-job-thousands-of-aussies-reject-job-offers-to-stay-on-benefits/news-story/9406583ae629023af264e10028c32006. Accessed 21 Aug 2018.

Bregman, R. (2017). *Utopia for realists and how we can get there*. London: Bloomsbury.

Cowburn, A. (2018, July 31). Labour set to include pilot of radical basic income policy in next manifesto, John McDonnell says. *Independent*. https://www.independent.co.uk/news/uk/politics/labour-universal-basic-income-john-mcdonnell-party-manifesto-corbyn-poverty-social-benefits-a8471616.html. Accessed 31 July 2018.

Cuthbertson, D. (2016, June 7). Arts for the dole? Greens propose living wage for creatives as part of election policy. *Sydney Morning Herald*. http://www.smh.com.au/entertainment/art-and-design/no-more-starving-artists-greens-propose-living-wage-for-creatives-as-part-of-arts-election-policy-20160607-gpddk6.html. Accessed 21 Aug 2018.

Daily Telegraph. (2017, March 6). Group within labor left are pushing for a universal basic income. *Daily Telegraph*. http://www.dailytelegraph.com.au/news/nsw/group-within-labor-left-are-pushing-for-a-universal-basic-income-which-is-not-meanstested/news-story/cc63da5f98a6d05cfee2976c95650bd4. Accessed 21 Aug 2018.

Di Natale, R. (2017). *Speech to National Press Club*. https://richard-di-natale.greensmps.org.au/articles/richard-di-natale-national-press-club. Accessed 21 Aug 2018.

Gillard, J. (2010, August 16). *Prime Minister, election speech, Brisbane*. http://electionspeeches.moadoph.gov.au/speeches/2010-julia-gillard. Accessed 21 Aug 2018.

Hollo, T., et al. (2016). *Can less work be more fair: A discussion paper on universal basic income and shorter working week*. The Green Institute. https://www.greeninstitute.org.au/publications/less-work-more-fair/. Accessed 21 Aug 2018.

Hollo, T., et al. (2017). *Views of a UBI: Perspectives from across Australia*. The Green Institute. https://www.greeninstitute.org.au/wp-content/uploads/2017/06/Views_of_a_UBI_Aust.pdf. Accessed 21 Aug 2018.

Keenan, M. (2018, May 8). *Tweet*. https://twitter.com/MichaelKeenanMP/status/993748763914133504

Leigh, A. (2017). *Speech – How can we reduce inequality – ANU Crawford School of Public Policy*. http://www.andrewleigh.com/speech_how_can_we_reduce_inequality_anu_crawford_school_of_public_policy. Accessed 21 Aug 2018.

Mason, P. (2015). *PostCapitalism: A guide to our future*. London: Allen Lane.

Megalogenis, G. (2010). *Quarterly essay, trivial pursuit: Leadership and the end of the reform era*. Melbourne, VIC: Black.

Moase, G. (2013, June 19). For a universal minimum income. *Overland*. https://overland.org.au/2013/06/for-a-universal-minimum-income/. Accessed 21 Aug 2018.

Murphy, K. (2017, June 9). Chris Bowen attacks universal basic income as 'payments to millionaires'. *Guardian Australia*. https://www.theguardian.com/australia-news/2017/jun/09/chris-bowen-attacks-universal-basic-income-as-payments-to-millionaires. Accessed 21 Aug 2018.

Novak, N. (2016, January 7). Welfare experiment may have applications in Australia. *Sydney Morning Herald*. http://www.smh.com.au/comment/welfare-experiment-may-have-applications-in-australia-20160106-gm0ukm.html. Accessed 21 Aug 2018.

O'Dwyer, K. (2010). *Maiden speech*. https://www.kellyodwyer.com.au/maiden-speech/. Accessed 27 Aug 2018.

Rundle, G. (2015, April 8). Spreading contagion of Greens Derangement Syndrome. *Crikey*. https://www.crikey.com.au/2015/04/08/rundle-spreading-contagion-of-greens-derangement-syndrome/. Accessed 22 Oct 2018.

Santens, S. (2018, May 2). *The future of the labor movement rests on the achievement of unconditional basic income*. Published online at medium. https://medium.com/basic-income/the-future-of-the-labor-movement-rests-on-the-achievement-of-unconditional-basic-income-217f26500d83. Accessed 28 Aug 2018.

Taylor, L. (2017, July 22). Alan Tudge waves his wand – And turns welfare debate upside down. *Guardian Australia*. https://www.theguardian.com/australia-news/2017/jul/22/alan-tudge-waves-his-wand-and-turns-welfare-debate-upside-down. Accessed 21 Aug 2018.

Tudge, A. (2016). *Speech – Welfare reform – Reducing dependency and setting higher expectations*. http://alantudge.com.au/Media/Speeches/tabid/72/articleType/ArticleView/articleId/940/language/en-US/Speech%2D%2DWelfare-Reform%2D%2DReducing-dependency-and-setting-higher-expectations.aspx. Accessed 21 Aug 2018.

Weeks, K. (2011). *The problem with work: Feminism, marxism, antiwork politics, and postwork imaginaries*. Durham, NC/London: Duke University Press.

Wilkie, A. (n.d.). http://andrewwilkie.org/project/social-services/. Accessed 28 Aug 2018.

8

Basic or Universal? Pathways for a Universal Basic Income

John Quiggin

Basic income (BI) concepts have been advanced in a number of different forms, and in support of radically different political agendas. As a result, it has acquired a highly disparate group of supporters, and also a disparate group of opponents. For example, the idea of a negative income tax (NET) is most commonly favoured by advocates of free markets, while the left has been more attracted to a universal payment or 'demogrant'. More incremental reform programmes have been associated with the concept of a guaranteed minimum income (GMI).

A crucial but not well understood starting point for analysis is that, when fully implemented, all of these proposals are equivalent in terms of their effects on the ultimate distribution of income. As this chapter will show, any universal payment financed by taxation can be replicated by a negative income tax, or by a means-test guaranteed minimum income.

The sharp differences between advocates of different versions of universal basic income reflect the broader political visions with which they are associated, and the rhetorical framing of the proposals. For a variety of reasons, many of the most ardent supporters of a universal basic income

J. Quiggin (✉)
University of Queensland, St Lucia, QLD, Australia

E. Klein et al. (eds.), *Implementing a Basic Income in Australia*, Exploring the Basic Income Guarantee, https://doi.org/10.1007/978-3-030-14378-7_8

are more excited by the first term, 'universal', than by the second 'basic', that is, by the idea that everyone should receive a payment, even if it is initially too small to support an adequate standard of living. However, this chapter will argue that any feasible route to a universal basic income (UBI) must begin by focusing on 'basic', that is, on ensuring all those whose market income is inadequate receive enough to provide a basic standard of living.

The chapter is organised as follows. Section 'Varieties of Basic Income' draws out the distinctions between different versions of basic income, and contrasts the age pension (unconditional, except for age, and adequate for a decent living standard) with other existing benefits. Most importantly, section 'Equivalence' demonstrates the equivalence claim made above, that any universal grant financed by taxation can be replicated by a negative income tax, or by a means-tested guaranteed minimum income. The core of the chapter is section 'Universal First or Basic First', which compares 'universal first' and 'basic first' approaches to UBI and argues that the 'basic first' approach is preferable. Section 'Utopianism, Managerialism and Reform' examines how the basic-first approach might work to transform the existing tax-welfare system, characterised by a patchwork of benefits and concessions, into a universal basic income. Section 'Utopianism, Managerialism and Reform' addresses political issues, beginning with the utopian nature of BI proposals. It is argued that the reintroduction of a utopian vision of the future is a necessary part of the restoration of a political left committed to radical reform in the short term. The section also deals with political issues and responds to a variety of common critiques of BI in the light of earlier discussion. Finally, some concluding comments are offered.

Varieties of Basic Income

This section begins by defining the three versions of basic income: a guaranteed minimum income, a negative income tax, and a universal grant. Section 'Universal First' begins with the observation that, except for the age requirement, Australia's retirement income system meets the requirements for a universal basic income. The age pension is set at a level sufficient to lift all people of eligible age out of poverty. Concessions on superannuation mean that virtually everyone receives public support equal to or greater than the value of the pension. In these respects, the age pension contrasts markedly with other existing benefits. Section 'Equivalence' provides the starting point for any comparative analysis, namely, a demonstration that any universal grant financed by taxation can be replicated by a negative income tax, or by a means-test guaranteed minimum income.

Definitions

The core feature of any basic income proposal is an unconditional commitment to ensure that all members of the community have an income sufficient to sustain a basic standard of living agreed by the community to be acceptable.

A universal basic income is an unconditional amount paid to everyone in the community The UBI could be paid to individuals or families and could be varied to take account of special needs such as disability.

A guaranteed minimum income is a policy that ensures that everyone in the community receives an income sufficient to sustain a basic standard of living. Although a UBI meets this criterion, a GMI is typically assumed to be paid only to those whose market income is inadequate.

A negative income tax is a specific way of implementing the GMI, with a tax schedule that includes a positive payment, equal to the guaranteed minimum for those with zero income. As income rises, the payment is reduced pro rata until income reaches the point where positive amounts of tax must be paid. The NIT is most closely associated with free-market economists such as Milton Friedman, with the primary appeal of replacing social welfare payments. Commonly, reflecting the general policy preferences of NIT advocates, the tax rate is assumed to be flat, but the scheme could be adopted to allow for a progressive scale,

Finally a universal grant, sometimes called a 'demogrant' is an unconditional payment to all members of the community. Advocates of universal grants commonly use the term universal basic income to describe this policy and claim that alternative versions such as GMI and NIT are not properly described as UBI policies. While rhetorically effective in some contexts, such a claim is not helpful as a starting point for analysis, since it constitutes an argument by definition, rather than a demonstration that a particular version of the policy is superior. Moreover, the fact that, as shown in section 'The Light on the Hill', all of these policies are (or may be made) effectively equivalent in terms of their effects on the distribution of income casts doubt on claims that seem to imply a fundamental difference between them.

A universal grant may be of any size, and need not be large enough to sustain a standard of living. The Alaska Permanent Fund Dividend (PFD), supported by oil revenues is an example. The Fund, which began operations in 1982, paid out about $2100 to every Alaskan resident in 2015, so it is not adequate enough for people to living on it with no other top up.

Retirement Income

As an example of a commitment to provide a basic income, consider retirement income. In Australia, as in most developed countries, everyone who has reached a sufficient age receives an income sufficient to keep them out of poverty, at least according to generally accepted measures such as the Henderson poverty line. The basic commitment is implemented through the age pension which is set, for an individual, at 27.7 per cent of Male Total Average Weekly Earnings (MTAWE). Further adjustments are made for differences in circumstances. Most importantly, recipients who rent privately receive assistance that depends on their household structure and rental payments.

The age pension is subject to a means test on income and assets. However, the thresholds are high enough and the clawback rates low enough that anyone for whom they are relevant can attain a standard of living comparable to that of typical working-age households. Moreover, taking superannuation concessions into account, the total value of the benefit provided to 'self-funded' retirees exceeds, in most cases, the value of the age pension. The means test simply limits 'double dipping'.

The social commitment to provision of a basic income does not extend to people of working age, or to children. Social security benefits for these groups are conditional on stringent tests for disability, active job search and so on, as well as income and asset tests that can only be satisfied by people below or near the poverty line. Moreover, most benefits are fixed at levels too low to keep recipients out of poverty. In particular, the unemployment benefit, now called NewStart allowance (the similarity to Orwell's Newspeak is presumably unintentional), has been frozen in real terms since 1994, and is well below the poverty line.

Equivalence

A crucial fact about the policies described in section 'Definitions' is that, in terms of their effects on the final distribution of income, after taxes and transfers, they are all equivalent. That is, any universal grant financed by taxation can be replicated by a negative income tax, or by a means-tested guaranteed minimum income. It follows that arguments about the appropriate form of a BI policy should not concern the effects of the policy on income distribution. Rather, they reflect secondary issues, such as the way in which policies are framed politically (see Lakoff, 2004), administrative issues such as 'churning' and income measurement or concerns about the way to move to a BI from our current starting point. The third of these issues is the primary concern of this chapter.

The equivalence of alternative forms of BI may be illustrated by a simplified example in which we disregard households and assume that everyone in the community is treated as a separate individual for the purpose of tax and welfare payments. Consider a community where average annual market income per person is \$100,000 and the acceptable basic income is set at \$25,000.

A universal payment of \$25,000 could therefore be financed by a proportional income tax set at a rate of 25 per cent. Someone with no market income would receive the payment and pay no tax, so that net income would be equal to \$25,000. Someone earning the average income of \$100,000 would receive \$25,000 in universal payment and pay \$25,000 in tax, ending up with an unchanged net income of \$100,000.

Someone earning $200,000 would pay $50,000 in tax, and have a net income of $175,000.

It is easy to see that the same outcome could be achieved with a negative income tax, also at a rate of 25 per cent, with the payment at zero income set at $25,000. This tax would raise zero net revenue, but would yield the same post-tax incomes as the universal payment described above.

Finally consider a means-tested guaranteed minimum income set at $25,000, with a clawback rate of 25 per cent. Everyone with incomes under $100,000 would receive a payment. The payment could be financed by a single-bracket income tax with a threshold of $100,000 and a marginal tax rate of 25 per cent.

These three policies would have identical effects on the distribution of income after taxes and transfers. Each would also imply that everyone in the community faced an effective marginal tax rate (the some of the marginal tax rate and the clawback rate for means-tested benefits) of 25 per cent. On the other hand, they would have radically different effects on the ratio of government revenue to national income. The universal payment would imply setting government revenue and expenditure equal to 25 per cent of income while, as noted, the negative income tax would raise no net revenue and require no expenditure.

The revenue and expenditure associated with a means-tested guaranteed minimum income would depend on how unequally incomes were distributed around the mean value of $100,000.

Based on plausible simplifying assumptions, the required expenditure and revenue would be between 7.5 and 12.5 per cent of national income. Polar cases include (a) a uniform distribution over the range (0, 100,000). This distribution implies a revenue and expenditure requirement equal to 12.5 per cent of national income; and (b) a three-point distribution, with 30 per cent receiving zero, 40 per cent receiving 100,000 and 30 per cent receiving 200,000. This distribution implies a revenue and expenditure requirement equal to 7.5 per cent of national income.

As these examples illustrate, the difference between means-testing and taxation is essentially arbitrary. This means that, in the present context, measures of the ratio of tax revenue and public expenditure to national income are largely uninformative. Depending on the administrative systems involved, the various proposals described above might have different implications for compliance and so on. However, in a fully integrated tax-welfare system, these distinctions would disappear.

However, this equivalence is only valid when the schemes are implemented in full. If we are considering a transition from the current situation to a universal basic income, there are genuine distinctions between the alternative approaches.

Universal First or Basic First

As a vision of the future, there's plenty of appeal in the idea of a society in which everyone has sufficient resources to meet their basic needs, regardless of their assets, abilities or the way they choose to live their lives. But once we return to the realm of electoral politics, the unavoidable question arises: how do we get there from here? Given the obvious impossibility of implementing a BI in one or a few terms of governments, what should be the first steps?

Universal First

Intuitively, a priority on universalism leads to the idea that we should begin with a small universal payment, which would gradually increase in value to the point where it becomes sufficient to meet basic needs. Alaska's Permanent Fund Dividend, paid out of the invested proceeds of oil royalties is often cited as an exemplar of this approach. The fund paid each Alaskan around \$2100 in 2015 (Widerquist, 2015), one of the highest amounts ever, reflecting high oil prices in the previous year.

Unfortunately, \$2100 a year is only about \$40 a week, a handy addition to the budget, but not nearly enough for a person to live on. In the absence of independent income (say, from private investments), the number of Alaskans who have been freed from the need to work, or meet the demanding conditions for unemployment benefits, is approximately zero.

Nor is there any real prospect that this will change. Even if the dividend were to double or triple, it would not provide a poverty line income as defined by the US government, let alone a decent living standard. And, in the absence of an unlikely oil bonanza, there's no reason to expect any increase at all.

In practical terms, a strategy of starting with a small universal benefit, and gradually increasing it, can yield no real impact for several decades. Over the course of such a period, it is likely that some real or imagined budgetary emergency would see the programme curtailed and ultimately scrapped. This has already happened in the case of Alaska's Permanent Fund. In 2017, the Alaskan legislature voted to allocate some of the fund to offsetting the state's budget deficit, rather than using it to finance the dividend. The result was to reduce the annual dividend to $1250 (Brooks, 2017).

To avoid these risks, a universal-first approach requires the immediate introduction of a universal payment substantial enough to support at least a minimal standard of living. This in turn would require a substantial increase in tax rates, introduced at a stroke. While the impact on net income would be offset by the existence of the universal grant, the difficulties in specifying a new tax scale, and adjusting tax concessions, in such a way as to spread the burden equitably, would be formidable. Political aspects of the problem are discussed in section 'Concluding Comments'.

Basic First

The alternative is to start with 'Basic' rather than 'Universal'. That is, begin by providing sufficient income to support a decent standard of living to those most in need, then expand it to the entire population. This approach is most naturally associated with a guaranteed minimum income.

Existing benefit systems potentially fall short of the GMI in three ways. First, each benefit in existing systems, such as that in Australia, is conditional on eligibility requirements such as disability or job search activity. Second, means-tested benefits such as those offered in Australia are subject to clawbacks that imply high effective marginal rates of taxation if people take work alongside the support. Finally, with exceptions such as the old age pension the benefits are typically insufficient to lift recipients out of poverty.

Over recent decades, access to basic incomes has become steadily more difficult in all these respects. The case of unemployment benefits, noted above, is typical. Similar cuts and restrictions have been imposed on disability benefits and supporting parents benefits in Australia and elsewhere in the world. These cuts have been driven by a combination of neoliberal drives to reduce public spending and conservative hostility to welfare recipients, reflected in the use of stigmatising terms such as Joe Hockey's distinction between 'lifters' and 'leaners'.

A 'basic first' approach would require reversing these trends and would therefore entail immediate and sharp political division between advocates of a basic income and supporters of the push to restrict welfare benefits to the 'deserving poor'. Political implications are discussed in more detail in section 'Concluding Comments'.

How to Get There

Assuming a 'basic first' approach is preferred, how might it be implemented? Three initial measures might be considered:

(i) increase unemployment benefits, at least to the poverty line;
(ii) replace the job search test for unemployment benefits with a 'participation' test;
(iii) fully integrate the tax and welfare systems

Increasing Unemployment Benefits

The basic old age pension in Australia is around 28 per cent of Male Total Average Weekly Earnings (MTAWE) for single pensioners and 42 per cent for couples. This income has proved sufficient to eliminate, almost completely, poverty among the olds, who were once the most exposed to privation. The same level applies to Service Pensions and Disability Support Pensions.

By contrast, unemployment benefits (now given the Newspeaky name Newstart) were briefly set equal to old age pensions at 25 per cent of MTAWE under the Whitlam government. However, a long series of cuts and freezes have reduced access to benefits and cut their relative value to around 18 per cent of MTAWE today.

Participation Income

While social acceptance for a completely unconditional basic income is a long way off, a 'participation income' as proposed by Atkinson would have many of the same effects. The criteria for earning a basic income would no longer be based on market production but on a social assessment of value. Participation in this context would include full-time study, raising children, and voluntary work.

The creation of a participation income would automatically raise the question 'what kinds of activities' are socially valuable. The default assumption, in a market society, is that the social value of any activity is reflected in the market income it generates. This assumption is explicit in neoliberal thinking about public policy, but it is also widely shared in the community in a more or less qualified form. Debate about a participation income would therefore involve fundamental changes to the assumptions underlying the neoliberal economic and social order.

On the one hand, supports of a BI would seek to extend the concept of participation to encompass commitments to artistic, cultural and sporting endeavours, even if these were not at a level sufficient to generate a market income, or to qualify for existing forms of public support, such as arts grants. On the other hand, debate over BI would focus attention on the fact that some activities generate large market incomes but yield little, or even negative, social value. The activities of the financial sector provide an example.

A Fully Integrated Tax-Welfare System

As discussed above, a fully implemented basic income would imply an integrated tax-welfare system, in which the distinction between means-testing and taxation would disappear. A step towards this goal would be the inclusion of benefit payments in taxable income, with a corresponding, or larger, reduction in clawback rates.

Completely integrating clawbacks into the tax system would clarify the high effective marginal tax rates currently faced by benefit recipients (commonly above 60 per cent). This would provide a counter-argument to the spurious claims that the marginal rate faced by high-income earners (less than 50 per cent) constitutes an unreasonable disincentive to work effort.

Utopianism, Managerialism and Reform

We've moved from a situation where the left offered a utopian vision that inspired people to a situation where centre-left parties offered a managerialist response to the Global Financial Crisis and the rise of inequality. That has proved insufficient to be enough to mobilise and engage people or to stave off the 'dominant identity politics' that has largely supplanted neoliberalism on the right. We need to recapture the kind of vision and language of utopia that used to be part and parcel of left politics.

The Light on the Hill

As the discussion above suggests, BI is not a short-term policy option but a vision to be realised over coming decades. So, the crucial issues are not those concerning the details of the design but the process and politics of getting there.

This distinction between a short-term policy platform and a long-term objective used to be normal for social democratic and socialist parties, and is still reflected in the unwillingness of members of the ALP to discard the Socialist Objective,[1] even after decades in which Labor governments were more likely to privatise than to nationalise.

For the future, we need more than a formal set of words in a policy platform. We need, in Chifley's words, a 'light on the hill' towards which we can climb year by year. In this context, it is useful to compare, once again, the 'basic first' and 'universal first' approaches.

A 'basic first' approach to universal basic income requires the reversal of long-standing trends that have tightened access to unemployment benefits and other forms of welfare. It therefore involves a direct assault on the policy directions that have prevailed for at least the past 25 years. It links an ultimate, currently unattainable, objective to immediate political struggles.

A 'universal first' approach is more explicitly utopian in its vision than the 'basic first' approach. However, there is no obvious starting point for a short-term 'fighting platform'.

Beyond the Labour Market

For most people, the central fact of economic life is the need to work for a living, by producing, or helping to produce, goods and services that can be sold in a market. That is true, not only of work for wages but of domestic work, mostly done by women, that must be done to make market work possible. It's also true of most of those who are formally classified as 'self-employed' and many small employers.

To put it simply, having a job is a vital economic necessity in late capitalism societies. To maintain a moderately comfortable life, we need not just a job but a full-time job, with good wages and reasonable security. Moreover, except for a relatively brief period in the mid-twentieth century (the Keynesian 'long boom'), the existence of enough jobs to provide

[1] The objective states 'The Australian Labor Party is a democratic socialist party and has the objective of the democratic socialisation of industry, production, distribution and exchange, to the extent necessary to eliminate exploitation and other anti-social features in these fields', and is followed by a list of principles associate with this objective. Even when disregarded in practice by the ALP, the Objective provides a point around which advocates of radical social change can rally'.

employment for the workforce has depended on the willingness and ability of owners of capital to provide those jobs (see Kalecki, 1943).

The critical feature of the labour market is that the owners of capital can choose whether or not to buy labour, but those whose only asset is labour have no choice but to sell it. This imbalance of power is inherent in capitalism.

The ultimate goal of socialism and social democracy should be a society and economy where work is a choice rather than an economic necessity.

A basic income, made universal over time, would play a central role in such a society. It would imply, for everyone, the possibility of maintaining an adequate standard of living without market work.

For this to be a real choice, the other side of the coin is a job guarantee, to ensure that everyone who wants to can work and earn a reasonable wage for doing so. The relationship between a UBI and a job guarantee is beyond the scope of this essay, but is discussed by Fitzroy and Jin (2018), Quiggin (2018) and Henderson and Quiggin (2019).

Political Obstacles

The political obstacles are substantial. The whole thrust of policy for decades has been to increase the intensity of work-testing for benefits of all kinds. And, unlike much of the neoliberal agenda, measures like 'work for the dole' have plenty of public support, despite the largely spurious nature of the work that can be required in such a scheme.

But the difficulty of the proposal is precisely the point. A BI represents both a long-term challenge to the entire organisation of work and labour and, in the short-term, a rallying point for a rejection of one of the central themes of neoliberalism, the critical importance of (paid) work. Conversely, advocacy of a BI focuses attention on the need to recognise the contribution made by unpaid work to society, including the formal economy. As the collapse of the neoliberal order accelerates under pressure from the political right, this mixture of utopian vision and immediate resistance is precisely what the left needs to offer.

It's not particularly challenging to take the first steps towards a BI using a universal payment approach. This may be done through a relatively modest payment, like the Alaska Permanent Fund Dividend. However, as noted above, the next steps in the transition are more problematic. Transition to a universal BI would require that the value of the universal grant should be increased over time. In reality, the opposite is happening. As Alaska's budget comes under stress, the grant is an obvious source of potential saving. Cuts have been proposed repeatedly.

Sustainability

Any discussion of the political sustainability of a full-scale BI is obviously speculative. Not only has nothing of the kind ever been attempted but also the implied social transformation is so radical as to make analysis a matter of conjecture rather than analysis.

Nevertheless, long-standing arguments about the superior political viability of universalism, compared to means-testing and targeting would seem to gain strength from the kinds of shifts required for such a policy.

As noted above, the difference between GMI and universal payments is one of form rather than substance. Hence, once a basic income was universally available, or nearly so, it would be possible to restructure the system to convert it to a universal payment.

Concluding Comments

When fully implemented, universal payments and GMI schemes are almost identical to each other (and to negative income taxes). To be more precise, in terms of the ultimate distribution of income and effective marginal tax rates, including the effects of means-testing basic payments, any universal payment is equivalent to a GMI with the same guaranteed payment and similarly progressive taxes, and vice versa. For wage earners operating under the Pay-As-You-Earn system, there would be no difference in net pay, just a different way of calculating it on the payslip. So, if we actually achieved a genuine GMI, transforming it to a universal payment would be largely a matter of definitions.

The critical question then is how to get there. Compared to 'Universal first' the 'Basic first' approach has the merit that we are already part of the way there, and the next steps involve clear, and feasible, political demands.

References

Brooks, J. (2017, April 12). Alaska House votes to lower permanent fund dividend. *Juneau Empire*. Retrieved from https://www.juneauempire.com/news/alaska-house-votes-to-lower-permanent-fund-dividend/

FitzRoy, F., & Jin, J. (2018). Basic income and a public job offer: Complementary policies to reduce poverty and unemployment. *Journal of Poverty and Social Justice, 26*, 191. https://doi.org/10.1332/175982718X15200701225179.

Henderson, T., & Quiggin, J. (2019). Trade unions and basic income. In M. Torry (Ed.), *Palgrave international handbook of basic income*. Melbourne, VIC: Melbourne University Press.

Kalecki, M. (1943). Political aspects of full employment. *The Political Quarterly, 14*(4), 322–330. https://doi.org/10.1111/j.1467-923X.1943.tb01016.x.

Lakoff, G. (2004). *Don't think of an elephant! Know your values and frame the debate – The essential guide for progressives*. New York: Chelsea Green.

Quiggin, J. (2018). Labour market policy and the future of work. In P. Saunders (Ed.), *Social security reform: Revisiting Henderson and basic income in Australia*. Melbourne, VIC: Melbourne University Press.

Widerquist, K. (2015). *Alaska, USA: 2015 dividend estimated to be near highest ever*. Basic Income Earth Network. Retrieved from http://basicincome.org/news/2015/08/alaska-usa-dividend-amount-estimated-to-be-near-highest-ever/

9

Stepping Stones to an Australian Basic Income

Ben Spies-Butcher and Troy Henderson

Introduction

Basic Income (BI) can be viewed as a "pragmatic-utopian reform" (Henderson, 2017) aimed at establishing a universal social right to a regular cash payment sufficient to meet basic needs. The high fiscal cost of such a policy, together with the cultural force of the "work ethic", and the specific institutional character of national tax and transfer systems, presents as significant obstacles to this reform. Therefore, we argue that a "stepping stones" approach may offer a way forward in terms of thinking through the intermediate steps between current institutional arrangements and the implementation of a truly universal and adequate BI.

B. Spies-Butcher (✉)
Macquarie University, Macquarie Park, NSW, Australia
e-mail: ben.spies-butcher@mq.edu.au

T. Henderson
University of Sydney, Sydney, NSW, Australia
e-mail: troy.henderson@sydney.edu.au

E. Klein et al. (eds.), *Implementing a Basic Income in Australia*, Exploring the Basic Income Guarantee, https://doi.org/10.1007/978-3-030-14378-7_9

Australia's system of targeted cash payments is one of the most redistributive in the world. An influential argument in Australia has been that by directing resources to those with limited means, more can be done to address inequality and poverty with limited resources. Given the targeted nature of the existing system, any move towards universalism is likely to reduce the degree of redistribution per dollar spent, and if done in isolation, may even reduce the total level of redistribution of social payments by only extending additional assistance to those with more resources.

There is, however, reason to believe that Australia's targeted payments system creates new problems, particularly by increasing tax resistance. The "paradox of redistribution" thesis (Korpi & Palme, 1998) claims that by targeting resources only to the poor, welfare programmes become stigmatised, middle class voters see little benefit, and thus the programmes lose the political support necessary to access fiscal resources. While the international evidence is mixed, the thesis is consistent with recent dynamics in Australia. The most targeted payments, especially the Newstart Allowance, have the greatest degree of stigma, have faced consistent erosion and have become subject to new punitive forms of conditionality. Alternatively, the more universal payments, the age pension and family benefits, have enjoyed much greater political support, have had much easier access and more generous indexation and have even seen discretionary increases in payment levels.

These existing institutional structures and cultural dynamics highlight opportunities—and likely points of resistance—in relation to shifting Australia's system of income support in the direction of BI. In this chapter, we first outline the "stepping stones" approach in general. Second, we examine how a combination of a more universal age pension and an unconditional Youth BI (YBI) might serve as an example of the "stepping stones" approach in practice. We conclude by noting how such an approach can help address emerging intergenerational inequalities.

Stepping Stones to Basic Income

The Basic Income Earth Network defines BI as "a periodic cash payment unconditionally delivered to all on an individual basis, without means-test or work requirement" (BIEN, 2016). One criticism of BI is that as soon as the payment reaches a non-trivial level its unconditional and universal character generates a high fiscal cost that renders the policy politically infeasible. There is a growing international body of literature focused on estimating the fiscal impact and static distributional effects of different levels—and models—of BI (see Martinelli, 2017; OECD, 2017; Reed & Lansley, 2016). The literature relies on microsimulations of the tax and transfer systems of various countries and regions.

There is a clear divide between "universal pension" or universal basic income (UBI) models in which everyone receives the same payment before tax and "negative income tax" (NIT) models in which only those individuals whose incomes fall below particular thresholds receive a full—or partial—payment. Harvey (2006) is not alone in concluding that "a UBI and an NIT designed to achieve the same redistributive effect would impose the same marginal rates of taxation on other sources of income, but that the overall tax burden required to fund an NIT would be much smaller than for an equivalent UBI" (Harvey, 2006: 17). Similarly, Honkanen, states that a UBI model "can be almost equal with an NIT model when we compare the distributional effects and net income flows" but that "If the difference between net and gross flows is not grasped, the large transfer flows create the appearance of very high costs" for the UBI model (Honkanen, 2014: 132–33).

Australian researchers have reached similar conclusions. A 1998 study modelled a range of BI/Flat Tax (FT) and NIT scenarios that might move Australia towards a more integrated and simplified tax and transfer system. The authors concluded that the "most radical change" of a BI/FT was "not likely to be feasible" but that scenarios that "involve the tapering out of tax credits, variable tax rates, and some selectivity in who receives tax credits make the idea of a negative income tax system look much more feasible" (Dawkins, Beer, Harding, Johnson, & Scutella, 1998: 254).

Scutella (2004) modelled a BI/FT model in which a "basic non-taxable level of income is introduced that replaces all existing basic social security benefits, and additional payments such as rent assistance, pharmaceutical allowance and family payments" and "the existing tax structure…is replaced with a constant marginal tax rate on all taxable income" (Scutella, 2004: 6). Scuttella concluded that a BI "coinciding with current benefit rates is costly, with a marginal tax rate of over fifty per cent required to ensure revenue neutrality in the first instance". While the system would be "more equitable and in certain circumstances social welfare enhancing" Scuttella found it would have negative effects on labour supply and efficiency and argued that "such a tax rate is almost certain political suicide for any government advocating such a system" (Scutella, 2004: 26).

We acknowledge that interpretations of "feasibility" differ, and that more radical models of BI may be more—or less—feasible in different economic and political contexts. Nonetheless, these concerns over the fiscal impact, incentive effects and political obstacles to moving straight to a full UBI suggest that a "stepping stones" approach could offer a way forward in terms of building political support for a more universal system of income support while improving the material circumstances of two groups with higher levels of vulnerability than the general population.

A Universal Age Pension

Australia's targeted social spending is a distinctive feature of an Antipodean social model developed around wage regulation during the early twentieth century (Castles, 1985). While arbitration is the central feature of this "wage earner" model of welfare, the use of flat-rate social payments is also distinctive. Unlike European contributory schemes, where payments are generally related to previous earnings and funded through social security contributions, or the highly targeted and stigmatised models of social payments in the United States, Australia pioneered a model of social protection that was inclusive but frugal. This initially developed through age pensions introduced at the turn of the twentieth century. The labour movement's ambivalence towards the state meant resistance to raising taxes on ordinary workers, significantly limiting the fiscal potential of social policy. Australia's model therefore tried to do a lot with limited revenues. The pension was set at a low flat rate, which provided reasonable "replacement" levels of income to low-income workers, but would be considered inadequate for the emerging middle class.

Australia's public pensions have (almost) always been means-tested; however, means-tests are qualitatively different to many other jurisdictions. Rather than using means-tests to restrict access to the very poor, the pension means-test is set at a level that ensures a substantial majority of those aged over 65 are eligible for at least a part pension, and a large minority receives the full pension. The use of means-tests to "exclude the rich" rather than to "target the poor" marks out the Antipodean model as a form of "affluence testing" as opposed to the more meagre tradition of "means testing". The distinction is not only a technical or economic one. Distinct political dynamics have emerged between those programmes in Australia that retain the structure of affluence testing—the age pension and family payments—and those that have been subject to more restrictive means-testing. The latter have seen their value stagnate in real terms, and fall as a proportion of average wages and incomes, and have become subject to increasingly paternalistic and stigmatising conditionality.

Alternatively, the age pension has enjoyed considerable political support. During the 2000s the Coalition widened access and the Labor Party then increased the rate. Similarly, the Coalition increased family payments; although targeting has been modestly tightened at times for both. In 2016, 69% (2.54 million) of eligible Australians received some level of age pension. Among recipients, 57.9% received the full pension (maximum rate payment) and 42.1% received a part pension. In 2015–2016, expenditure on the age pension was around $42 billion or 2.6% of gross domestic product (GDP) (Department of Human Services, 2016).

The political resilience of Australia's public age pension suggests an important advantage of universalism. However, this model has come with two significant problems. First, the model is based on a very particular understanding of the life course. Means-tests operate as "affluence testing" largely because most older Australians earn relatively low incomes from the labour market. While retirement is not mandated, the "pension age" has a strong cultural role in determining retirement. The income test for the pension, which reduces payments by 50c in the dollar for earnings over $168 per fortnight, creates challenges for encouraging labour force participation.

Second, the Australian model has given rise to a dualistic pensions system based on inconsistent treatment of various forms of investment (Spies-Butcher & Stebbing, 2011: 46–9). The early politics of public pensions focused on providing for blue collar workers and was funded by taxes on the affluent (the initial tax base was highly progressive). This produced a compromise where those on higher incomes could adopt private pension arrangements exempt from taxation. Tax concessions survived the expansion of private pension savings to an employer-funded, compulsory mass system, called superannuation, in the 1980s and 1990s. Tax concessions were then expanded in the 2000s by a conservative government.

In addition, a separate set of tax concessions was introduced for owner-occupied housing as part of the "democratisation" of home ownership (Ibid.). Home ownership has effectively been built into the Australian pension model, with the rate reflecting low housing costs, and owner-occupied housing being exempt from the pension asset means-test.

The dualistic system creates challenges and opportunities for reformers. The tax concessions now have a substantial fiscal impact, potentially creating funds that could be directed towards a BI, while improving the incentives and distributive impacts of the tax system. Super tax concessions amounted to $33 billion in 2016–2017 (with more rapid growth than the age pension), while housing-related tax concessions total to over $60 billion (Treasury, 2017: 9).

A universal pension would eliminate the assets means-test, simultaneously eliminating the current exemption of the family home. Combined with eliminating the current tax exemptions for the family home, this would address one of the most significant distortions in the Australian housing market, assisting younger households currently locked out. Eliminating tax concessions for superannuation would close another distortion to current savings.

The combined effects would very likely improve equity amongst older households too. Both the superannuation and housing tax concessions are radically inegalitarian. The level of benefit is a function both of how much a person invests and a person's marginal tax rate, both of which *increase* with income. Grudnoff estimates over 70% of the benefits of the main housing tax concession, from the capital gains tax, are received by the top 10% of income earners (2015). Such a change would substantially increase the tax revenue available, allowing either a substantial reduction in eligibility age or support for other spending, such as the model for a Youth BI (YBI) we propose below.

However, the complexity of the dualistic pension system also presents challenges. Superannuation income, for example, is not taxed, but is included in the pension means-tests. This creates immense complexity for older households, who can opt to take some work income as superannuation contributions (reducing the tax paid) but potentially reducing public pension income.

Responding to the incentive problems created by these tax concessions, governments have gradually introduced work arounds. There is a special tax credit for older Australians earning labour market income, and limited exemptions for the proceeds of selling a home from the pension asset test. Ostensibly, this complexity reinforces the case for simplification; however, it also creates the potential for new losers. A recent announcement by the Labor Party to simplify the treatment of another concession granted to dividend income highlighted the potential for scare campaigns. While the reform improved equity overall, adverse media coverage of a small number of low-income losers caused the Labor Party to create a new set of exemptions of pensioners.

Australia has a history of converting tax concessions into related social spending. In the 1970s, tax concessions for private health insurance were converted into funding for universal public health care. In the 1980s concessional tax arrangements for dependent spouses were converted into benefits paid to primary carers. Ingles and Denniss (2014) have explored a similar conversion of superannuation tax concessions into a universal age pension. They found foregone tax revenue would not only fund a universal pension payment but also allow the eligibility age to be modestly lower. A BI model would be marginally more expensive, because it would eliminate the lower rate for individuals in a couple.

A universal pension is likely to increase workforce participation for older Australians. New Zealand is often taken as an Australian comparator, given similar histories, political institutions and policy settings. New Zealand also has a flat-rate pension, but one that is universal and non-means-tested for all over 65. While Australia's workforce participation rate of 12.9% for those aged 65 and over is considerably higher than many European countries, it is much lower than the New Zealand figure of 20% (AIHW, 2017), suggesting Australia's complex means-tests create work disincentives.

Rather than universalising the pension and lowering the eligibility age through the complete elimination of tax concessions, we propose a more modest and gradual route. A "stepping stones" model would ease the means-test, integrating the withdrawal of benefits with the marginal tax rates in the income tax system to produce a more consistent form of affluence testing. This approach promises to substantially reduce the cost of universalising the payment, while maintaining the incentive effects of universalism. It is also consistent with recent policy changes that have gradually reduced access to tax concessions, rather than eliminating them entirely.

However, the complexity of the current pension and housing tax arrangements makes any transition complicated. To explain how such a transition would work, we therefore focus on reforming the current youth benefit—Youth Allowance. We suggest that similar changes can be made to the age pension, allowing a gradual process of joining up these systems, a point we return to below.

A Youth Basic Income

We have argued that the age pension creates a useful model for a potential BI by adapting an "affluence tested" payment into a more universal payment consistent with labour market participation. Here we examine how a highly targeted "means-tested" payment might be transitioned into an affluence-tested payment. Creating a common policy architecture for youth and aged payments may foster policy competition towards genuine universalism. Incrementally extending payments to new age cohorts over several election cycles would reduce the fiscal cost of each step to the range of other election commitments, creating a viable political pathway.

As we have said, the targeted nature of Australia's existing payments systems means it is hard for reforms to increase progressivity or redistributive effect while also universalising access. An exception to this is where, as with our proposal for the pension, universalism is funded by removing regressive tax concessions. The benefits of universalism, however, also lie elsewhere. An important benefit claimed for the BI is that it might support workers in the context of riskier and less standardised labour markets by providing a partial form of social protection. This emphasises the insurance and incentive functions of a BI, rather than its redistributive effect. Following this logic, we focus on young people, a particularly vulnerable labour market segment, where we would expect workers to be making numerous transitions and to work variable hours across the year. Focusing on age also complements our initial discussion of pensions, which can be framed as a political bargain aimed at addressing emerging intergenerational inequalities.

Aspects of this approach are already evident in reforms to cash payments for working age people over the past 40 years. Originally, the unemployment benefit had a 100% withdrawal rate. This reflected Australia's breadwinner labour market, in which the clear majority of jobs were full-time, meaning that employment could be sensibly viewed as a binary variable (employed/unemployed). As part-time and casual forms of employment have proliferated since the 1980s, so policy makers have focused attention on effective marginal tax rates. Likewise, this complicates assumptions about "dependency", as groups unable to maintain full-time employment, such as those with a disability or caring responsibilities, gain non-standard employment.

The focus on effective marginal tax rates also highlights the partial equivalence of tax rates and benefit withdrawal rates. Each creates identical incentive effects because they have the same effect on marginal income gains from work. Yet they have profoundly different budgetary implications, and thus political implications.

Imagine two ways of funding an increase in spending on cash payments. One is to raise marginal tax rates; the other is to increase benefit withdrawal rates. The first increases aggregate taxation and maintains higher social spending—giving the appearance of "big government". The later reduces spending and maintains taxation—giving the appearance of "small government". While the incentive and distributional impacts of the two schemes may be identical, and the *net* fiscal impact is also the same, the politics differ. In the context of market ascendency since the 1980s, we argue it is unsurprising Australian governments frequently opted for the later strategy; and indeed note that Australia's highly targeted welfare system in many ways underestimates the effective size of the state.

Drawing on this logic, we propose a model tax and benefit withdrawal scale designed to re-create the Newstart Allowance for Australians age 20–24 as an "affluence tested" Youth Basic Income (YBI).[1] We operate on the following principles:

(i) Effective marginal tax rates should only increase with income
(ii) High income earners should receive no net benefit from moves towards universalism
(iii) No below average income earner should be left worse off (i.e. have a lower net income for any given market income)
(iv) The current tax scale and payment level should largely be taken as given

There are a range of payment rates, eligibility requirements and benefit withdrawal rates for Youth Allowance and the Newstart Allowance (see Department of Human Services, Australian Government, 2017a, 2017b). For the purposes of illustrating this model, we have chosen to set the YBI at $14,068 per annum, marginally above the single Newstart rate, while creating supplements for parents, carers, those with disability and some others to maintain existing payment levels. This ensures the proposal meets our four principles. Our intention is not to eliminate all other payments, but to create a new floor. We also note a minor New Zealand political party, TOP (Top Opportunities Party) recently proposed "an Unconditional Universal Basic Income and pay $200 a week (AUD188.33) to all New Zealanders aged 18–23" (Hayton, 2017).

Newstart Allowance recipients face high effective marginal tax rates as they take on paid work. Withdrawal of benefits starts at 50c in the dollar after earning only $52 a week, and rise to 60c before the benefit cuts out. The withdrawal rates for Youth Allowance are both less severe, and allow recipients to earn more income before benefits are withdrawn. Youth Allowance recipients can receive approximately $11,000 per annum in earned income without losing any benefit. As stated above, our proposal raises the YBI to $14,068 but begins withdrawals at $10,000, slightly

[1] The lower age bound was largely chosen for data reasons, and the upper bound reflects, we believe, a logical transition point.

Table 9.1 Proposed "affluence tested" universalism for Youth Allowance

Market income	Current marginal tax rate	Proposed withdrawal rate of payment	Effective marginal tax rate	Benefit received at top of income bracket
0–$10,000	0	0	0	$14,068
$10,001–$18,200	0	37c	37c	$11,034
$18,201–$37,000	19c	18c	37c	$7650
$37,001–$87,000	32.5c	5.5c	38c	$4650
$87,001–$180,000	37c	5c	42c	$0
$180,001+	45c	0c	45c	$0

Source: Authors' calculations

earlier than the current Youth Allowance withdrawal threshold. As can be seen below, this allows the combination of withdrawal and marginal tax rates to integrate more easily with the existing policy settings. Note also that given the higher base payment, all current Youth Allowance beneficiaries would be left better off. The proposed scales are presented in Table 9.1.

The labour force status of young people is strikingly dissimilar to the core working age population in Australia, primarily reflecting engagement in education. However, younger people are also overrepresented in terms of precarious and low-income work. According to analysis by the Australian Institute of Health and Welfare, young workers (aged 15–24) were twice as likely to be casual as any other age group in 2013 and youth unemployment was twice the national unemployment average, leaving young people with much lower incomes (AIHW, 2015).

An estimate of the net cost of a YBI along the lines we are proposing could be generated using a microsimulation of Australia's tax and transfer system. Here we provide only a rough estimate of the gross cost of our proposal to provide an indicator of the likely sums involved based on AIHW data (2013a: 57, 2013b: 10). Using conservative assumptions for earnings, we estimate a gross cost of approximately **$17.5 billion** (for full details, see Henderson & Spies-Butcher, 2017). While a substantial figure, it represents less than 1% of Australia's GDP and less than double the current cost of all unemployment assistance.

We are well aware this proposal faces significant challenges. While much cheaper than a fully universal BI, it remains a significant budgetary outlay. This is particularly because the current eligibility rules make it difficult for many young people to qualify, and force them instead to rely on their parents' income. It is difficult to estimate the saving produced by current spending this proposal would replace, given that it spans two payments; however, it is unlikely to be much over $1 billion. Removing the independence test, we argue, is both administratively and ethically sound, but expensive. However, the fiscal gap is substantially lower than the cost of regressive housing tax concessions.

Young workers do face some of the most frequent and precarious labour market transitions, but are also often perceived as less deserving than other social groups. This may be somewhat mitigated by two features of the system. First, this proposal is focused on effective marginal tax rates and so emphasises work incentives, and so can be seen as consistent with encouraging work effort. Second, given that the current system creates high barriers for young people to be deemed independent, in practice much of the additional spending is likely to ultimately result in reduced financial burden on many parents, as the demands on them to fund the consumption of their adult children diminish. Third, a YBI may go some way towards reducing intergenerational inequality by providing young Australians with the means to pursue a range of goals, such as concentrating on education and training, saving for a house deposit or starting their own business.

Many would argue that our base payment is still far from adequate. We agree. Here we make two notes. First, even though low, our proposal would increase the current incomes of the lowest income young people. Second, both this proposal and more generous proposals can be funded through small increases in the top two tax rates. This would allow a higher withdrawal rate for those earning $87,001–$180,000, meaning a higher base payment could be fully phased out by $180,000 while meeting our other principles. A higher base payment would also allow withdrawals to start earlier, ensuring only those on the lowest income received any benefit from the change, and reducing the total cost. We decided to leave some portion of income without any withdrawal to mimic the incentive effects of the current Youth Allowance payment; however, beginning withdrawals earlier has the potential to significantly reduce the cost of the proposal.

Finally, we draw attention to the logical equivalence between this scheme and a universal BI of the same amount introduced alongside a rescaling of the tax system so that marginal tax rates equal the effective marginal tax rates given in Table 9.1. Both proposals would involve the same incentive structure, the same distributional pattern and same net fiscal impact. However, a universal payment would involve substantially higher social spending, would necessarily involve higher headline tax rates and thus increase recorded levels of taxation. As each of these three consequences is likely to create additional political resistance, we argue our proposal presents a more plausible strategy for advancing the aims of a UBI, targeted at people of working age. Once in place, we also believe an affluence-targeted measure is less likely to suffer the political resistance associated with means-testing, while also constructing a larger constituency of beneficiaries. Thus, while initially modest, this may offer a politically realistic strategy to develop a more adequate payment over time.

Conclusion

Social scientists have an important role to play in helping to bridge the gap between the "big idea" of Basic Income and existing institutional, economic and cultural contexts. We argue that a "stepping stones" approach contributes to this end. Our proposal involves two steps and infers a third. First, transforming the age pension to mimic a universal payment. Second, to create a Youth Basic Income for those aged 20–24 based on an application of Australia's current use of "affluence testing". Finally, we argue these measures would create the political conditions for expansion, as citizens enjoyed the benefits of more universal payments and parties competed for support by expanding access to other age cohorts. Starting with young people focuses on citizens most supportive of BI, aiding political mobilisation. While adopting incrementalism, and modifying universalism through the principle of "affluence testing", we believe this proposal is consistent with appeals to a transformative politics, which clearly lays out a commitment to universalism. The proposal could be feasible over time by adapting the age pension to an "affluence tested" model, lowering the threshold at which the YBI is "clawed back" and by rolling back Australia's regressive system of tax expenditures. Unwinding these tax expenditures alongside a more universal pension also promises to address distortions in the housing market, offering the possibility of a new generational bargain for young people locked out of secure housing.

References

AIHW. (2013a). *Australia's welfare* 2013. *Australia's welfare no. 11. Cat. no. AUS 174*. Canberra, ACT: AIHW. Available at http://www.aihw.gov.au/publication-detail/?id=60129543825

AIHW. (2013b). Additional material Appendix A supplementary tables: Australia's welfare 2013 Appendix tables—Chapter 4 Children and young, *Australia's welfare* 2013. *Australia's welfare no. 11. Cat. no. AUS 174*. Canberra, ACT: AIHW. Available at http://www.aihw.gov.au/WorkArea/DownloadAsset.aspx?id=60129544251

AIHW. (2015). *Young people (15–24), Australia's welfare 2015*. Canberra, ACT: AIHW. Available at http://www.aihw.gov.au/australias-welfare/2015/young-people/#t7

AIHW. (2017). *Employment and economic participation: Work and retirement*. Canberra, ACT: AIHW. Available at http://www.aihw.gov.au/ageing/older-australia-at-a-glance/engagement/employment-and-economic/

BIEN. (2016). *About basic income*. Basic Income Earth Network. Available at http://basicincome.org/basic-income/

Castles, F. G. (1985). *The working class and welfare: Reflections on the political development of the welfare state in Australia and New Zealand, 1890–1980*. Wellington, NZ/Sydney, NSW: Allen & Unwin.

Dawkins, P., Beer, G., Harding, A., Johnson, D., & Scutella, R. (1998). Towards a negative income tax system for Australia. *The Australian Economic Review, 31*(3), 237.

Department of Human Services. (2016). *Age pension payment trends and profile report*. Canberra, ACT: Australian Government. Available at http://data.gov.au/dataset/4ccff587-4a46-4ab9-8833-76dadaa10ebe/resource/2b4f711b-c9a6-48d2-a47d-3cfeb268d693/download/age-pension-payment-trends-and-profile-report-june-2016.pdf

Department of Human Services. (2017a). *Newstart allowance*. Canberra, ACT: Australian Government. Available at https://www.humanservices.gov.au/customer/services/centrelink/newstart-allowance

Department of Human Services. (2017b). *Youth allowance*. Canberra, ACT: Australian Government. Available at https://www.humanservices.gov.au/customer/services/centrelink/youth-allowance

Grudnoff, M. (2015). *Top gears: How negative gearing and the capital gains tax discount benefit the top 10 per cent and drive up house prices*. Canberra, ACT: Policy Brief, Australia Institute.

Harvey, P. (2006). The relative cost of a universal basic income and a negative income tax. *Basic Income Studies, 1*(2), 1–24.

Hayton, M. (2017, September, 23). *MAX HAYTON. New Zealand's general election*. John Menadue pearls and irritations. Available at http://johnmenadue.com/may-hayton-new-zealands-general-election-september-23-2017/

Henderson, T. (2017). Real freedom for all revisited. *Basic Income Studies, 12*(1), 1–9.

Henderson, T., & Spies-Butcher, B. (2017). *Pathways to an Australian basic income*. Paper presented to an Australian Research Council workshop, Melbourne, VIC. Available at https://basicincome.org/wp-content/uploads/2015/01/Troy_Henderson_Basic_Income_in_Australia.pdf.

Honkanen, P. (2014). Basic income and negative income tax: A comparison with a simulation model. *Basic Income Studies, 9*(1–2), 1–17.

Ingles, D., & Denniss, R. (2014). *Sustaining us all in retirement: The case for a universal age pension. Policy brief no. 60*. Canberra, ACT: The Australia Institute. Available at http://www.tai.org.au/sites/defualt/files/PB%2060%20Sustaining%20us%20all%20in%20retirement.pdf

Korpi, W., & Palme, J. (1998). The paradox of redistribution and strategies of equality: Welfare state institutions, inequality, and poverty in the Western countries. *American Sociological Review, 63*, 661–687.

Martinelli, L. (2017, March 2017). *The fiscal and distributional implications of alternative universal basic income schemes in the UK* (IPR working paper). Bath, UK: Institute for Policy Research, University of Bath.

OECD. (2017). *Basic income as a policy option: Can it add up?* (Policy brief on the future of work). Paris: OECD.

Reed, H., & Lansley, S. (2016). *Universal basic income: An idea whose time has come?* London: Compass. Available at http://www.compassonline.org.uk/wp-content/uploads/2016/05/UniversalBasicIncomeByCompass-Spreads.pdf

Scutella, R. (2004). *Moves to a basic income-flat tax system in Australia: Implications for the distribution of income and supply of labour* (Melbourne Institute working paper no. 5/04).

Spies-Butcher, B., & Stebbing, A. (2011). Population ageing and tax reform in a dual welfare state. *Economic and Labour Relations Review, 22*(3), 45–64.

Treasury. (2017). *Tax expenditure statement 2016*. Canberra, ACT: Treasury.

10

What About Young People? Why a Basic Income for Young People Matters

Jenny Kaighin

A basic Income (BI) is proposed to be a modest income paid to all, at regular intervals, with lower rates paid to children (Standing, 2011). This chapter seeks to trouble the idea of a lower payment for children, with regard to payments to young people. This chapter argues that young people aged 16[1] and above should receive a BI amount that is equivalent to adults. A BI has the potential to be transformational, it can transform people's lives through the choices they can make, and it can transform how we see ourselves as a society. However, when considering paying young people an equivalent BI to adults some tensions emerge. These tensions arise from societal constructions of young people as dependent, unskilled and inexperienced, which are reflected in junior wages and lower rates of income support. This chapter will analyse the discourses

[1] Although many states have no restrictions on the legal age to begin work, most states have work restrictions for young people below 15 years of age. Young people can receive a Centrelink payment at 16. Most states have compulsory school attendance up to age 16 (or upon completion of year 10).

J. Kaighin (✉)
Queensland University of Technology, Brisbane, QLD, Australia
e-mail: j.kaighin@qut.edu.au

E. Klein et al. (eds.), *Implementing a Basic Income in Australia*, Exploring the Basic Income Guarantee, https://doi.org/10.1007/978-3-030-14378-7_10

and policies which both reflect and enable these constructions of young people. Ultimately, this chapter argues that an equitable BI will better enable young people to plan for their future, to shift out of survival mode if unemployed, and to enact their responsibilities and contribute to society as the responsible and active citizens that they already are.

Youth incomes are generally structured around maintaining young people's dependence on their families, and/or implying that young people have lower living costs, as well as being supported by assumptions about young people's skill levels and experience regardless of the actual value of their labour output (White, Wyn, & Robards, 2017). In Australia, 16-year-old wages sit at around 50 percent of adult (21+years) wages, and 18-year-old wages at 70 percent of adult wages. Yet young people might contribute to family incomes and young people who live independently have the same costs as adults but receive lower wages.

This creates challenges for considerations around BI because it will either perpetuate the dependent construction by being fixed at a lower rate for young people (especially those under 18 years), or be a payment that exceeds current junior wages, which then feeds into concerns around income support promoting dependence, or assumptions of 'laziness concerning job seeking (White et al., 2017). Australia's income support system, managed through the Centrelink, is tightly targeted, especially in relation to young people, with strict eligibility requirements, and strongly enforced mutual obligation responsibilities (Centrelink, 2018b). Within this climate, young people who are on income support measures are constructed as "dole bludgers"', too lazy to work and at risk of never developing a strong work ethic. These constructions will be examined later in this chapter. BI debates are about ethical justifications concerning equity and social rights (Mays & Marston, 2016). Pilot programmes, including Mincome in Canada, clearly demonstrate that receiving a BI does not build dependence or a handout mentality, in fact people want to work, or study (Forget, 2011) The intent of the BI isn't about supporting people to stay out of work, rather it's about providing a base income, as a right, to ensure a capacity to engage in the economy, to promote health and well-being, to foster innovation because people aren't just in survival mode, and to potentially reduce crime, particularly survival related crime.

Resolving these tensions will take a re/imagining, re/constructing of young people as active participants in society now, not just in the future. It will require valuing young people's contributions now, not just for what they might contribute in the future. Specifically, there needs to be recognition that young people, particularly those who are living independently, have the same basic living costs as adults and therefore, when upheld as a right, should receive a BI that is equal to that of adults. This chapter will engage in an analysis of discourses and the policy positions arising from these discourses in considering the issues arising in relation to the inclusion of young people in an equitable BI.

It is widely recognised that *youth* is a social construction (Nilan, Julian, & Germov, 2007; Sercombe, 2010; Wyn & White, 1997). A widely held construction is the idea that youth is a time of transition. The transition from child to adult, from school to work, from dependent to independent is deeply embedded in common sense thinking, and in policy language about young people. Granville Stanley Hall (1904) in his seminal text *Adolescence*, saw this stage as a time of storm and stress; a time where young people experienced high rates of conflict with parents, mood disruptions and risky behaviours. Arnett and Hughes (2012) state that although much of the detail of Hall's construction of youth as a time of storm and stress has been critiqued, a modified view of storm and stress has become widely accepted. Erikson (1968) posited that adolescence is a time of identity searching, whereby young people are trying to integrate their independent and dependent selves, and that a poor resolution of this crisis results in role confusion (Arnett & Hughes, 2012). Again, these notions of adolescence have been critiqued, yet the idea that young people don't know who they are yet, and therefore cannot be left to make critical decisions, has become part of the hegemonic discourse of adolescence (White et al., 2017). The prevailing belief that youth is a stressful and conflictual time has crept into common sense thinking, and shapes policy and interventions directed at young people.

Nilan et al. (2007) highlight that youth is a social construction that is historically linked to the birth of modern capitalism and the expansion of mass education. Functionalist constructions of young people highlight the need for young people be socialised in order to become citizens who will contribute to the workforce and economy (Parsons, 1951). Family and schools are identified as key institutions responsible for the socialisation of young people. Many of the problems attributed to young people such as early school leaving and juvenile crime are linked to poor socialisation, particularly by parents (Cunneen & White, 2011). Nilan et al. (2007) argue that an outcome of conservative constructions of young people as potentially disruptive and a threat to social order has resulted in interventions seeking to guide and control young people. As Sercombe (2010, p. 17) states 'if young people are qualitatively different from adults, and are particularly susceptible to trouble, they need different treatment and different models of governance'. He argues that most frequently these different models draw on principles of containment and control, and that policy and practice that emerge from this reinforce youth as the problematic 'other'.[2]

Transition approaches suggest that moving from childhood to adulthood is a universal developmental process that has a defined beginning and end point (White et al., 2017). They also argue that transition approaches almost exclusively focus on the transition from education to work. However, what becomes clear is that the nature of both education and of work are shifting, and therefore the transitional markers, that is, school being an indicator of childhood, and work being an indicator of adulthood, are shifting (Nilan et al., 2007). In Australia, we see an extended period of education and training, a highly casualised job market that requires increasing flexibility and capacity to shift between jobs (FYA, 2018). The extension of education and training is a product of neoliberal ideology which seeks to shift the onus of responsibility onto individuals to be 'job ready'. Neoliberal ideals create a hegemonic discourse that values individualism, competition, merit, consumerism and materialism, and these values are embedded in the ways people think about and treat themselves and others (Hosken, 2016). Nilan et al. (2007, p. 9) pose that neoliberal governmentality sees citizens as human capital with market value. Therefore, the transition from child to adult is a transition into 'high value human capital'. They argue that young people experience this as a lack of interest in them as people with value in the

---

[2] 'Through "othering" dominant groups in society maintain their dominance by assuming that their own features, characteristics and circumstances are the yardstick by which all others should be judged' (Couch & Cooper, 2016, p. 257). The practice of 'othering' is the exclusion of people who do not fit the dominant social norms.

present, rather than for their potential future value as a human capital resource. One outcome of the focus of young people as 'human capital' is that other issues young people may be dealing with such as mental health issues, alcohol and substance misuse, or homelessness are seen through the lens of these issues diminishing a young person's capacity to engage with the world of work (Sercombe, Omaji, Drew, Cooper, & Love, 2002).

Mainstream constructions of young people position them in two key ways. Firstly, young people are seen as dependent on parents and social institutions to both guide and protect them from themselves and from others (White et al., 2017). Secondly, young people are seen as problematic, evidenced by a range of moral panics created around young people as threats to law and order, threats to social capital and lazy and self-centred (Sercombe, 2010). The mainstream media ensure these constructions are front and centre in the public imagination, and the public uncritically accept these constructions, even when it does not match reality (Sercombe, 2010). The inherent harms in these negative constructions are that they perpetuate a positioning of young people as 'other'. As Giroux (2009, p. 16) in writing about the ideological and resulting policy threats facing young people in America laments:

> Youth have been increasingly removed from the register of public concern, civic commitment and ethical responsibility – viewed as a bad social investment. They linger in the public imagination as dim- witted, if not dangerous, ingrates, unworthy of compassion, and so justifiably relegated to the civic rubbish pile.

Giroux (2009) argues that within these constructions it is forgotten that young people are a product of the society that created them. The neoliberal individualising of risk (Furlong & Cartmel, 1997) sees young people being blamed for issues that, in reality, are created through social processes and structures (White et al., 2017). For example, young people are blamed for their own unemployment, accused of not trying hard enough to seek work, or being too picky about job opportunities. The reality, however, is that young people are the victims of an increasingly precarious labour market (Standing, 2011), as will be discussed further on in this chapter. The pressure is placed on young people to actively shape their lives under a neoliberal illusion which posits that obstacles can be overcome by hard work and a commitment to strive towards an independent future. As Giroux (2009) claims, within this narrow notion of individualism, all that matters is one's ability to compete and to win. However, as Furlong and Kelly (2005) point out, such logic discounts the ways multiple social divides including age, class, gender, ethnicity, sexual and gender identity, dis/ability and geography, structure life courses, chances and choices. White et al. (2017) argue that young people's social contexts are changing, as evidenced by extended education and precarious work. Therefore, they claim, the experiences of young people today must be viewed through the lens of these changing social contexts, rather than as a different (and problematic) generation. It is to the changing contexts of work and youth incomes that this chapter will now turn.

Work is a key structural institution shaping everyday life. Work is both a source of income and also as a source of identity (Sercombe et al., 2002). However, global capitalism and the rise of digital technologies are changing the nature of work and the way it is experienced. Since the Industrial Revolution, with the expansion of work to the majority it became seen as a natural and necessary part of life (Humphry, 2016). Humphry (2016, p. 268) suggests that work is a 'social negotiation that occurs within specific historical periods, but those who are most powerful preserve the right to direct and define the future of work'. In Australia, there has been an increase in the average hours of paid work, resulting in employees reporting feeling overloaded and experiencing poor work/life balance (Skinner & Pocock, 2010). Not only are we working harder, but also we are working longer, as seen by the removal of a fixed retirement age, and an increase to 65 years and 6 months in the age that a person can receive the Age Pension (Centrelink, 2018a). However, the availability of full-time permanent work, particularly at the entry level of the jobs market, has all but disappeared. A 2017 report by The Brotherhood of St Laurence (BSL) notes there has been a reduction in more than 50 percent in entry-level jobs since 2006. In Australia the youth labour market is characterised by higher levels of job mobility, lower average incomes and a different occupational profile to the rest of the working population (Davidson, Saunders, Bradbury, & Wong, 2018). For young people work is primarily located in the retail and food service industries, and this work is highly casualised and insecure (Foundation for Young Australians, 2013). The increasing insecurity of work, largely driven by global capitalism, and neoliberal policies arising from this demonstrate the critical importance of a BI. A BI provides some protections for all people, but particularly those least able to negotiate the peaks and troughs of a changing work landscape.

The term precarious work describes a combination of low pay, employment insecurity and working time insecurity (Campbell, 1997). For young people, low pay is a feature of junior wages, where young people are paid at a lower rate than adults. Yet young people often perform the same tasks with the same responsibilities for less pay. Junior wages present a crucial barrier in consideration of an equitable BI. Employment insecurity and an erosion of workers' rights and power are features of neoliberalism and deregulation (Australian Council of Trade Unions, 2011). The evidence of this can be seen in highly casualised and non-permanent work where employees can be dismissed or laid off without costs to the employer (ACTU, 2011). Unsafe or risky work can also add to employment insecurity. The third feature of precarious work is insecurity of hours, where an employee may be self-employed, working in the 'gig' economy (Arthur, 2016), or forced to change their spread of hours beyond the norm (White et al., 2017). The impacts of precarious work are in part mediated by class. White et al. (2017) note that precariousness signals a form of intergenerational inequality, and also intra-generational inequality based on class and family of origin.

The precarious nature of work, combined with an increasing expectation to engage in post school education. can result in a mismatch between educational credentials and workforce opportunities. This can lead to frustration for young people who, faced with increasing education debts, are unable to find full-time or permanent employment in their field of study (White et al., 2017). Standing (2011) identifies two precarity traps for young people emerging from tertiary education, one a debt trap, the other is being torn between the need for an income and a desire to follow their aspirations. This precarity can lead to a greater risk of exploitation, whereby employers are aware of young people's indebtedness and can use this to leverage a higher degree of compliance. As an example of this precarity, Standing (2011) notes the rise of internships as extremely problematic.

Young people, often during or post university studies compete for unpaid or low paid work in the hope of gaining skills and an entry into potential future professional work (Standing, 2011). Internships are promoted as opportunities to gain real-world experience according to the Australian Internships website (2018, para 3) 'an internship is the transition from study to work and is a necessary component to develop a student's skills, making them more advanced and diligent when they finally have the opportunity to be part of the working world' The rise of the internship as a 'necessary component' is evidence of a shifting of the goalposts in the transition from school to work, from youth to adult. The Australian Internships website (2018, para 4) goes on to say that 'the internship program is unpaid as the main aim is for the intern to meet their objectives', these objectives being skill development and training. However, it is difficult to imagine that earning an income would not somehow be an important objective, in order to survive. Standing (2011) argues that being an intern disguises unemployment. Internships provide a form of employment, which removes a person from the unemployment register, as they are no longer actively seeking work. This results in an apparent reduction in the unemployment figures, yet the work is unpaid and short term, a person cannot survive as an intern. Yet the government can trumpet their success in reducing unemployment (see current Prime Minister Scott Morrison's comments on this when he was Treasurer. As reported by the ABC Letts, 2018). Standing (2011) further states that internships are a threat to young people, because work is intended to be cheap. This exerts downward pressure on wages and opportunities of others who might otherwise be employed (Standing, 2011, p. 130). What is clear is that internships remove entry-level jobs out of the paid labour sphere and serve to create a pathway into work that is only accessible by those who have the support and resources to engage in unpaid labour. If unpaid labour, whether through internships or volunteering, is constructed as the new entry into paid work, then BI can help to facilitate this process. This is particularly true for those young people who may not have parental support and resources to draw while undertaking unpaid work.

Where precarious work is a significant issue for young people, there is the added complication of unemployment. The BSL (2018) states that one-third of all unemployed people in Australia are aged 15–24 years of age. Australia's overall unemployment rate is currently 5.3 percent, the lowest jobless rate since 2012 (Trading Economics, 2018). The government proclaims that it has created '1100 jobs a day' (Tehan, 2018). Yet many of these jobs fall into the realm of precarious employment, and young people are not necessarily the beneficiaries of this apparent jobs' growth as highlighted by the BSL (2018). The BSL (2018) while noting that the youth unemployment rate has decreased since 2014, it is still, at 12.2 percent, more than double the overall unemployment rate. However, the rate of youth unemployment is not evenly experienced across the country. BSL identifies 20 high youth unemployment hotspots, including the Queensland outback, a region which incorporates the mining towns of Mt. Isa and Weipa which have a youth unemployment rate of 67.1 percent. As argued by BSL in their 2017 report *Reality Bites* (BSL, 2017, p. 2) 'blaming young people for their predicament is simply not supported by the facts'.

Youth wages are set at levels below adult wages. White et al. (2017) state that low youth wages are related to entrenched social judgements about the value of youth labour. 'The acceptance of youth wages contradicts the longstanding principle of equal pay for work of equal value' (NSW Young Labor, 2012, p. 2) Young people as employees are seen as inexperienced and in need of training and extra supervision. Yet, these claims are not borne out in the responsibilities given to young people, who often perform the same work as their adult counterparts. This was highlighted in the submission to the Fair Work Review by NSW Young Labor (2012, p. 2) 'An 18 year old who has been employed in a job for two years can be paid less than a 22 year old who has been doing the same job for 2 weeks'. Two areas of the labour market that have high rates of young people working in them are the retail and the fast food industries. When looking at the awards rates of pay in these industries across those aged 15–21+ years, the wage differentials are significant. A 15-year-old under the Fast Food Industry Award (level 1 Casual) in 2018 receives AUD $10.39 per hour (weekday rate), by 17 years of age, this rate increases to AUD $15.59 per hour and the full adult (21+) wage is set at AUD $25.99 per hour (weekday rate) (Fair Work Ombudsman, 2018a). The rates are similar under the Retail Award (Fair Work Ombudsman, 2018b). Youth wages have an impact on youth unemployment. Nilan et al. (2007) highlight that employers employ young people due to low youth wage rates for employers. However, the anecdotal experience of young casual employees is that this changes as they age out of youth wages and into adult wages. Clearly, young people are excluded from wage justice simply because they are young, not because they are less responsible or more inexperienced. As stated earlier, this chapter argues that young people aged 16 years and above should be paid a BI at an equivalent rate to adults. The lack of appropriate remuneration for work, rather than justifying a lower BI, emphasises the importance an equitable payment.

Low youth wages then impact Youth Allowance,[3] the youth unemployment benefit. As stated earlier, the Commonwealth government continues to use targeted measures for income support, especially in relation to young people. Unemployment benefits have historically been set at a level below the minimum wage to provide an incentive for people to seek paid work (Mendes, 2003). For young people, this then sees the rate of income support set at well below adult income support payment levels and poverty line (Davidson et al., 2018). In the June quarter of 2018 the poverty line, inclusive of housing costs for a single person was AUD $409.20 per week. A single young person under 18 on Youth Allowance, living at home, receives $244.10 per fortnight and a single young person aged 16–21 and living away from home receives AUD $445.80 per fortnight (Centrelink, 2018b), just over half of the poverty line rate. Newstart Allowance begins at 22 years of age with the rate for a single person with no children set at AUD $545.80 per fortnight (Centrelink, 2018a). All of these rates are well below the adult minimum wage as set by the Fair Work Ombudsman (2018c) of AUD$719.20 per week. In 2013, Homelessness Australia did a comparison of the mean cost of living with Youth Allowance rates. Homelessness Australia (2016) included the maximum Rent Assistance rate, which bought the total amount to AUD $526 per fortnight. At the end of paying for rent, food, transport, utilities, internet and mobile phone, the difference was a deficit of AUD

[3] Youth Allowance is Government financial assistance paid to people 24 and under who are students, and 21 and under who are looking for work. The Adult equivalent is called Newstart. Allowance There are strict eligibility requirements for receiving Youth Allowance and recipients must be actively seeking work or in full-time study.

$94.16 and this model did not include study costs. While these figures are from 2013, the discrepancy in wages and cost of living still holds true. Indeed the cost of living has increased since 2013, and Youth Allowance has not increased at the same rate (Davidson, 2018). In 2018, the Anglicare Rental Affordability Snapshot (Anglicare Australia, 2018) found only **two** affordable (less than 30 percent of income) rental options for a person on Youth Allowance across Australia. Undoubtedly, Youth Allowance is insufficient to cover the very basics. The low rate of income support for young people rests upon two dominant assumptions: one that income support settings should be conducive to continuing engagement with family of origin; and two that young people have lower living costs (Wyn & White, 1997). Some young people do have lower living costs; however, many others do not have parental support, they may live independently, and some may have dependent children. Young people living independently receive junior rates of income support or wages, but pay the same rates for rent, utilities, and groceries, as do adults. An equitable BI on top of youth wages may at least open up more housing opportunities and potentially lift people out of simply surviving. This might then allow young people to consider further study, make different work choices, and even plan a career path.

Discussion of the systemic precarious conditions young people face is clearly important in considering the need for a BI. The Foundation for Young Australians (FYA, 2014) expresses the concern that this generation of young people will be the first generation of Australians to do worse than their forebears. In a capitalist, consumer society the importance of a regular adequate income is highly significant (White et al., 2017). Life chances are closely linked to the capacity of young people to be proactive in the planning of their futures. An adequate income is central to this aim. A BI, which is 'an income paid by a political community to all its members on an individual basis, without means test or work requirement' (Van Parijs, 2004, p. 7) is a simple solution (Arthur, 2016; Van Parijs, 2004). However, there are points of difference about the universality of such a scheme regarding young people. Some argue that the scheme should be paid to adult members of society (see Arthur, 2016; Murray, 2006), others propose a lower payment to children (see arguments in Mays, Marston, & Tomlinson, 2016) and others propose a scale that takes into account cost of living and earning capacity, resulting in lower payments to children and higher payments to people aged 18–24, reducing down again until the age of 65 due to increased earning capacity, and then increasing at 65 to act as a guaranteed aged pension (see Bruenig, 2015). Others propose that it be paid to all, regardless of age (see Van Parijs, 2004).

A BI is important as a response to the effects of global capitalism, as described above in relation to young people's precarious work and reduced wage justice. However, as argued by Ferguson (2010), it could also be consistent with neoliberal aims towards individual responsibility and reliance on the market. A BI provides a capacity for people to engage with the market and to set career goals and work towards them through participation in study. Detractors of a BI typically express concerns that if the government gives people money, they will work less (see Lewis, 2018 for discussion of the 'something for nothing' debate). Arthur (2016) highlights concerns expressed that the BI's lack of reciprocity weakens people's social obligation to work and pay taxes. However, Mays et al. (2016) claim BI provides a better way forward from the neoliberal trends that have dominated recent political thinking and policy. Indeed, it is these neoliberal forces that have created an economic and social environment that makes a BI even more necessary and more urgent for young people.

As discussed earlier, young people are constructed as needing guidance and control, as having a poor work ethic and as simply being different to other generations. Three key challenges arise when considering young people and BI. These three challenges link to these negative constructions of young people discussed throughout this chapter. The first challenge is the idea that young people should be dependent on family, and BI could be construed as giving young people the capacity to leave the parental home. The same concerns were expressed at the introduction of Young Homeless Allowance in 1986 (O'Connor, 1989). What was found was that the Young Homeless Allowance provided a pathway for young people to leave unsafe homes; however, it did not encourage young people to leave home simply because they didn't want to live with parental rules (O'Connor, 1989). The evidence is clear that where home is a safe environment, then young people will choose to stay there. The Annual *Mission*

Australia Youth Survey (Bullot, Cave, Fildes, Hall, & Plummer, 2017) consistently records that young people value family relationships very highly (80 percent) and that parents (78 percent) and friends (84 percent) are the most common sources of support. A BI provided to young people will contribute to the overall family income, thereby reducing some of the financial stress that families experience in raising young people (Phillips, Li, & Taylor, 2013). Financial stress can result in increased family conflict, and potential early home leaving by young people (National Youth Commission, 2008) Therefore, a BI could have the opposite effect. Rather than encouraging young people to leave home, it could reduce financial stress and the resulting family conflict and potential early home leaving.

A second concern is about incentives and assumptions that young people will not look for work if they are receiving a BI. These claims, made by conservative commentators and politicians (see Tehan, 2018),[4] reflect dominant discourses that young people without proper guidance (and penalties) will drift into a life of video game playing and crime. Discourses such as these result in tightly targeted and punitively delivered mutual obligation income support strategies. It is argued that these measures ensure that young people who are on income support develop a work ethic and become work ready (Tehan, 2018) These claims are countered by evidence that young people engage in work while at school (White et al., 2017). The *Longitudinal Study of Australian Children* (Australian Institute of Family Studies, 2017) found that 40 percent of 14–15 year olds had worked in the previous year. Young people are also engaged in volunteering (Walsh & Black, 2015), are active community members and digital citizens (Vromen, 2017) and many take on caring responsibilities in their families (Carers Australia, 2018). Young people want to work. Australia has the fourth highest employment rates of those aged 15–24 years old in the OECD (2018). White et al. (2017) claim that while young people undoubtedly experience precarious work, for some young people this is not necessarily perceived as a problem. They argue

[4] See also recently revealed reports that former Australian Prime Minister Tony Abbott planned to cut unemployment benefits for people under 30 in the 2014 Budget (McGhee & McKinnon, 2018).

that young people are active agents, who are engaging with the world as they find it and are therefore more able to respond to flexible work opportunities. Yet, at the same time Andreas and Wyn (2010) liken young people's experiences of work to the metaphor of a side show game of duck shooting where the benefits never seem to line up, resulting in simultaneous advantages and disadvantages, particularly where the demands on their lives are less flexible than their work opportunities might provide. They found that young men from lower socio-economic families find it most difficult to meet their goals, and education debts place them at higher risk because they have fewer resources in the first place. For many of the young people in their study, 'entrapment in inferior life chances' is a reality (Andreas & Wyn, 2010, p. 235). These challenges, which both draw on and perpetuate the devaluing of young people, highlight the criticality of the need for BI for young people. White et al. (2017) suggest that life chances are closely linked to the ability of young people to be proactive in the planning of their futures. Rather than a BI providing a 'something for nothing' benefit (Lewis, 2018), a BI provides a capacity for young people to be flexible, to engage in study and to manage the increasing precariousness of work. A BI makes it possible to survive while undertaking an internship, if that is the entry point into paid work. And importantly, a BI can help facilitate long-term career and life goal planning.

A third challenge, and potentially the most difficult to navigate, is that of the low rate of youth incomes. As discussed throughout this chapter, this chapter argues strongly that a BI for young people should be set at the same rate as for adults. A review of BI literature indicates that few BI proponents explore the wage level for young people. Consideration of this is important given the potential vulnerabilities for young people. This chapter identified that for many young people, youth wages do not cover the basic costs of living (Homelessness Australia, 2016). If a BI is set below that of the adult rate, and is not accessible by young people who are of working age and may be living independently, then the potential for further entrenching of inequalities increases. Further, it would reproduce the constructions of young people as dependent on their families. Lower rates of youth wages, rather than justifying a lower BI rate, provide a stronger argument for an equitable BI to try to mitigate at least some of the harms that come from the lack of wage justice experienced by young people. Troy Henderson and Ben Spies-Butcher's chapter in this collection provides a possible pathway to consider how BI can respond to inequities for older young people (see Chap. 11). The challenge remains for inclusion of young people 16–20 years of age.

Rather than a targeted and punitive income that constructs recipients in terms of dole bludgers and ingrates as discussed above, a BI, in contrast, provides an income to live with dignity; a positive freedom, the freedom to live a 'good life' (Mays et al., 2016). Van Parijs and Vanderborght (2017, p. 159) argue that 'A BI will empower those with most constraints, enable them to be choosier among possible occupations, taking full account of what they like to do and what they need to learn'. In writing about BI and disability, Mays (2016, p. 241) contends that 'a BI aligns with an appropriate, ethically sound alternative'. A BI has the potential to be transformational, not just for young people, but for all, and how we see ourselves as a society, essentially the basis of what makes a good society. This is supported by Giroux (2009, p. 21) who argues that 'youth provide a powerful touchstone for a critical discussion about the long-term consequences of neoliberal policies, which undermine any viable notion of justice, equality and freedom' A BI disrupts the neoliberal narrative of individual gain and individualised risks. It provides a pathway to a more egalitarian society, more egalitarian values. A society that accepts the principles behind a BI, that is, equality and liberty (see Mays et al., 2016), is a society that rediscovers the social in social capital. A BI is indeed a simple solution with transformative potential.

The critical issue is that society must be ready to let go of the neoliberal discourses that structure how we view employment and income. Even more challenging, however, is that an equitable BI for young people requires a major transformation in the ways we see young people more broadly. As a society we need to let go of inherently damaging discourses about young people. We need to accept that young people are not Hall's dangerous barbarians, or Erikson's lost souls unsure yet of whom they are. Ultimately, we need to trust young people as Bamber and Murphy (1999, p. 230) state:

> Young people can be responsible for and capable of making a valued contribution to society. They need to be helped to make such a contribution which, in the end, means that they have the power to make and take significant decisions with social consequences

Society needs to accept a new reality, one which positions young people as both responsible citizens and rights holders. In this new reality, an equitable BI is just one of those rights that will help young people make the contribution we know they can. The time for that reality is now.

References

Andreas, L., & Wyn, J. (2010). *The making of a generation: The children of the 1970's in adulthood*. Toronto, ON: University of Toronto Press.

Anglicare Australia. (2018). *Rental affordability snapshot 2018*. Canberra, ACT: Anglicare Australia.

Arnett, J., & Hughes, M. (2012). *Adolescence and emerging adulthood: A cultural approach*. Edinburgh, UK: Pearson Education Limited.

Arthur, D. (2016). *Basic Income; a radical idea enters the mainstream* (Research paper series 2016–2017). Canberra, ACT: Parliamentary Library.

Australian Council of Trade Unions. (2011). *The future of work in Australia: Dealing with insecurity and risk*. Melbourne, VIC: ACT.

Australian Institute of Family Studies. (2017). *The longitudinal study of Australian children annual statistical report 2016*. Melbourne, VIC: AIFS.

Australian Internships. (2018). http://www.internships.com.au/hosts/what-is-an-internship/. Accessed 14 Aug 2018.

Bamber, J., & Murphy, H. (1999). Youth work: The possibilities for critical practice. *Journal of Youth Studies, 2*(2), 227–242. https://doi.org/10.1080/13676261.1999.10593037.

Brotherhood of St Laurence. (2017). *Reality bites; Australia's youth unemployment in a millennial era*. http://library.bsl.org.au/jspui/bitstream/1/10341/1/BSL_Reality_bites_Australias_youth_unemployment_Dec2017.pdf. Accessed 20 Sept 2018.

Brotherhood of St Laurence. (2018). *An unfair Australia? Mapping youth unemployment hotspots*. http://library.bsl.org.au/jspui/bitstream/1/10573/1/BSL_Unfair_Australia_Mapping_youth_unemployment_hotspots_Mar2018.pdf. Accessed 27 Aug 2018.

Bruenig, M. (2015, September 15). A universal basic income approach. *Policyshop*, Demos website. Accessed 1 Sept 2018.

Bullot, A., Cave, L., Fildes, J., Hall, S., & Plummer, J. (2017). *Mission Australia's 2017 youth survey report*. Sydney, NSW: Mission Australia.

Campbell, I. (1997). Beyond unemployment; the challenge of increased precarious employment. *Just Policy, 11*, 4–20.

Carers Australia. (2018). *Young Carers*. http://www.carersaustralia.com.au/about-carers/young-carers2/. Accessed 30 Aug 2018.

Centrelink. (2018a). *Newstart allowance*. https://www.humanservices.gov.au/individuals/services/centrelink/newstart-allowance/how-much-you-can-get. Accessed 14 Aug 2018.

Centrelink. (2018b). *Youth allowance*. https://www.humanservices.gov.au/individuals/services/centrelink/youth-allowance-job-seekers/how-much-you-can-get. Accessed 14 Aug 2018.

Couch, J. & Cooper, T. (2016). 'Deviance and moral panics' In J. Arvanitakis (Ed.) *Sociologic: analysing everyday life and culture* (pp. 241–261). South Melbourne Oxford.

Cunneen, C., & White, R. (2011). *Juvenile justice: Youth and crime in Australia*. South Melbourne, VIC: Oxford University Press.

Davidson, P. (2018). *Faces of unemployment. ACOSS/Jobs Australia*. Sydney, NSW: ACOSS.

Davidson, P., Saunders, P., Bradbury, B., & Wong, M. (2018). *Poverty in Australia, 2018* (ACOSS/UNSW poverty and inequality partnership report no. 2). Sydney, NSW: ACOSS.

Erikson, E. H. (1968). *Identity: Youth and crisis*. New York: Norton.

Fair Work Ombudsman. (2018a). *Pay Guide – Fast Food Industry Award 2010 [MA000003]* Published 28 June 2018. Accessed 29 July 2018.

Fair Work Ombudsman. (2018b). *Pay Guide – General Retail Industry Award 2010 [MA000004]*. Published 28 June 2018. Accessed 29 July 2018.

Fair Work Ombudsman. (2018c). *Minimum wages*. https://www.fairwork.gov.au/how-we-will-help/templates-and-guides/fact-sheets/minimum-workplace-entitlements/minimum-wages#current-national-minimum-wage. Accessed 29 July 2018.

Ferguson, J. (2010). The uses of neoliberalism. *Antipode, 41*(S1), 166–184. https://doi.org/10.1111/j.1467-8330.2009.00721.x.

Forget, E. (2011). The town with no poverty: The health effects of a Canadian guaranteed annual income field experiment. *Canadian Public Policy – Analyse de politiques, xxxvii*(3), 283–306.

Foundation for Young Australians. (2013). *How young people are faring*. Melbourne, VIC: Foundation for Young Australians.
Foundation for Young Australians. (2014). *Renewing Australia's promise*. Melbourne, VIC: Foundation for Young Australians.
Foundation for Young Australians. (2018). *The new work reality* (FYA new work order report series). Melbourne, VIC: Foundation for Young Australians.
Furlong, A., & Cartmel, F. (1997). *Young people and social change: individualization and risk in late modernity*. Buckingham, UK: Open University Press.
Furlong, A., & Kelly, P. (2005). The Brazilianisation of youth transitions in Australia and the UK? *Australian Journal of Social Issues, 40*(2), 207–225.
Giroux, H. (2009). *Youth in a suspect society: Democracy or disposability?* New York: Macmillan.
Hall, G. S. (1904). *Adolescence, its psychology and his relations to physiology, anthropology, sociology, sex, crime, religion and education*. New York: Appleton.
Homelessness Australia. (2016). *Homelessness and young people*. Fact Sheet. https://www.homelessnessaustralia.org.au/sites/homelessnessaus/files/2017-07/Young percent20People.pdf. Accessed 27 Aug 2018.
Hosken, N. (2016). Social work, class and the structural violence of poverty. In B. Pease, S. Goldingay, N. Hosken, & S. Nipperess (Eds.), *Doing critical Social work: Transforming practices for social justice* (pp. 104–120). Crows Nest, NSW: Allen and Unwin.
Humphry, J. (2016). Work and society. In J. Arvanitakis (Ed.), *Sociologic: Analysing everyday life and culture* (pp. 254–277). South Melbourne, VIC: Oxford.
Letts, S. (2018, July 19). Employment regains its mojo with booming growth in June. *ABC News website*. https://www.abc.net.au/news/2018-07-19/unemployment-and-employment-june-2018/10012434. Accessed 24 Sept 2018.
Lewis, M. (2018). *Basic income and the something for nothing objection*. Opinion the USBIG Blog. Accessed 2 Sept 2018.
Mays, J. (2016). Disability, citizenship, and basic income: Forging a new Alliance for a non-disabling Society. In J. Mays, G. Marston, & J. Tomlinson (Eds.), *Basic income in Australia and New Zealand: Perspectives from the neoliberal frontier* (pp. 207–252). New York: Palgrave Macmillan.
Mays, J., & Marston, G. (2016). Reimagining equity and egalitarianism; the basic income debate in Australia. *Journal of Sociology and Social Welfare, 43*(3), 9–25. Available at https://scholarworks.wmich.edu/jssw/vol43/iss3/3
Mays, J., Marston, G., & Tomlinson, J. (2016). Neoliberal frontiers and economic insecurity: Is basic income a solution? In J. Mays, G. Marston, & J. Tomlinson (Eds.), *Basic income in Australia and New Zealand: Perspectives from the neoliberal frontier* (pp. 1–28). New York: Palgrave Macmillan.

McGee, A., & McKinnon, M. (2018, January 29). Tony Abbott's razor gang considered welfare crackdown on 'job snobs' under 30. *ABC News website*. https://www.abc.net.au/news/2018-01-29/tony-abbotts-razor-gang-considered-welfare-ban-for-under-30s/9352888?section=politics. Accessed 20 Sept 2018.

Mendes, P. (2003). *Australia's welfare wars: The players, the politics and the ideologies*. Strawberry Hills, NSW: UNSW Press.

Murray, C. (2006). *In our hands: A plan to replace the welfare state* (pp. 130–139). Washington, DC: American Enterprise Institute.

National Youth Commission. (2008). *Australia's homeless youth: A report of the National Youth Commission inquiry into youth homelessness*. Brunswick, VIC: NYC.

Nilan, P., Julian, R., & Germov, J. (2007). *Australian Youth: Social and cultural issues*. Frenchs Forest, NSW: Pearson Education Australia.

NSW Young Labor. (2012). *Youth wages*. Submission to the Fair Work Act Review.

O'Connor, I. (1989). *Our homeless children; their experiences*. Report to the National inquiry into homeless children by the Human Rights and Equal Opportunity Commission.

OECD. (2018). *Employment rate by age group (indicator)*. https://doi.org/10.1787/084f32c7-en. Accessed 11 Sept 2018.

Parsons, T. (1951). *The social system*. Abingdon, UK: Routledge & Kegan Paul.

Phillips, B., Li, J., & Taylor, M. (2013, May). *Cost of kids: The cost of raising children in Australia*. AMP.NATSEM Income and Wealth Report, Issue 33, Sydney, NSW, AMP.

Sercombe, H. (2010). *Youth work ethics*. London: Sage.

Sercombe, H., Omaji, P., Drew, N., Cooper, T., & Love, T. (2002). *Youth and their future: Effective youth services for the year 2015*. Hobart, TAS: Australian Clearinghouse for Youth Studies.

Skinner, N., & Pocock, B. (2010). Work, life, flexibility and workplace culture in Australia. Results of the 2008 Australian Work and Work Life Index survey. *Australian Bulletin of Labour, 36*(2), 133.

Standing, G. (2011). *The precariat: The new dangerous class*. New York/London: Bloomsbury Publishing PLC.

Tehan, D. (2018, February 28). *Government renews plan to drug test unemployed welfare recipients*. Interview on Radio National Breakfast.

Trading Economics. (2018). https://tradingeconomics.com/australia/unemployment-rate. Accessed 14 Aug. 2018.

Van Parijs, P. (2004). Basic income: A simple and powerful idea for the twenty-first century. *Politics and Society, 32*(1), 7–39. https://doi.org/10.1177/0032329203261095.

Van Parijs, P., & Vanderborght, Y. (2017). *Basic income : A radical proposal for a free society and a sane economy*. Cambridge, MA: Harvard University Press.

Vromen, A. (2017). *Digital citizenship and political engagement; the challenge from online campaigning and advocacy organisations*. London: Palgrave Macmillan.

Walsh, L., & Black, R. (2015). *Youth volunteering in Australia: An evidence review* (Report prepared for the Australian Research Alliance for Children and Youth). Canberra, ACT: ARACY.

White, R., Wyn, J., & Robards, B. (2017). *Youth and society* (4th ed.). South Melbourne, VIC: Oxford University Press.

Wyn, J., & White, R. (1997). *Rethinking youth*. St Leonards, NSW: Allen and Unwin.

11

Situating a Basic Income Alongside Paid Work Policies

Andrew Scott

Introduction

This chapter considers the Basic Income (BI) debate and in so doing compares the employment and social policies pursued in Australia with the policies pursued in the four main Nordic countries (Sweden, Finland, Denmark and Norway). Esping-Anderson's well-known work has identified clear differences between social democratic welfare states and liberal welfare states. Social democratic welfare states, as exemplified in Nordic countries, have positively 'decommodified' labour to a greater extent than the liberal welfare states exemplified in English-speaking countries. 'De-commodification occurs when a service is rendered as a matter of right, and when a person can maintain a livelihood without reliance on the market' (Esping-Anderson, 1990: 21–22).

The social democratic Nordic welfare states have achieved comparative decommodification, in part by establishing universal welfare provision to

A. Scott (✉)
Deakin University, Burwood, VIC, Australia
e-mail: a.scott@deakin.edu.au

E. Klein et al. (eds.), *Implementing a Basic Income in Australia*, Exploring the Basic Income Guarantee, https://doi.org/10.1007/978-3-030-14378-7_11

a much greater extent than the liberal welfare states. While there are criticisms of Esping-Anderson's typology, including about how neatly Australia fits or does not fit into it, his essential argument is helpful for highlighting key policy differences between countries which are relevant to the debate over a Basic Income.

Proponents of a BI explicitly aim to more thoroughly decommodify labour in the long term. However, in the short and medium term, better policies to support job creation, work/life balance, improved quality of working life and skills retraining will be needed alongside any steps towards a BI. The Nordic nations have by no means completely decommodified people's labour but the leading steps which they have taken in this direction are valuable for Australia and other countries to consider and learn from.

Constructive Scepticism About a BI

Discussing implementation of a BI assumes that a BI is an inherently desirable destination and that it is just a matter of working out the best way to get there. That assumption needs to be carefully tested. Even those who are committed to transitioning towards a BI need to effectively outline strategies to reach—and face the potential barriers in the way of arriving at—what they regard as a desirable destination.

The arguments for a BI assert a rightful share for all members of society. Proponents of a BI variously critique: the way in which labour commodifies people; the limitations of paid work in the current labour market; and how women are particularly disadvantaged by current economic arrangements. Discussion of a BI has become more prominent in Australia recently in connection with somewhat apocalyptic predictions of a massive decline in jobs as a result of pending automation. These predictions have been particularly associated with a working paper by two Oxford academics (Frey & Osborne, 2013). That kind of crisis talk is very demotivating and disempowering. There is also, rightly, quite a deal of healthy scepticism about whether it is accurate (Wajcman, 2017).

Scepticism about whether such 'end of work' predictions are accurate arises in part because similar past predictions have failed to come true.

It is important that policy measures which better tackle the actual continuing experience of intermittency, and inequality, of paid work opportunities experienced by people in Australia and other wealthy nations be discussed, in addition to a BI. These other policy measures include unemployment insurance drawing on Danish successes and precedents.

Trials of a BI in Nordic nations have taken place in a context in which paid work continues to be valued highly and where work/life balance is the focus. In those countries, there are higher rates of paid workforce participation than Australia. On average, the four main Nordic nations' workforce participation rates are 1.5 percentage points higher than Australia's (OECD, 2017, Table C). These high rates of workforce participation crucially underpin the payment of the relatively high taxes which create the revenue base for their comparatively universalist welfare provision. Australia needs to look particularly at those countries' approaches as it reconsiders its current policy: which is actually to make people work longer, not less.

Denmark was a nation in which discussions of a 'citizen's wage' first prominently arose following the return of high unemployment in the 1970s (Meyer, Petersen, & Sørensen, 1978, 1981). Ideas for a guaranteed minimum income were canvassed widely across many rich nations from that time. This was due to escalation of entrenched structural unemployment to levels that had not been seen for many decades. Some predicted that many more jobs overall would disappear as a result of new technology and that this would usher in an age of comparative leisure (Gorz, 1983, 1985). There were ideas for people's self-sufficiency and for types of work not negotiated through the labour market to be encouraged and supported more. Those ideas were largely not pursued, however, and they were also criticised from many different perspectives: including that, if implemented, they would marginalise many of the people who did not receive income from paid employment (Pixley, 1993).

A general age of leisure did not materialise. However, greater inequalities emerged between those with too much paid employment and those with too little. This occurred in part because Keynesian policies to wholeheartedly tackle the rise in unemployment were abandoned in favour of monetarist policies to 'fight inflation first'. Now, with similar pessimism about future widespread job losses as a result of new technology, ideas for a basic minimum income are being discussed more prominently again. However, there is valid scepticism about whether there will, in fact, be such a general decline in paid work; and, to the extent that paid job opportunities may decline, about whether those will decline differently from how they have previously, which has been with very unequal effect.

Proposals and Policy Trials

The idea of a BI envisages a payment to be provided to all adults to allow them to meet their basic needs, which will not be means-tested and for which people will not be required to do anything in exchange. In Australia, these proposals were advanced when the Greens Party Leader said (Di Natale, 2017, 15 March), in a speech to the National Press Club in Canberra, that:

> We want to kick off a conversation about the future of work and start by questioning the entrenched political consensus that a good life can only come from more work.
>
> ...As part of that discussion, let's also talk about guaranteed adequate income.
>
> Many other countries are trialling models...[for that which are] designed to look after everyone in a 21st century economy where work has changed radically.
>
> We...[need to] seriously discuss the outcomes of the international trials examining universal basic income.
>
> A secure income could drive research, innovation and creativity and reset what is meaningful in our lives, rather than assuming we are all just units of economic output.
>
> Pair this with greater investment in education, re-skilling those in declining industries and a focus on Australia's natural strengths in services, in health and aged care, in renewable energy – and we have all the ingredients we need to re-think the future of work in a way that takes care of people and the planet that we depend on.
>
> [Conservative employers] want you to believe that you don't have a choice, that we can't change course, because it serves their own narrow self-interest.

Those ideas put forward by the Australian Greens Party Leader are welcome and thought-provoking and they should certainly be included as part of a broad discussion. It is always very valuable to open up questions about where money comes from, and on what basis money is made available. One country which has explored these questions is Finland, as it now concludes a two-year trial of a payment which has some features of a BI. Finland commenced this in January 2017 to explore, with rigorous evaluation, in a particular local area, the idea of a basic income support payment to replace existing benefits.

During the Finnish experiment, a total of 2000 unemployed persons between 25 and 58 years of age have received a monthly payment of €560, unconditionally and without means testing. The stated purpose of Finland's basic income experiment has been to find ways to reshape the social security system in response to changes in the labour market. The experiment has also explored how to make the system more empowering and—it is important to note—how to make the system more effective in terms of providing incentives for work. Further objectives include the reduction in bureaucracy and streamlining the complicated system for providing welfare benefits (Kela, 2017). Finland has decided, however, to not proceed further than this two-year local trial, which indicates that a BI is only a very distant possibility even in that Nordic nation whose advanced social policies are widely praised.

Better Work/Life Balance as an Alternative Scenario to the Disappearance of Paid Work

The higher rates of productivity in nations of northern Europe—together with, at the same time, their shorter working hours than in Australia—have long provided evidence that an attitude which better balances life with work does not result in the economies of prosperous countries grinding to a halt. Work/life balance is very highly valued and very well guarded in the Nordic nations. Gender equality is also much more advanced in those nations than elsewhere. This is partly because those nations have a 'dual earner' policy based on a norm of both men and women undertaking paid work. The Nordic countries combine welfare universalism with an employment orientation. Dual earner support is designed to allow both mothers and fathers to participate similarly in paid employment, through the provision of a long period of paid parental leave and extensive high quality, affordable, publicly-provided early childhood education and care (Scott, 2014: 66–67).

Australia, by contrast, has a one and a half breadwinner model which assumes a family structure of a male full-time worker and a female part-time worker. This is partly the legacy of the Harvester Judgement of 1907, handed down by Australia's unusual system of industrial arbitration tribunals, which defined family incomes according to male wage levels. The proportion of employed women who still work only part-time, instead of full-time, in Australia is considerably more than double that of Sweden: 38 per cent compared with 17.5 per cent (OECD, 2017, Table H). Women in Australia pay a price for tending to be so heavily in part-time work, rather than full-time work, in the form of downgraded career options and less pay and other benefits. The prospects of working women will be improved if Australia becomes one of the 'dual earner' policy nations—with more women working in full-time jobs which have reasonable, regulated hours, or in more secure, better paid and higher quality part-time jobs which have better career prospects—like Sweden (Scott, 2014: 67). This will achieve greater economic equality between women and men in one likely future scenario whereby paid work does continue to be crucial in determining most people's financial positions, and that therefore a BI does not become widespread.

Organisation for Economic Co-operation and Development (OECD) data indicates that Australian workers overall spend more hours a year working (1676) than do workers in Sweden (1612), Switzerland (1570), the Netherlands (1433), Norway (1419) Denmark (1408) and Germany (1356). Therefore, in Germany, one of the world's powerhouse economies, workers spend on average nearly 6 hours a week less at work than Australians; yet in the same year Germany had a significantly lower unemployment rate (at just 3.8 per cent) than Australia. Australia does not have a higher proportion of people in paid jobs than any of those six countries; and Australia's official current unemployment rate (5.6 per cent) is higher than the average current unemployment rate (5.0 per cent) of those six countries (OECD, 2017, Tables L, A, and C). These findings are significant because they indicate that it is possible to achieve a more equal distribution of paid work opportunities than in Australia and other English-speaking countries without introducing a radical change towards a Basic Income.

The six northern European nations listed above are, in turn, consistently rated as among the most economically prosperous and innovative nations in the world (World Economic Forum, 2017). All of them are ranked much higher on the current rankings than Australia: with Switzerland at number 1, The Netherlands at number 4, Germany at number 5, Sweden at number 7, Norway at number 11, Denmark at number 12—whereas Australia is at number 21 in global 'competitiveness'. Clearly therefore there are strong arguments, and exemplar nations, for a better balance between paid work and other aspects of life than is currently achieved in the English-speaking countries.

Improving the Quality of Working Life

Finland's trial of a Basic Income for research purposes has taken place in a context in which paid work continues to be valued highly. Further, in the Nordic nations, quality of working life is emphasised. Sweden, Finland, Denmark and Norway have long been leaders in better workplace design. This requires participatory design of technology, taking into account aesthetics, ergonomics and nature—including at the very least having natural light in people's work environments, but, preferably, fully expressing the principles of 'biophilia' in order to improve employees' mood and therefore their productivity as part of expressing employees' imaginative impulses and fostering their personal fulfilment at work.

The Nordic nations' emphasis on positive work design and industrial democracy starts from the premise that it is part of human nature to be active; that people want self-expression in their working lives, and not to merely work as a tedious necessity in order to have 'a life' which exists totally outside work. Employees, with their unparalleled experience and insights, are also recognised in those countries as the greatest source of potential upon which to draw to achieve innovation. 'Employee-Driven

Innovation' involves, from a basis of employment security, democratic participation by workers and cooperative encouragement of their informed insights into problem-solving (Aasen, Amundsen, Gressgård, & Hansen, 2012). The Nordic nations have not abolished, but they have reduced, the extent of instrumentalised, alienating paid work compared to other countries; and those reform achievements need to be considered by other countries.

Properly Supporting the Unemployed to Find Jobs

When social security and housing payments made to people in their first year of unemployment in different countries are compared, it emerges that Australia pays the lowest in the OECD for a single person who has recently lost her or his job. Australia provides an unemployed single person who has no children only 39 per cent of a low full-time wage, compared with the OECD median of 68 per cent. That OECD median is equalled or exceeded by all the four main Nordic nations, with Denmark providing one of the developed world's highest rates of support at 85 per cent (OECD, 2015).

In Australia currently, therefore, if you lose your job it is catastrophic because you then fall below the poverty line. People who are unemployed in Nordic nations, by contrast, can afford to spend time retraining and then move into another, sustained career benefiting, during their time of transition, from the higher social security payments, and unemployment insurance, which are provided in those nations. There is much merit in, and feasible applicability to Australia of, the Danish approach to 'Flexicurity'. This provides a basis of economic security for workers to move between particular jobs. Considerable attention is given in Denmark to the significant transitional phases in the life cycle such as when people enter middle age and may need to change jobs or careers.

To jump from where Australia is now, with one of the lowest and most shamefully inadequate unemployment payments in the developed world, to a BI, seems unrealistic. It is first necessary to take new steps to enable as many people as possible, when they lose one job, to retrain for another job without falling into poverty.

Pressure to Make People Work Longer, Not Less

We also need to contend with the reality that Australia is currently moving to make people work longer, not less. Other countries are doing this too, but Australia has officially proposed not only the longest working lives but also to bring that extension in before any other country. This derives from the fear of what has for some time been referred to in international social policy debates as a rising 'dependency ratio'. Fear of a rising dependency ratio is based on expectations of a higher proportion of retirees in the population, as the 'baby boomers'—that is, those people born from the end of the Second World War up to and including the year 1961—move into their later years in life.

That fear led to a decision by the government of the former Australian Labor Prime Minister, Kevin Rudd, to put up the age pension eligibility to 67 years, across the board, with little discussion. That decision, taken in 2009, was to phase in the higher age of pension eligibility from July 2017 to July 2023. The Liberal Party Coalition Government in its 2014 Budget then decided to further lift the age pension eligibility to 70 by 2035 and that remained Australian government policy until a sudden announcement in September 2018 reversing that, following another change of prime ministership a fortnight earlier. Although other developed countries are also beginning to raise the age of retirement, Australia is the only developed country which committed to increasing it to age 70. If Australia's pension age is increased to 70, it will very likely be the highest in the developed world by 2035 (Chomik & Whiteford, 2017, February 15).

Supporting Mature-Age Workers Who Want or Need to Stay in Paid Employment

The alterations to the existing, almost universal age pension payment in Australia which began on July 1, 2017 saw the age of eligibility start to rise towards 67 years. The reality and implications of this are starting to bite. The people who will be most affected by this are those who do hard physical work, such as construction workers and nurses who struggle to stay in paid work once they are aged in their 60s (Irving, Kulik, Pocock, & Charlesworth, 2017: 25, 29, 32).

Australia's Productivity Commission, however, is focused only on an agenda of people working longer. This is despite research from Household, Income and Labour Dynamics in Australia (HILDA) data in its own publications which indicates that nearly half of all Australians who retire between the ages of 45 and 70 do so involuntarily and those who retire involuntarily mostly do so due to adverse health outcomes or an inability to maintain or find a job (Productivity Commission, 2015: 211). These trends lend support to the idea that more resources need to be invested to give workers who lose their current job, before reaching their superannuation preservation or pension eligibility age, substantial new skills retraining opportunities which will equip them to take up other, different jobs before they permanently leave the paid workforce.

There is a need for a clearer focus on the problems faced by workers who are not in a position to work as long as is being officially contemplated; and for sensitivity to the needs of mature-age workers who are losing jobs before they reach the current official pension and superannuation access ages. Those mature-age workers who are seeking to stay in paid employment longer need positive policy interventions to give them skills retraining and other job opportunities which will take them through to those ages. It is very important that we now identify more ways to retain experienced workers in paid employment, through better skills retraining possibilities for workers aged in their 40s.

There needs to be particular support for skills retraining for workers in occupations which involve a high level of physical labour to move into new and different employment opportunities in middle age, building upon the proven, successful, concrete examples of 'Flexicurity' which already now operate in some parts of Australia, as a result of the leadership actions of funds such as Incolink which are associated with trade unions (Incolink, 2018). In addition, deficiencies in employment services which affect mature-age workers through varying forms of age discrimination, and not enough personalised case management orientation, need to be rectified (Wickramasinghe & Bowman, 2018). Younger people are currently more likely to confidently prepare resumés, and formally apply for jobs, than are mature-age unemployed workers, for instance. Many measures are needed to tackle the serious problem of discrimination against employing mature-age workers in Australia.

Training, Jobs and Transitions to Retirement

It is of course essential to ensure that there is not training just for training's sake. Training needs to be for meaningful jobs and for other real prospects. It is true that no amount of extra education and training will enable all the unemployed to participate in paid employment given that there are not enough paid jobs. It is for people in that situation, and for those who do vital unpaid work and creative work which is not adequately recognised and remunerated, that a BI seems most logically needed and pressing. There also needs to be particular programmes and distinct payment options for particular places in which there are not jobs: for example, and especially, in remote parts of Australia where many Indigenous Australians live.

However, there is scope to considerably increase participation in paid employment for very many people through better education and training in Australia, because some other countries have demonstrated that this is possible. A high first priority is for displaced mature-age workers to receive secure and more adequate income support as a basis for broader-minded skills retraining possibilities for them.

A more optimistic and measured view of Australia's employment future, amidst its currently naturally ageing population, has recently been put forward by Don Edgar, a respected, progressive sociologist and the first Director of the Australian Institute of Family Studies, who writes (Edgar, 2017, 3 July) that:

> If you look at the stats, two things stand out: First, those in middle age (50–75) make up the largest group in Australia (7.1 million). They are mature, well-educated, working productively and caring (often simultaneously) for their offspring (often young adults still in education) and their ageing parents (who are living longer than ever).

> Second, the influx of younger migrant workers and families makes for a growing cohort of future workers who will give the lie to notions of a higher dependency ratio because of an ageing population. We have a middle-ageing society, where dependent old age doesn't really start until after 80 for most of us.
>
> The proviso is that our work structures and our education system will have to become more adaptable as technology shifts the ground from under our feet. Age discrimination starts at 50, when most people are at their peak. They want and need to keep working and earning.

The key to enabling these objectives to be met, he argues, is an adaptable workplace allowing for reduced hours, job sharing and part-week or part-year work for people over the age of 60 (see further Edgar & Edgar, 2017). Achievement of those policy objectives would contribute to reforms which make a BI less necessary.

Negotiating the policy landscape in Australia to achieve these objectives means engaging with the prominent presence of superannuation provision, in which industry superannuation funds with trade union participants are important players and policy actors. The current 'transition to retirement' (TTR) arrangements offered by industry superannuation funds are relevant to, and could even form a concrete beginning for, the innovative, hybrid approaches which some may seek as part of moving towards a BI in Australia. However, TTR is much more common among white-collar than blue collar workers because the former can more readily envisage an affordable reduction of paid working hours than can blue collar workers. Advocates of a BI therefore need to engage in more detail with the particular experiences, needs and aims of blue collar workers.

There is no longer a clear, classical pathway into retirement. Instead there are different pathways, and frequent fitful stop-start transitions, including interruptions to paid employment, before many workers reach retirement age. There needs to be leadership to formulate a policy response to those prematurely forced out of the workforce to enable their effective, dignified retirement and to reduce the tendency for 'early retirement', in countries like Australia, to actually mean poverty in old age. People's perspectives on retirement, including the extent to which some of them desire to stay occupationally active, can also help to inform further discussion about the merits or otherwise of a BI.

Conclusion: Reform or Revolution?

Steady incremental reforms do need to be pursued, rather than not pursued because they may fall short of one revolutionary big idea. The introduction of unemployment insurance in Australia has previously been proposed, drawing on Danish successes and precedents in employment policy (Scott, 2016). That is one of the other ideas—besides a BI—which is now out there.

It is appropriate to be sceptical about—but not to be sectarian against—ideas for a BI. There is a parallel in the debates between sceptics and proponents of a BI with past debates between 'reformist' and 'revolutionary' policy positions. In Australia, the BI sceptics are more associated with the Labor Party while its proponents are more associated with the Greens Party. It is important to look in these debates for the possibilities for some shared, so-called Red/Green coalition policy space, of the kind which has led to major and valuable reforms in northern Europe.

Critics of a BI (e.g. Dawson, 2018, 5 April) have not acknowledged the problems created by Australia having such a highly targeted welfare system which enables very few areas of universal provision. Neither do these critics offer solutions to the fact that some long-term unemployment is so intractable that much more money may indeed need to be paid to many people who cannot get paid work, in order to build on the current inadequate levels, and excessive conditionality, of Australia's unemployment payments. For these reasons a nuanced debate does need to continue about a BI.

It is essential, however, that, in the continuing debate about a BI, ideas for such a new payment are realistically situated alongside policies to enhance balanced opportunities for paid work, particularly for those people who need it most. Those policies, in turn, should draw on the details of successful Nordic policies for job creation, work/life balance, improved quality of working life and skills retraining, which have helped to partially decommodify labour in those countries and which can offer similar benefits and progress if now pursued in English-speaking countries.

References

Aasen, T. M., Amundsen, O., Gressgård, L. J., & Hansen, K. (2012). In search of best practices for employee-driven innovation: Experiences from Norwegian work life. In S. Høyrup, M. Bonnafous-Boucher, C. Hasse, M. Lotz, & K. Møller (Eds.), *Employee-driven innovation: A new approach* (pp. 57–74). Basingstoke, UK: Palgrave Macmillan.

Chomik, R., & Whiteford, P. (2017, February 15). FactCheck. *The Conversation.*

Dawson, E. (2018, April 5). Plan for universal basic income ignores the value of work. *The Age*, Melbourne, VIC.

Di Natale, R. (2017, March 15). National Press Club address. http://richard-di-natale.greensmps.org.au/articles/richard-di-natale-national-press-club. Accessed 21 Oct 2018.

Edgar, D. (2017, July 3). The demographic truth. *The Age*, Melbourne, VIC.

Edgar, P., & Edgar, D. (2017). *Peak: Reinventing middle age*. Melbourne, VIC: Text.

Esping-Anderson, G. (1990). *The three worlds of welfare capitalism*. Cambridge, UK: Polity Press.

Frey, C. B., & Osborne, M. A. (2013). *The future of employment: How susceptible are jobs to computerisation?* Oxford, UK: Oxford Martin Programme on Technology and Employment.

Gorz, A. (1983). *Les Chemins du Paradis: L'Agonie du capital*. Paris: Editions Galilée.

Gorz, A. (1985). *Paths to paradise: On the liberation from work* (M. Imrie, Trans.). London: Pluto Press.

Incolink. (2018). *Redundancy, insurance, wellbeing*. http://www.incolink.org.au. Accessed 21 Oct 2018.

Irving, J., Kulik, C., Pocock, B., & Charlesworth, S. (2017). *Work well; retire well. Findings from the work, care, health and retirement: "Ageing Agenders" project*. Adelaide, SA: University of South Australia.

Kela. (2017). *Objectives and implementation of the basic income experiment*. https://www.kela.fi/web/en/basic-income-objectives-and-implementation. Accessed 21 Oct 2018.

Meyer, N. I., Petersen, K. H., & Sørensen, V. (1978). *Oprør fra midten*. Copenhagen, Denmark: Gyldendalske Boghandel, Nordisk Forlag AS.

Meyer, N. I., Petersen, K. H., & Sørensen, V. (1981). *Revolt from the center* (C. Hauch, Trans.). London: Marion Boyars Publishers.

OECD. (2015). *Benefits and wages database*. http://www.oecd.org/els/benefits-and-wages-statistics.htm. Accessed 21 Oct 2018.

OECD. (2017). *Employment outlook statistical annex*. http://www.oecd.org/els/emp/employment-outlook-statistical-annex.htm. Accessed 21 Oct 2018.

Pixley, J. (1993). *Citizenship and employment: Investigating post-industrial options*. Cambridge, UK: Cambridge University Press.

Productivity Commission. (2015). *Superannuation policy for post-retirement* (Vol. 2). Canberra, ACT: Productivity Commission.

Scott, A. (2014). *Northern lights: The positive policy example of Sweden, Finland, Denmark and Norway*. Melbourne, VIC: Monash University Publishing.

Scott, A. (2016). *A proposal for unemployment insurance*. Melbourne, VIC: Jobs Australia.

Wajcman, J. (2017). Automation: Is it really different this time? *British Journal of Sociology, 68*(1), 119–127.

Wickramasinghe, S., & Bowman, D. (2018). *Help, but not real help: Mature age jobseeker perspectives on employment services in Australia*. Melbourne, VIC: Brotherhood of St Laurence.

World Economic Forum. (2017). *The global competitiveness report 2017–2018*. Geneva, Switzerland: World Economic Forum.

12

Social Work, Human Services and Basic Income

Phillip Ablett, Christine Morley, and Michelle Newcomb

Introduction

Economic inequality is increasing throughout the world, leading to greater social injustice (WID, 2018). Consistent with the global trend, Australia has one of the fastest growth rates in income inequality (IMF, 2017), exposing inhabitants to economic insecurity and social distress. As professions formally committed to promoting social justice, social work and human services (SWHS) can potentially make important contributions in addressing economic inequality. Social workers in particular have been encouraged by their international professional body to "become

P. Ablett (✉)
University of the Sunshine Coast, Sippy Downs, QLD, Australia
e-mail: pablett@usc.edu.au

C. Morley
Queensland University of Technology, Brisbane, QLD, Australia
e-mail: c3.morley@qut.edu.au

M. Newcomb
Griffith University, Brisbane, QLD, Australia

E. Klein et al. (eds.), *Implementing a Basic Income in Australia*, Exploring the Basic Income Guarantee, https://doi.org/10.1007/978-3-030-14378-7_12

more political" in combatting inequality (Horton, 2014). At the same time, there has been a revival in the idea of a basic income (BI) from diverse perspectives concerned with economic and social futures. However, exploration of how SWHS can contribute to addressing economic inequality through engaging with basic income proposals and campaign initiatives has received limited attention. This chapter explains the role that SWHS have played, and may yet play, in publicly supporting a basic income, as one redistributive mechanism amongst others, for addressing economic inequality and poverty.

Social work emerged historically as a response to what was once called "the social question" (Lorenz, 2016) or "the social problem" (Stuart, 2013), understood as "the extreme stratification in wealth distribution and consequently, in standards of living" (Lengermann & Niebrugge, 2018: 185) created by industrial capitalism. However, that response was formed in the struggles between liberalism and socialism. Therefore, social work has always been divided between practitioners who diagnose the source of poverty in individual character deficiencies which they seek to regulate; and those emphasising "structural inequalities" which can only be redressed through egalitarian social transformation (Mendes, 2009: 17). Human services emerged in the 1960s as an interdisciplinary field, challenging elitism within the established social professions and advocating social change (Dumont, 1970), but is similarly conflicted between individualist and structural responses to inequality. Unfortunately, for much of their contested history, the liberal tradition has been "mainstream" in SWHS, while critical perspectives stressing economic justice are typically subordinate (albeit not without impact). Contemporary neoliberal discourses reinforce this, having colonised the Australian social assistance sector, treating social problems as matters of individual responsibility (Marston, 2014) yet failing to reduce inequality (ACOSS, 2018) or poverty (ACOSS, 2016). However, a range of structural SWHS understandings and responses to inequality continue to flourish (Baines & McBride, 2014; Goldberg, 2012; Krumer-Nevo, 2015; Morley & Ablett, 2016b, 2017; O'Brien, 2011; Pease, Goldingay, Hosken, & Nipperess, 2016; Webb, 2010).

The recent renewal of "critical social work" (Ferguson, 2016; Fraser, Beddoe, & Ballantyne, 2017; Gray & Webb, 2013; Morley & Ablett, 2016a), variously labelled "radical", "structural" or "anti-oppressive", is reclaiming and advocating policy and social reform rather than individualised "band-aid" solutions to economic inequality as central to SWHS practice. So, this chapter begins with an overview of current trends in economic inequality, followed by an assessment of how a basic income might counter its adverse distributive effects in contrast to the current design of the Australian social assistance system. We argue that a basic income, one that is equity-promoting and adequate, can be an effective means for addressing the problems of economic inequality and that SWHS can make positive contributions to this project. Indeed, we show that historically (in Australia) and in contemporary practice in other countries (e.g. Canada), SWHS practitioners can play a useful role in promoting basic income through practitioner activism, professional advocacy and critical pedagogy.

Economic Inequality

The growing global wealth divide is highlighted by Oxfam (2018) who reported that the 42 richest people in the world now own as much as the poorest half of humanity (3.7 billion people). Moreover, in the past year the richest 1% obtained 82% of all wealth generated, while the bottom 50% received no increase (Credit Suisse, 2017; Oxfam, 2018). This increasing inequality has occurred disparately. In the United States and Russia, for example, the growth in inequality has been extreme, whereas in Europe it has been relatively moderate (WID, 2018). What these variations demonstrate is that wealth inequality and poverty can be reduced by different social policies. While Australia's wealth inequality remains closer to European rather than American levels, current policy regimes and inequality trajectories are not encouraging (Sheil, 2017).

The past 40 years has witnessed a major decline in wage-earner's share of national income, from a peak of 62.5% in 1975 to 53.4% by 2014 (Mitchell, 2015). This decline has coincided with increased productivity and company profits since the 1990s, facilitated by global competition, automation, casualisation and industrial legislation designed to deter redistribution by limiting the bargaining power of workers (Stanford, 2018). Unequal ownership and wage stagnation, combined with increasing underemployment and benefits held below the poverty line, prevent redistribution and increase inequality. Economic inequality can also be directly linked to a broad range of social issues that SWHS deal with daily, such as intergenerational poverty, poor education, increased violence, substance abuse, increased physical and mental health issues, and suicidality (Wilkinson & Pickett, 2010).

Historically, Western societies have reduced inequalities in wealth and income via various welfare and labour market regimes. Economic inequalities decreased in Australia from the 1920 to 1970s (Perry, 2014; Leigh, 2013). However, current policies favouring market liberalisation and reductions in social provision exacerbate inequality. Additionally, many governments, (including in Australia) have introduced austerity measures, punitively affecting the most disadvantaged. Increased profits and productivity, combined with decreased business taxes, wages growth and social provision, are all part of an inequality-promoting matrix that will further concentrate wealth and amplify social problems without significant redistributive intervention.

Basic Income?

A basic income, understood as "an unconditional grant that is paid by the government to all permanent residents at regular intervals" (Mays, Marston, & Tomlinson, 2016: 3), is one possible redistributive response to economic inequality. Proponents argue that such a grant must be "adequate" in providing "a material foundation on which life can firmly rest, promoting real freedom for all…" (2016: 3). This means it must be ensured that it leaves nobody below the poverty line, thereby providing an opportunity for people to engage in creative activities without the coercive fear of destitution. Such a proposal is advocated from diverse ideological perspectives (egalitarian and libertarian) with various motives. This attempt at combining traditionally opposed values may help alleviate, some tensions in the ethical statements of most national and international social work associations, which promote both social justice and self-determination. That is, a basic income could provide a non-authoritarian form of distributive justice if it provides an adequate floor upon which all people could stand to optimise their individual and collective freedoms. A basic income cannot achieve this if it removes other social protections and subsidises employers to pay below poverty-line wages (Ruckert, Huynh, & Labonté, 2018).

Proponents maintain that a basic income would have clear redistributive effects (Santens, 2016) countering economic inequality. Direct effects would occur provided a basic income is part of a broader redistributive suite (Klein, 2016), including a genuinely progressive taxation system and additional wealth taxes. The latter could include a combination of taxes on rentier wealth, such as natural resources, corporate stock, land-value or transaction taxes (Santens, 2016) and may involve the use of a sovereign wealth fund (Standing, 2017). Indirect impacts would be observable through poverty relief, allowing people to engage in entrepreneurship, education and the exercise of power as citizens and workers (Santens, 2016). Erik Olin Wright (2005) argues that a basic income would strengthen the bargaining power of workers, reduce the commodification of labour and increase the power of civil society over the economy for meeting social and environmental needs that markets and governments cannot address.

Alternatively, opponents believe it may discourage job seekers from finding work, reducing labour supply and work ethic (IMF, 2017). To date, there has been no full-scale national implementation of a basic income at subsistence level to test this claim. The closest approximation would be the small annual dividend paid to Alaskan residents from the oil-derived, Alaska Permanent Fund (ADRPFDD, 2017), where researchers have found no evidence of work disincentives (Jones & Marinescu, 2018). Most other basic income trials have been limited to particular sub-populations and paid at varying rates. Research does not support significant work reduction, but points rather to people using their free time in productive activities that are not normally paid such as volunteering, childcare and education (Forget, 2011; Pasma, 2014). These activities have the capacity to enrich communities, potentially reducing a range of social problems that neoliberal governments then require providers in the social assistance sector to police rather than advocating for those in need.

The Australian Social Assistance Sector

The development and implementation of social policy is largely born by governments, but also public/private partnerships and non-government organisations (NGOs). A vast range of agencies tasked with delivering social services (including avowedly equity-enhancing) programmes broadly constitute the Australian "social assistance" sector. This workforce is now Australia's largest industry (ABS, 2017), compromising more than a million workers or 12.6% of all employed people. SWHS constitute a strategic group within this sector, whose educational standards (AASW, 2012) and ethical conduct statements, publicly commit them to address social injustice. However, our political environment constrains such aims and so there is a question over whether practitioners are equipped to address unfair social policy.

For over three decades, SWHS practitioners have existed under a regime of neoliberal government policies, which have denied the social-structural causes of poverty (Marston, 2014; Mullaly, 2010). This regime has emphasised "individual responsibility" for poverty and pursued the "activation" of problematic unemployed people (Marston, McDonald, & Bryson, 2014). Payments within this system are highly conditional, targeted and, low by Organisation for Economic Co-operation and Development (OECD) standards (Marston, 2014). In the view of many economists, like Richardson and Denniss (2014), such polices exacerbate inequality and its attendant social problems.

These working environments place SWHS practitioners in a difficult conundrum. Many service contracts, since the conservative Howard Government (1996–2007), contain clauses prohibiting criticism and advocacy by service providers (Marston, 2014). What's more, as the sector is increasingly privatised, many fields of practice become commercial industries. This includes employment services, prisons and parts of the child protection system. Within these fields, case management has dominated SWHS practice, and this can lead to further surveying and policing of welfare recipients as mere "cases" and again side lines the structural issues of inequality and poverty (Marston & McDonald, 2008: 262). The contention here is that, SWHS can provide a critical response which aims to address inequality through structural change, and that response should include advocating a basic level of income.

Critical SWHS and Basic Income: Venues and Strategies

Critical approaches to SWHS aim not only to relieve individual suffering but also to abet changing unjust structures that give rise to it. This means they seek to link micro-level relief with macro-level change. Critical practitioners collaborate with "non-professional" alliances within and beyond the welfare sector; with their fellow residents; and with service users and constituent communities. Therefore, SWHS activism, professional bodies and education may provide important venues and strategies for promoting a basic income policy in Australia, and that is what we will consider in this section.

Practitioner Activism

While any professional can engage in activism for social justice, SWHS formally claim this commitment in their disciplinary and professional mission statements throughout the world (Greenslade et al., 2015: 423). This stems from a radical tradition going back to Jane Addams in the American Progressive era (1890–1920), where social activism was integral to early versions of social work, albeit later marginalised by conservative and liberal, case-management traditions (Ferguson, 2008). In Australia, despite conservative origins, a social activist, SWHS stream emerged in the 1970s (Healy, 1993). A recent collection (Noble, Pease, & Ife 2017) is replete with examples of radical social-work activists participating in and instigating social justice campaigns as an extension of their practice (e.g. in defending Medicare, conducting public inquiries into poverty and disadvantaged schools, campaigning for indigenous land-rights, co-founding community health and sexual assault services). Some of these activists pioneered the first and only Australian experiment with a guaranteed basic income scheme.

In the early 1970s, in the wake of the Henderson Inquiry into poverty, the Australian Council of Trade Unions (ACTU) hired social worker Connie Benn (1926–2011), to research family costs of living to bolster their wage cases. This led her to advocate for a guaranteed income for low-income families in her subsequent role at the Brotherhood of St Laurence as Director of Policy and Research (AASW Interview, 1996: 5). Benn was part of the radical shift in social work from a liberal, case-management approach, to a focus on structural issues, necessitating community development, social policy activism and reform. The Brotherhood of St Lawrence, with Benn as research director, initiated the Family Centre Project (FCP), which centred on an income supplement (Keen, 1996: 12). It demonstrated that poverty was rooted in the power structures of society, rather than dysfunctional individuals. Benn (1981) believed that by changing the economic conditions much suffering would be resolved.

The FCP, according to Mendes (2009: 21), was the "first and perhaps most successful attempt in Australia to translate macro-structural ideas into micro-practice". It provided 60 Melbourne-based families, who had been long-term welfare recipients, with a Guaranteed Income Supplement for three years (1972–1975). The weekly supplement was based on the minimum wage to take families up to the Henderson poverty line (Bowman, Mallett, & Cooney-O'Donoghue, 2017: 12–13). The project involved participants in making informed decisions about their own welfare rather than just surviving from day to day (Keen, 1996: 13).

The FCP results were too small to generalise. Some retrospective analysis, however, suggests that the income significantly alleviated economic insecurity, positively impacting gender asymmetries due to income being paid to female household heads (Gilley, 1990; Bowman et al., 2017). Benn's own view was: "the trouble with poor people is that they don't have any money. So, with a guaranteed minimum income many of those people did really well" (AASW Interview, 1996: 6). Benn's contribution was pivotal in re-directing social work away from its traditional liberal bias for case-managing individuals into dealing with the socio-economic sources of poverty.

Another radical social work pioneer, John Tomlinson, has advocated for a basic income for decades and researched a doctorate on *Income*

Maintenance in Australia: The Income Guarantee Alternative (1989). Tomlinson initiated the Basic Income Guarantee Australia (BIGA) research site at the Queensland University of Technology (renamed Basic Income (2018)), where he lectured in SWHS. BIGA has since been coordinated by Greg Marston and Jennie Mays, promoting a basic income as an alternative to poverty and insecurity. BIGA is affiliated with the international Basic Income Earth Network (BIEN). These, along with Tomlinson's own website (http://johntomlinsoncollectedworks.com/incomemaintenance/basic-income/), remain invaluable resources for practitioner activism promoting basic income.

Benn and Tomlinson were part of an attempt to fundamentally reframe the trajectory of SWHS in Australia. One that some argue has failed, though this is a contestable point. Numerous SWHS practitioners still engage in policy practice and advocacy, union action, lobbying government, community development, supporting political campaigns or joining a protest "off-duty" (Greenslade et al., 2015; Moniz, 2018). In addition to practitioner activism, SWHS professional associations also valorise activism and advocacy for social justice in their various codes of ethics and mission statements (Greenslade et al., 2015: 423). Professional bodies, like the Australian Association of Social Workers (AASW), are more often preoccupied with inward looking policies around standards and credentials, yet remain sites of contestation for mobilising professional power in the public sphere. The role of the Canadian Social Work Association in promoting a basic income is exemplary in this respect.

Professional and Interprofessional Advocacy

Canada, like Australia is an Anglophone welfare state, whose social payments are likewise, conditional, targeted and subject to similar neoliberal policies over recent decades (Marston, 2014; Mulvale, 2008). As in Australia, Canada has a growing gap in economic inequality (Heisz, 2016; Macdonald, 2018) and the basic income idea has been in circulation for over 50 years. A pilot programme called Mincome ran almost contemporaneously (1974–1978) with the Brotherhood of St Lawrence's FCP, but with much larger numbers (1300 residents of the town of

Dauphin) in Manitoba (Bowman et al., 2017). This experiment followed with fluctuating but wider public and political interest than in Australia. It has also had its structural social work advocates, who have assembled research and campaigned to keep equity issues and the basic income on the political agenda. They have written numerous articles, and along with their allies within and beyond the welfare sector, have been effective political lobbyists. Furthermore, after a process of consultation beginning in 2012, the Canadian Association of Social Workers (CASW) adopted a formal policy in 2014, advocating a basic income, becoming the first social work association in the world to do so (Drover, Moscovitch, & Mulvale, 2014).

The report underpinning the policy states that, "It is the position of CASW that such an initiative would make a very significant contribution to the reduction of income inequality and the negative consequences of high levels of poverty" (Drover et al., 2014). This position has inspired further advocacy amongst practitioners, who have developed information kits, online resources and presentations promoting a basic income through the internet and public venues. The activism of this professional body has also been supported by allied professional bodies, such as the Canadian Public Health Association and Canadian Medical Association, who provided similar endorsements of a basic income (Hyndman & Simon, 2015: 9) proving something of an exemplar for the possibilities of interprofessional activism. The CASW has further strengthened its policy position in subsequent publications (Kennelly, 2017: 12), which relate it to healthcare outcomes and specify that, "This universal demogrant [basic income] model will foster social cohesion and decrease stigmatization. Building a sense of community involves … having true equal access to income and services." This latest CASW statement also clarifies that a universal basic income is not a panacea and must not be misused to jettison other social assistance programmes:

> Social workers know that economic, health, and social well-being are intertwined. As such, CASW favours proactive approaches to wellness. We believe that the transformative potential of a uBIG has not been fully realized from an economic, health, or social perspective. We encourage con-

> solidation… but do not condone the elimination or privatization of social programming. (Kennelly, 2017: 10)

This policy further acknowledges that income alone is not the sole source of poverty, that "more must be done to address intersecting forms of oppression", and that a basic income "would provide all Canadians with a floor to stand on" (Kennelly, 2017: 3).

In Australia the response of peak SWHS bodies has been quite different, with the AASW appearing reticent in publicly addressing rising economic inequality; apart from a short submission to the Australian Senate's Standing Committee on Community Affairs (2014). Rather than agenda-setting in the manner of the CASW, the AASW cautiously shadows government policy in its public pronouncements on inequality. For example, in response to government policies of individualised and compulsory "income management", the AASW (2011) endorses voluntary income management for those in economic distress and its selective compulsory use in child protection and domestic violence cases (AASW, 2011). In terms of advancing a redistributive policy vision addressing inequality and poverty, the contrast between the AASW and the CASW is profound. The Canadian Association's support for a basic income was articulated under the Conservative Harper Government, whereas the AASW statement on income management was formulated under a national Labor Government. However, the new national President of the AASW, Christine Craik (in Morley, Ablett, & Macfarlane, 2019: 8) has recently endorsed the critical SWHS position that "practice is as much about… structural change as it is about… particular situations".

While the AASW has no current position on basic income, this is a contestable terrain. The renewal of the basic income conversation in Australia is also in its infancy and the neoliberal responses to increasing inequality and poverty are failing. In July 2018, the Queensland Branch of the AASW, in opposing the Federal Government's attempts to introduce a Cashless Debit Card to intensify compulsory income management, cited the work of Mays et al. (2016) on basic income in its submission (AASW, 2018) to the Senate. This is the first time an AASW branch has drawn on basic income research. Whether this is incidental or anticipates further engagement with social policy alternatives by SWHS professional bodies in Australia remains to be seen.

It should be noted, that simply having a basic income policy on the books will achieve little without an educated membership base. Structural social work and anti-oppressive practice are prominent in Canada, where university SWHS programmes pride themselves with these orientations. Critical social work education in Australia by contrast struggles to break the stranglehold of market-driven, task-centred, technical definitions of the discipline.

SWHS Education

Educators in SWHS, like other critical social scientists, hold an important responsibility in challenging wealth inequality and exploring reforms like a basic income through their role in the formation of future practitioners. This can only occur if educators employ critical approaches to social issues, particularly inequality and poverty. While most studies show that a strong social-structural analysis of poverty in social work curricula produces graduates who view inequality as systemic, rather than blaming individuals for their poverty, the colonisation of curriculum by psychological approaches and individualised, case-management strategies, confuses students in their response (Hill, Toft, Garrett, Ferguson, & Kuechler, 2016), especially if social justice is ambiguously defined (Dahl, 2016) and not integrated in field education (Rupaleem, Raluca, & Daphne, 2017). In other words, SWHS graduates are often left without a strong skill-set in critical policy practice despite the social justice goals of SWHS education. For critical SWHS educators, the challenge is to constantly renew the pedagogy of economic justice with feasible utopian proposals like a basic income that are already in play in experimental forms.

The standards set by the AASW in relation to tertiary education state that social workers should "work towards the elimination of social inequalities in society to facilitate a more equitable distribution of resources" (2012: 8). However, they do not currently require any examination of poverty and wealth inequality or policy alternatives. The research of scholars who investigate economic inequality, its impacts and possible policies provides rich resources to respond to wealth inequality in Australia (ACOSS, 2016, 2018; Baines & McBride, 2014; Habibis & Walter, 2015; Hosken, 2016; Marston et al., 2014; Mays et al., 2016). However, their influence on SWHS curricula is uneven and appears to have had minimal impact on the newly proposed 2017 draft educational standards of the AASW. These proposed standards again define social work as advancing social justice, but in contrast to the 2012 standards, reduce reference to material inequality, mentioning it only once (in relation to Aboriginal and non-Aboriginal Australians). On the other hand, the draft standards do provide an opportunity for critical social work educators to contest the terrain when they specify knowledge of "Power, Oppression and Exploitation" as required curricula (AASW, 2017: 17). Even more promising is that the ability to "Critically analyse… social context and barriers as foundational to understanding individual/community issues and change efforts" (2017: 21) is proposed as an assessable graduate attribute.

Critical social analysis is the cornerstone of critical SWHS practice and pedagogy (Pease, 2013). Originally inspired by Marx, critical analysis in SWHS education has been employed to expose the unequal social outcomes produced by unregulated global capitalism and the possibilities for transformation (Parrott, 2014: 33). This remains foundational but more recent critical theories recognise the multiplicity of different yet intersecting forms of oppression; many of which are compounded by, yet cannot be reduced to, the inequality-generating dynamics of capitalism (Habibis & Walter, 2015; Weinberg, 2008). The differences within critical social work education between these emphases should present no barrier to the propagation of basic income models, provided the differing faces of oppression, including economic inequality, are given due attention. Socio-economic analysis is constantly updated. The research of contemporary economists like Piketty (2014) on global inequality (and its mutability) or Standing's (2014) work on the rise of a precarious workforce (the precariat) displaced by technology into a constant state of income insecurity and anxiety contributes to a critical awareness that is essential for practice in an uncertain and divided world. Unfortunately, the knowledge base and policy application of critical analysis are threatened by moves towards a more managerial and individually therapeutic-based

SWHS curricula (Hanesworth, 2017; Morley, Macfarlane, & Ablett, 2017). However, as we have indicated and the Canadian case demonstrates, critical SWHS educators can effectively contest this space and the basic income conversation is part of their repertoire.

Conclusion

Addressing economic inequality and its social impacts through redistributive strategies are central imperatives for SWHS if they are to remain credible as self-identified, social justice professions. We have noted the contested nature of these professions, caught between the competing imperatives of individual and structural approaches to economic justice. We have also explored what the SWHS professions have contributed and might contribute in future to the promotion of a basic income in Australia (and elsewhere) as a means for combatting inequality and poverty. While dominant trends in SWHS are not promising, neither are they irreversible and the recent renewal of "critical social work" in marshalling socio-economic analyses to promote social policy activism demonstrates a constituency for alternative models and practice. The conversation around a basic income is timely because it offers a viable redistributive response to structural inequality, which critical SWHS could support provided it is adequate for subsistence and part of an equity-promoting social policy suite. To this end, we have outlined three modes of engagement through which SWHS could be an ally in promoting an equitable and adequate basic income: practitioner activism, professional advocacy and critical pedagogy. For its part, the equity-promoting potential of SWHS practice and education to bolster the emancipatory possibilities of a basic income will hinge on the retention of critical socio-economic analyses and curriculum. In this, we heed Foucault's (1979: 308) sobering advice at the end of *Discipline and Punish*, that we must "Hear the distant roar of battle."

References

AASW. (2011). Income management position paper. *Australian Association of Social Workers*. https://www.aasw.asn.au/document/item/2213

AASW. (2012). *Australian education and accreditation standards (ASWEAS) 2012 v1.4* (Rev. 2015). Canberra, ACT: AASW National Office. Retrieved from http://www.aasw.asn.au/document/item/3550

AASW. (2014). *Australian Association of Social Workers*. Submission to the Senate Standing Committee on Community Affairs Re: Inquiry into the extent of income inequality in Australia. http://www.aasw.asn.au/document/item/6727

AASW. (2017). *Australian education and accreditation standards (ASWEAS) May 2017 (Draft Only)*. North Melbourne, VIC: AASW National Office.

AASW. (2018). *Australian Association of Social Workers*. Submission to the Senate Standing Committee on Community Affairs Re: Social Services Legislation Amendment (Cashless debit card trial expansion) Bill 2018. https://www.aasw.asn.au/document/item/11183

AASW Interview. (1996). Transcript of interview – Connie Benn. *50th anniversary oral history project*. Australian Association of Social Workers (Victorian Branch). https://www.aasw.asn.au/document/item/8023

ABS. (2017). Healthcare and social assistance our largest industry. Australian Bureau of Statistics. Media Release. http://www.abs.gov.au/ausstats/abs@.nsf/mediareleasesbyReleaseDate/B611DFF5E8590F8ACA2581BF001F743B?OpenDocument

ACOSS. (2016). *Poverty in Australia 2016, poverty and inequality in Australia*. Australian Council of Social Service, in partnership with Social Policy Research Centre (SPRC), University of New South Wales, Sydney, NSW. https://www.acoss.org.au/wp-content/uploads/2016/10/Poverty-in-Australia-2016.pdf

ACOSS. (2018). *Inequality in Australia 2018*. Australian Council of Social Services, in partnership with the University of New South Wales. https://www.acoss.org.au/wp-content/uploads/2018/07/Inequality-in-Australia-2018.pdf

ADRPFDD (Alaska Department of Revenue Permanent Fund Dividend Division). (2017). *About us, State of Alaska*. Juneau, AK. https://pfd.alaska.gov/Division-Info/About-Us

Baines, D., & McBride, S. (2014). Introduction: Context and fight-back. In D. Baines & S. McBride (Eds.), *Orchestrating austerity: Impacts & resistance* (pp. 1–8). Black Point, NS: Fernwood Publishing.

Benn, C. (1981). *Attacking poverty through Participation*. Bundoora, VIC: PIT.

Bowman, D., Mallett, S., & Cooney-O'Donoghue, D. (2017). *Basic income: Trade-offs and bottom lines*. Fitzroy, VIC: Brotherhood of St Laurence. https://www.bsl.org.au/knowledge/browse-publications/basic-income-trade-offs-and-bottom-lines/

Craik, C. (2019). 'Practitioner perspectives'. In C. Morley, P. Ablett, & S. Macfarlane, *Engaging with social work: A critical introduction* (2nd ed.). Cambridge, UK: Cambridge University Press.

Credit Suisse. (2017). *Global wealth report*. https://www.credit-suisse.com/corporate/en/research/research-institute/global-wealth-report.html

Dahl, N. (2016). The impact of social work education on social justice practice behaviors. *Master of Social Work Clinical Research Papers* (Paper 573). http://sophia.stkate.edu/msw_papers/573

Drover, G., Moscovitch, A., & Mulvale, J. (2014). *Promoting equity for a stronger Canada: The future of Canadian Social Policy*. Canadian Association of Social Workers (CASW). https://www.casw-acts.ca/sites/default/files/policy_statements/promoting_equity_for_a_stonger_canada_-_the_future_of_canadian_social_policy_0.pdf

Dumont, M. (1970). The changing face of professionalism. *Social Policy, 1*, 26–31.

Ferguson, I. (2008). *Reclaiming social work: Challenging neoliberalism and promoting social justice*. London: Sage.

Ferguson, I. (2016). The new social work radicalism. *Social Alternatives, 35*(4), 90–95. https://search.informit.com.au/documentSummary;dn=872394158068859;res=IELAPA

Forget, E. (2011). The town with no poverty: The health effects of a Canadian guaranteed annual income field experiment. *Canadian Public Policy, 37*(3), 283–306. http://utpjournals.metapress.com/content/xj02804571g71382/fulltext.pdf

Foucault, M. (1979). *Discipline and punish: The birth of the prison*. New York: Vintage Books.

Fraser, H., Beddoe, L., & Ballantyne, N. (2017). 'Is there a renaissance of radical social work?' [online]. *Aotearoa New Zealand Social Work, 29*(2), 1–5. https://search.informit.com.au/documentSummary;dn=337733995061596;res=IELFSC

Gilley, T. (1990). *Empowering poor people: A consumer view of the family centre project*. Melbourne, VIC: Brotherhood of St Laurence.

Goldberg, G. (2012). Economic inequality and economic crisis: A challenge for social workers. *Social Work, 57*(3), 211–224.

Gray, M., & Webb, S. (2013). *The new politics of social work*. Basingstoke, UK: Palgrave Macmillan.

Greenslade, L., McAuliffe, D., & Chenowith, L. (2015). Social workers' experiences of covert workplace activism. *Australian Social Work, 68*(4), 422–437.

Habibis, D., & Walter, M. (2015). *Social inequality in Australia: Discourses, realities and futures*. South Melbourne, VIC: Oxford University Press.

Hanesworth, C. (2017). Neoliberal influences on American higher education and the consequences for social work programmes. *Critical and Radical Social Work, 5*(1), 41–57.

Healy, B. (1993). Elements in the development of an Australian radical social work. *Australian Social Work, 46*(1), 3–8.

Heisz, A. (2016). Trends in income inequality in Canada and elsewhere. In D. A. Green, W. C. Riddell, & F. St-Hillaire (Eds.), *Income inequality: The Canadian story* (pp. 77–102). Montreal, PQ: Institute for Research on Public Policy.

Hill, J., Toft, K., Garrett, K., Ferguson, S., & Kuechler, C. (2016). Assessing clinical MSW students' attitudes, attributions, and responses to poverty. *Journal of Poverty, 20*(4), 396–416.

Horton, C. (2014). Social workers "should be more political in tackling inequality. *The Guardian, Social Care Network*. Retrieved from https://www.theguardian.com/social-care-network/2014/jul/09/social-workersmore-political-inequality

Hosken, N. (2016). Social work, class and the structural violence of poverty. In B. Pease, S. Goldingay, N. Hosken, & S. Nipperess (Eds.), *Doing critical social work: Transformative practices for social justice*. Crows Nest, NSW: Allen & Unwin.

Hyndman, B., & Simon, L. (2015, October). *Basic income guarantee backgrounder*. Ontario Public Health Association. http://www.opha.on.ca/getmedia/bf22640d-120c-46db-ac69-315fb9aa3c7c/alPHa-OPHA-HEWG-Basic-Income-Backgrounder-Final-Oct-2015.pdf.aspx?ext=.pdf. Accessed 22 July 2016.

IMF. (2017, October). *IMF fiscal monitor: Tackling inequality*. http://www.imf.org/en/publications/fm/issues/2017/10/05/fiscal-monitor-october-2017

Jones, D., & Marinescu, I. (2018). *The labor market impacts of universal and permanent cash transfers: Evidence from the Alaska permanent fund* (NBER Working paper no. 24312). http://www.nber.org/papers/w24312.pdf

Keen, S. (1996). *Non-profit organisations and public policy: Exploring the research role of the brotherhood of St Laurence* (Working Paper 67). Program on Nonprofit Corporations. Queensland University of Technology, Brisbane, QLD. https://eprints.qut.edu.au/53417/. Accessed 12 Aug 2017.

Kennelly, C. (2017). Universal basic income guarantee: The next 'BIG' thing in Canadian Social Policy. *Canadian Association of Social Workers (CASW)*. Ottawa. Ontario. https://www.casw-acts.ca/sites/casw-acts.ca/files/attachements/universal_basic_income_guarantee_-the_next_big_thing_in_canadian_social_policy_0.pdf

Klein, E. (2016). Universal basic income. *Arena Magazine, 142*(6), 6–8.

Krumer-Nevo, M. (2015). Poverty aware social work: A paradigm for social work practice with people in poverty. *British Journal of Social Work, 46*(6), 1793–1808.

Leigh, A. (2013). *Battlers and billionaires: The story of inequality in Australia*. Melbourne, VIC: Redback.

Lengermann, P., & Niebrugge, G. (2018). Settlement sociology. In A. Treviño (Ed.), *The Cambridge handbook of social problems* (pp. 185–202). Cambridge, UK: Cambridge University Press. https://doi.org/10.1017/9781108656184.012

Lorenz, W. (2016). Rediscovering the social question. *European Journal of Social Work, 19*(1), 4–17. https://doi.org/10.1080/13691457.2015.1082984

Macdonald, D. (2018). Born to win: Wealth concentration in Canada since 1999. *Canadian Centre for Policy Alternatives*. https://www.policyalternatives.ca/sites/default/files/uploads/publications/National%20Office/2018/07/Born%20to%20Win.pdf

Marston, G. (2014). Welfare for some, illfare for others: The social policy agenda of the Abbott government. Australian Review of Public Affairs. October. Available at: www.australianreview.net/digest/2014/10/marston.html

Marston, G., & McDonald, C. (2008). Feeling motivated yet? Long-term unemployed people's perspectives on the implementation on workfare Australia. *The Australian Journal of Social Issues, 43*(2), 255–269.

Marston, G., McDonald, C., & Bryson, L. (2014). *The Australian welfare state: Who benefits now?* South Yarra, VIC: Palgrave Macmillan.

Mays, J., Marston, G., & Tomlinson, J. (Eds.). (2016). *Basic income in Australian and New Zealand: Perspectives from the neoliberal frontier*. London, UK: Palgrave Macmillan.

Mendes, P. (2009). Tracing the origins of critical social work practice. In J. Allan, L. Briskman, & B. Pease (Eds.), *Critical social work: Theories and practices for a socially just world* (2nd ed., pp. 17–29). Crows Nest, NSW: Allen & Unwin.

Mitchell, W. (2015, February 24). Punishment dished out to unemployed is on par with our treatment of refugees. *The Guardian*. Retrieved from http://www.theguardian.com/commentisfree/2015/feb/24/punishment-dishedout-to-unemployed-is-on-par-with-our-treatment-ofrefugees?CMP=soc_568

Moniz, C. (2018). Social workers and policy practice: Affecting policy and achieving policy action. In C. Moniz & S. Gorin (Eds.), *Behavioral and mental health care policy and practice*. New York: Routledge.

Morley, C., & Ablett, P. (2016a). The renewal of critical social work. *Social Alternatives, 35*(4), 3–6.

Morley, C., & Ablett, P. (2016b). A critical social work response to wealth and income inequality. *Social Alternatives, 35*(4), 20–26.

Morley, C., & Ablett, P. (2017). Rising wealth and income inequality in Australia and New Zealand: A radical social work critique and response. *Aotearoa New Zealand Social Work, 29*(2), 6–18.

Morley, C., Ablett, P., & Macfarlane, S. (2019). *Engaging with social work: A critical introduction* (2nd ed.). Cambridge, UK: Cambridge University Press.

Morley, C., Macfarlane, S., & Ablett, P. (2017). The neoliberal colonisation of social work education: A critical analysis and practices for resistance. *Advances in Social Work and Welfare Education, 19*(2), 25–40.

Mullaly, B. (2010). *Challenging oppression and confronting privilege: A critical approach to anti-oppressive and anti-privilege theory and practice* (2nd ed.). Toronto, ON: Oxford University press.

Mulvale, J. (2008). Basic income and the Canadian welfare state: Exploring the realms of possibility. *Basic Income Studies, 3*(1), 1–25.

Noble, C., Pease, B., & Ife, J. (Eds.). *Radicals in Australian social work: Stories of lifelong activism*. Redlands Bay, QLD: ConnorCourt Publishing.

O'Brien, M. (2011). Equality and fairness: Linking social justice and social work practice. *Journal of Social Work, 11*(2), 143–158.

Oxfam. (2018). *Reward work, not wealth: To end the inequality crisis, we must build an economy for ordinary working people, not the rich and powerful*. https://d1tn3vj7xz9fdh.cloudfront.net/s3fs-public/file_attachments/bp-reward-work-not-wealth-220118-en.pdf

Parrott, L. (2014). *Social work and poverty: A critical approach*. Bristol, UK: Policy Press.

Pasma, C. (2014). *Basic income programs and pilots*. Ottawa, ON: Basic Income Canada Network. http://www.niagaraknowledgeexchange.com/wp-content/uploads/sites/2/2014/05/Basic_Income_Programs_and_Pilots.pdf

Pease, B. (2013). A history of critical and radical social work. In M. Gray & S. Webb (Eds.), *The new politics of social work*. Basingstoke, UK: Palgrave Macmillan.

Pease, B., Goldingay, S., Hosken, N., & Nipperess, S. (2016). *Doing critical social work: Transformative practices for social justice*. Crows Nest, NSW: Allen and Unwin.

Perry, B. (2014). *Household incomes in New Zealand: Trends in indicators of inequality and hardship 1982 to 2013*. Wellington, New Zealand: Ministry of Social Development.

Piketty, T. (2014). *Capital in the twenty-first century*. Cambridge, MA: Harvard University Press.

Richardson, D., & Denniss R. (2014). *Income and wealth inequality in Australia* (Policy Brief No. 64). Canberra, ACT: Australia Institute. Retrieved from http://www.tai.org.au/system/files_force/PB+64+Income+and+wealth+inequality+FINAL.pdf

Ruckert, A., Huynh, C., & Labonté, R. (2018). Reducing health inequities: Is universal basic income the way forward? *Journal of Public Health, 40*(1), 3–7. https://doi.org/10.1093/pubmed/fdx006

Rupaleem, B., Raluca, B., & Daphne, J. (2017). Social workers' perspectives on social justice in social work education: When mainstreaming social justice masks structural inequalities. *Social Work Education, 36*(4), 373–390.

Santens, S. (2016). Inequality and the basic income guarantee. In C. Oestereich (Ed.), *What do we do about inequality?* Wicked Commons Collaborative. CreateSpace Independent Publishing Platform. https://medium.com/basic-income/inequality-and-the-basic-income-guarantee-c8f84d936640

Basic Income. (2018) Faculty of Health, Queensland University of Technology. Retrieved from https://www.qut.edu.au/health/about/schools/school-of-public-health-and-social-work/basic-income

Sheil, C. (2017). The cutting edge of inequality. *Evatt Foundation, News*. Retrieved from https://evatt.org.au/news/cutting-edge-inequality.html

Standing, G. (2014). *The precariat: The new dangerous class*. London: Bloomsbury.

Standing, G. (2017). *Basic income: And how we can make it happen*. London: Penguin.

Stanford, J. (2018). *Wages crisis has obvious solutions*. The Australia Institute. Opinion. http://www.tai.org.au/content/wages-crisis-has-obvious-solutions

Stuart, P. (2013). Social work profession: History. In *Encyclopedia of social work*. Oxford, UK: NASW Press/Oxford University Press. Retrieved 7 September, 2018, from http://socialwork.oxfordre.com/view/10.1093/acrefore/9780199975839.001.0001/acrefore-9780199975839-e-623

Webb, S. (2010). (Re)Assembling the left: The politics of redistribution and recognition in social work. *British Journal of Social Work, 40*(8), 2364–2379.

Weinberg, M. (2008). Structural social work: A moral compass for ethics in practice. *Critical Social Work, 9*(1). Retrieved from http://www1.uwindsor.ca/criticalsocialwork/structural-social-work-a-moral-compass-for-ethics-in-practice

WID. (2018). *World inequality report 2018*. World Inequality Database. https://wir2018.wid.world/

Wilkinson, R., & Pickett, K. (2010). *The spirit level: Why equality is better for everyone*. Hammondsworth, UK: Penguin.

Wright, E. (2005, March 4–6). *Basic income as a socialist project*. Paper presented at the Annual US-BIG Congress. https://www.ssc.wisc.edu/~wright/Basic%20Income%20as%20a%20Socialist%20Project.pdf

13

Basic Income in Canada: Lessons Learned and Challenges Ahead

James P. Mulvale and Sid Frankel

Introduction

In this chapter, we will analyse the quest to put in place a basic income (BI) in Canada. We will outline past attempts to establish this approach to economic security, draw some lessons from them and examine issues to do with design and implementation of BI in Canada.

Canada is an interesting comparator to Australia when it comes to social programmes. Both countries have broadly similar political histories as white settler dominions of the former British Empire. Both were created as federated nations (Canada in 1867, Australia in 1901) that amalgamated smaller, distinct colonies. Both countries have a liberal democratic model of governance in the Westminster parliamentary model. Both countries were established through the dispossession of Indigenous peoples of their lands, and both attempted to erase Indigenous cultures and identity. The two nations have been populated by successive

J. P. Mulvale (✉) • S. Frankel
Faculty of Social Work, University of Manitoba, Winnipeg, MB, Canada
e-mail: James.Mulvale@umanitoba.ca; Sid.Frankel@umanitoba.ca

E. Klein et al. (eds.), *Implementing a Basic Income in Australia*, Exploring the Basic Income Guarantee, https://doi.org/10.1007/978-3-030-14378-7_13

waves of immigrants from Britain, Europe and other parts of the globe, with many of these newcomer groups being confronted with discrimination and racism. Both have similar, and relatively high, poverty rates (OECD, 2018).

One important difference pertains to how the two countries assign jurisdiction for social welfare programmes between the national and subnational levels of government. The Australian Constitution (Part V, 51, secs. xxii & xxiiA) delegates responsibility for a broad range of these programmes to the Commonwealth (national) government. Conversely, Canada's *Constitution Act* (1982) makes provinces responsible for the delivery of social programmes—although during welfare state expansion in the 1960s, the federal government carved out a more prominent role for itself in social insurance (for retired and unemployed workers, co-funded by employer and employee contributions) and in co-funding social programmes delivered by the provinces (Finkel, 2006).

Another difference is that the 1982 version of the Constitution of Canada incorporates the *Charter of Rights and Freedoms*, and the Constitution of Australia does not have an equivalent declaration of fundamental rights. That said, it can be argued that the Canadian Charter has had only limited impact in advancing rights to social welfare in areas such as income security, adequate housing and child care (Young, 2007, pp. 2–4).

With this context in mind, let us examine the history, contemporary discourse and key design and implementation questions in regard to BI in Canada. We hope that this discussion will be a useful point of comparison for those working to achieve a progressive version of BI in Australia.

The Political History of Basic Income in Canada

One of the earliest manifestations of interest in BI in Canada arose during the Great Depression. The Social Credit Party led by William Aberhart was elected as the government of the province of Alberta in 1935. That party proposed to pay a "social credit" or regular dividend to all citizens. This proposal never came to fruition due to a lack of funds in the provincial treasury, as well as the federal government's opposition to Aberhart's attempts to intrude into federal jurisdiction over currency and banking (Young & Mulvale, 2009, p. 12).

Broad political and public discussion of basic income faded in Canada over the following decades. But in 1967, the Liberal federal government introduced the Guaranteed Income Supplement as part of the Old Age Security programme, in order to reduce poverty among seniors. In 1970, the Royal Commission on the Status of Women recommended that a "guaranteed annual income be paid by the federal government to the heads of all one-parent families with dependent children" delivered through a negative income tax scheme (Young & Mulvale, 2009, p. 13). In 1971, a Senate Committee chaired by David Croll recommended a negative income tax version of a federal guaranteed annual income for non-seniors that "provides adequate income, … preserves the incentive to work, and … is fiscally possible" (Senate of Canada, 1971). Croll's proposal garnered considerable interest, but was not implemented due to perceptions of its high cost and inadequate work incentives.

In 1974, the federal government and the provincial government of Manitoba agreed to undertake an extensive real-life experiment of a negative income version of BI that was dubbed "Mincome" (Mulvale & Frankel, 2016, pp. 35–36). While initially envisioned by at least the Manitoba government as a simple and relatively inexpensive trial, Mincome evolved into a complicated pilot project with a focus on the issue of whether or not a guaranteed income would be a disincentive to recipients engaging in paid work. The Mincome project involved 1300 Manitoba families drawn from both urban and rural communities and randomly assigned into "experimental" and "control" groups (similar households that respectively received one of nine versions, or did not receive the Mincome benefit). One Mincome site, the town of Dauphin, was a "saturation" site in which all those whose income fell below a set level could receive the benefit.

By 1979, the Mincome experiment had lost political support and was cancelled. There had been recent elections, and new Conservative governments had replaced the Liberals federally and the New Democratic Party (NDP) provincially in Manitoba. The abrupt cancellation of the Mincome project resulted in no official findings or recommendations being issued at that time. But later analysis of the Mincome saturation site in Dauphin by Forget (2011) demonstrated that that hospitalizations, accidents, injuries, and mental health problems declined, and that the high school completion rate increased, during the Mincome experiment in that community. Forget also found that Mincome participation led to very little decline in labour market participation. Calnitsky (2016) has shown that Dauphin residents receiving Mincome payments did not see them as stigmatizing, in contrast to the very negative perception of social assistance payments. He (Calnitsky, 2016) concludes that the "bright line dividing the deserving and undeserving poor turned fuzzy" (p. 64), and sees this as removing an impediment to social solidarity (p. 65).

Discussion of a form of guaranteed income resurfaced again in the mid-1980s in Canada. The Royal Commission on the Economic Union and Development Prospects for Canada (Royal Commission, 1985) recommended the implementation of a Universal Income Security Program (UISP) (Mulvale & Frankel, 2016, pp. 36–38). It was billed as a reform that would be "radical, not cosmetic, and wholesale rather than tinkering at the margin." The Commission's guaranteed income proposal was designed to replace much of the then existing financial safety net, and would pay benefits below the poverty line on the assumption that provincial or municipal social assistance would top-up the amounts for families.

Critics of the UISP saw it as a scheme that would effectively institutionalize poverty, setting income security benefits for many at even lower levels than existing programmes. The UISP also met with strong opposition from the Canadian labour movement (Haddow, 1994). The federal Conservative government ignored the UISP recommendation of the Royal Commission. For many in Canada with an interest in progressive social policy, the UISP proposal came to symbolize the risk that the introduction of BI in Canada would leave poor people worse off.

In 1994, a discussion paper tabled in the House of Commons by Human Resources Minister Lloyd Axworthy dismissed the idea of a formal guaranteed income programme. The paper argued (speciously) that Canada's mix of social assistance and tax credit programmes was a "de facto guaranteed minimum income" (Young & Mulvale, 2009, p. 15). Guaranteed income schemes then fell off the political radar for several subsequent years in Ottawa.

The Conservative Party under Prime Minister Stephen Harper governed Canada from 2006 until 2015. This government was dedicated to downsizing federal expenditures and federal responsibility for social programmes (Porter, 2015). For the first five years of this period, the Harper Conservatives had to govern with a minority of seats in the House of Commons, meaning that there would be a majority of Opposition members on parliamentary Committees. As a result, progressive MPs and Senators were able to make recommendations for improved social supports, even though the governing Conservatives were not likely to support these ideas. During this period support for BI surfaced in at least two significant fora. A Senate Committee (Senate of Canada, 2009) recommended that the federal government study "the costs and benefits of current practices with respect to income supports and of options to reduce and eliminate poverty, including a basic annual income based on a negative income tax," taking into account the results of the Mincome trial in Manitoba (Recommendation 5). It also recommended the implementation of "a basic income guarantee at or above LICO [low income cut-off[1]] for people with severe disabilities" (Recommendation 53). A House of Commons Committee also recommended that the government "create a federal basic income program for persons with disabilities and support a disability-related supports program to be delivered by the provinces and territories" (House of Commons, 2010, p. 143). On the other hand, this Committee "decided not to make a recommendation regarding a universal GAI [guaranteed annual income], considering it preferable to take one step at a time and begin with a program benefitting only persons with a disability" (p. 194).

One of the most prominent basic income advocates during this period was "red Tory" Senator Hugh Segal (2012) from the Conservative Party. He very publicly and repeatedly called for the introduction of BI, arguing that Canada could afford it. In February 2008, he introduced a notice of motion in the federal Senate calling for "a fulsome study on the feasibility of a Guaranteed Annual Income … or Negative Income Tax as a means of reducing poverty."[2]

---

[1] A semi-relative measure of poverty described further below.

[2] Quoted from a "Communique" and "Notice of Motion" released by the Office of Senator Hugh Segal, Senate of Canada, 6 February 2008.

The federal Liberals were re-elected to government in 2015 under Justin Trudeau. In recent years, the Liberal Party membership has been expressing positive interest in BI. The party adopted resolutions calling for basic income at its national policy conventions held in 2014 and 2016 (Liberal Party of Canada, 2014, 2016). At their convention in April 2018, the Liberal Party members again approved a resolution calling on the government of Canada to "work with the provinces to develop a universal, equitable and sustainable guaranteed minimum income model for the benefit of all Canadians" (Liberal Party of Canada, 2018).

To date the Liberal government has not moved to implement these convention resolutions on BI. But it has made significant positive changes to existing programmes that resemble BI. These changes include increases to unconditional (but income-tested) payments to families with children through the Canada Child Benefit (Department of Finance, 2018). The Liberals have also reversed the decision of the previous Conservative government to raise the age of eligibility for the Old Age Security programme from 65 to 67 (Stone, 2016), and made some improvements to Canada Workers Benefit for the working poor (Canada, 2018b). The current Minister of Families, Children and Social Development, Jean-Yves Duclos, has expressed the view that "the [BI] concept has merit as a policy to consider after the government implements more immediate reforms" (Curry, 2016, p. Al).

In August 2018, the Liberal government announced the first-ever federal Poverty Reduction Strategy (Canada, 2018a). There are positive features in the Liberals' strategy, including setting poverty reduction targets of 20% by 2020 and 50% by 2030. The plan set out as an aspiration that Canadians "would have enough income to meet their basic needs" (p. 9). However, no new money was committed to reduce poverty beyond commitments already made in income support and housing, no detailed action plans were specified, and no mention was made of BI as a policy direction moving forward.

Canada's social democratic party is the New Democratic Party (NDP). New Democrats have until recently been uninterested, sceptical, and even antipathetic towards the BI model of economic security for all. One factor in this regard has been the NDP's close alliance with Canadian labour unions, and the latter's strong orientation to "good jobs" with union protection as the bedrock of economic security. As mentioned above, the Canadian labour movement strongly opposed the minimalist model of guaranteed income recommended by a Royal Commission in the mid-1980s (Haddow, 1994). But a positive step towards acceptance of the basic income model was taken by the NDP at its national convention in April 2016. A resolution (No. 3-45-16) was adopted that "affirm[s] the principle of a Basic Income Guarantee" and that "endorses informed discussion within the party to explore potential options for a basic income guarantee for all in Canada" (NDP, 2016).

The NDP had a federal leadership race in 2017. One of the candidates was Guy Caron, a Member of Parliament from the province of Quebec, who made a negative income tax version of BI a primary plank in his leadership campaign platform. Although Caron was not the successful candidate, he put BI on the NDP agenda in a way that garnered a considerable amount of discussion and debate within the party.

Non-governmental social policy advocacy organizations in Canada have until recently ignored or been sceptical about the BI model. However prominent groups in this sector, such as the Canadian Centre on Policy Alternatives (Khanna, 2016; Macdonald, 2016), Campaign 2000 (2017, p. 13), and the Tamarack Institute (Seth, 2017, p. 7) have recently indicated some support for BI. The non-governmental organization that has been the most prominent in advocating for BI in Canada has been the Basic Income Canada Network (BICN).[3] It was established in 2008 as a Canadian affiliate of the Basic Income Earth Network[4] and has worked since then to advance knowledge and support of BI in Canada through conferences, public education, and political advocacy. BICN has also addressed the concern of some on the political left (e.g. Raphael, Bryant, & Mendly-Zambo, 2018) who worry that BI could provide a justification for neo-liberal forces to cut or eliminate "in-kind" social programmes of the welfare state, such as universal health care, social housing, and child care. BICN has crafted a document entitled "The Basic Income We Want" (BICN, 2016) that calls for BI to be embedded in a broad range of public services in order to effectively address poverty and social

[3] See https://www.basicincomecanada.org/

[4] See https://basicincome.org/

inequality. BICN has also promoted a letter signed by 100 CEOs of Canadian businesses objecting to the cancellation of the Ontario BI pilot, and calling for the broad implementation of a universal basic income as a response to "[a]ccelerating technological job displacement due to advances in automation, software, and AI."[5]

Provincial Government Initiatives

Recently some provincial governments in Canada have given serious consideration to BI as a potential new model of economic security. For instance, in late 2017 the Government of Quebec announced a programme labelled as basic income that would incrementally increase benefits for "an estimated 84,000 Quebecers .... largely those with physical and intellectual disabilities" (Shingler, 2017). The provincial advocacy group for BI, Revenu de base Québec, said that the announcement was "a move in the right direction" (ibid). During the 2018 provincial election campaign, the left-wing party Québec solidaire (QS) committed to a Basic Income Pilot project in their first mandate if elected, and stated that in "a second QS mandate, the system would be installed across Quebec, to replace the welfare system" (Presse Canadienne, 2018). However, the QS plan was premised on the idea that "a well-paid job remains the best way to get out of poverty," and that basic income should be targeted specifically to "vulnerable people" (ibid). The right-wing Coalition Avenir Québec won the election of October 2018, and the CAQ advances the neo-liberal orthodoxy that "the fight against poverty" should be carried out not by government but by "concerned community organizations" assisting those not in the work force.[6] So it appears that a BI programme model in Quebec is not a likely development in the near future.

The provincial NDP in British Columbia formed a minority government in 2017 with support pledged by the provincial Green Party. One of the Greens' conditions for their support was that the NDP govern-

[5] See https://ceosforbasicincome.ca/letter-from-100-ceos-to-doug-ford/

[6] See https://coalitionavenirquebec.org/en/blog/enjeux/solidarity/. The target group identified in the French version is "les personnes ayant des contraintes sévères à l'emploi."

ment would "design and implement a basic income pilot" (BC Green Caucus and BC New Democrat Caucus, 2017, pp. 7–8). In July 2018 the NDP government announced their "pilot"—which was not an actual demonstration project, but "independent research to test the feasibility of a basic-income pilot in British Columbia" that would be conducted by a team of three university researchers (BC Gov News, 2017).

In April 2017 the provincial government of Ontario, led by Liberal Premier Kathleen Wynne, announced that it was launching a Basic Income Pilot project (Ontario, 2017). This pilot enrolled over 4000 low-income people in three areas of the province to participate in the pilot for a three-year period. These participants were to receive enhanced and unconditional monthly benefits at levels significantly above social assistance or disability allowance rates, and to have their benefits reduced by only 50% (as opposed to dollar-for-dollar) if they earned income from paid work. The pilot participants were to be compared to a similar group not receiving the basic income, to determine if there were differences in a range of factors including food security, mental and physical health, housing, employment, and enrolment in education.

The provincial election of June 2018 was lost by the Liberals, and resulted in a new Conservative Party government led by Doug Ford. Within two months the new government cancelled the Basic Income Pilot, despite its commitment during the election campaign to let the project run its three-year course and to examine the results. This precipitous cancellation led to a very strong wave of protest, including from grass roots organizations (including the Basic Income Canada Network and the Ontario Basic Income Network), social policy advocates, major media outlets (Globe and Mail, 2018; Monsebraaten, 2018; Toronto Star, 2018), and researchers from around the world (Cooke & De Wispelaere, 2018; Forget et al., 2018).

The cancellation of the Ontario pilot was a very disheartening development for BI advocates in Canada. But the strong and diverse opposition to this cancellation suggests an underlying and broad openness to consideration of the BI model in Canada, which can be seen as a positive shift compared to the past.

Implementation of Basic Income in Canada

In this section we explore Canadian experience with implementation of full and partial BI schemes. At least four implementation approaches are available in the policy literature. The first is the conventional approach of full implementation. This approach requires rigorous implementation planning (Caputo, 2014), ideally involving simulations to work out implementation issues. It also requires careful monitoring of implementation to detect any difficulties as early as possible; and the marshalling of technical resources to take immediate action. The main advantage of this approach is that, once the programme is adopted, there is little space for detractors to stop its implementation. The main disadvantages are that the inevitable implementation problems must be worked out quickly, may be highly visible and can engender considerable political risk.

A second option is to conduct one or more pilot studies (Fraser & Galinsky, 2010). As opposed to experiments, pilot studies focus not on effects, but on testing the performance of administrative and delivery systems and making necessary improvements. They provide an opportunity to work out the bugs, but may also create an opportunity for opponents to delay or stop implementation. Several challenges are involved in implementing pilots. For example, if pilot beneficiaries are selected on a geographic or population sub-group basis there is less opportunity to build broad support and those not selected may feel that the pilot confers unfair advantages on its beneficiaries. Therefore, those not selected should be promised compensation when full implementation occurs, and the outcomes of the pilot should be strategically communicated to future beneficiaries and their supporters.

A third approach involves incremental changes to existing programmes that are gradual and reversible (Offe, 2001) to promote learning and preference change through action and experience. This is seen as a means to avoid a frontal attack on affordability and predicted erosion of work effort through gradual movement toward a comprehensive basic income. The key disadvantages are that gradualism may not develop sufficiently broad support to encourage full implementation and that a long timeline is provided for opponents to mobilize against the policy change.

A fourth approach involves the use of experiments and quasi-experiments to estimate effects and gather support on the basis of these effects. Individual effects can be rigorously measured with a true experimental design, and quasi-experiments can be mounted to study community-level and local economy-level effects. Support is more likely if positive and negative effects are comprehensively assessed. Causal inferences in basic income experiments may be limited by threats to construct validity (short term and high profile) and threats to internal validity (sampling and response bias) (Simpson, Mason, & Godwin, 2017). Quasi-experimentation leaves more room for divergent interpretation (Cook, Campbell, & Shadish, 2001). In both cases, effective communication strategies are required (Simpson et al., 2017; Widerquist, 2005) if progress is to be made in completing the (quasi) experiment, and translating the findings into new policies and programmes.

Canada has relevant experience in the first and fourth approach. As described above, in 2016, the Government of Canada introduced the Canada Child Benefit (CCB), an income-tested subsidy for families with children (Tollstam, 2016). It was not described as a partial BI for families with children, but it has the characteristics of a negative income tax, requires no conditions of parental work or educational attendance, and is received by approximately 90% of Canadian families with children. Therefore, implementation of this benefit involves useful lessons relevant to implementation of a basic income.

Level of payment of the CCB is based on income tax reporting (Revenue Canada, undated). The benefit was implemented through a full implementation approach. Media coverage has reflected broad support for the benefit as a large portion of Canadians experience its effects (e.g. Carrick, 2016). The merit of the programme has not generally been questioned; but some implementation issues have raised criticism. These involve problems with the delivery system which result in under-enrolment of Indigenous families (Canada, 2018a) and women with children in intimate partner violence shelters (Office of the Taxpayers Ombudsman, 2018). In addition, onerous documentation requirements render demonstration of eligibility difficult for divorced and separated parents (Robson, 2016).

BI is often justified on the basis of its administrative simplicity. However, Canadian experience confirms that considerable care must be taken in designing eligibility standards, structures and procedures to locate and distinguish eligible beneficiaries, and systems to regularly pay benefits to these recipients (some of whom have limited bureaucratic skills) in a great variety of changing circumstances (De Wispelaere & Stirton, 2012, 2013; Mulvale & Frankel, 2016).

Lessons Learned from Canadian Experience

Based on Canada's experience with basic income—both in advocacy for its adoption, and in projects to test implementation—we can offer ten lessons that may be helpful for Australia and the international community. Five lessons focus on the political issues involved in adoption of a basic income, and five are related to implementation issues.

Adoption

First, a universal demogrant model of BI is not politically feasible because of the greater initial expenditures compared to a negative income tax model, even if substantial recovery through income taxation decreases its net costs. These higher expenditures could contribute to greater growth in the size of public expenditures, annual deficits and the accumulated debt (Frankel & Mulvale, 2014). In addition, the net cost of a demogrant will be higher because tax expenditures (deductions and loopholes) accessible to high income earners will limit the recapture of the demogrant through income taxation (Bird & Zolt, 2015).

Second, in arguing for the feasibility of a BI advocates should point to existing income security programmes that already contain partial BI (income top-up) mechanisms, and that enjoy broad public support. As discussed above, Canada already has such programmes for seniors, young families, and the working poor.

Third, the palatability of the cost of basic income can be increased in three ways. First, advocates must present their own carefully prepared cost estimates to counter opponents of BI who often present unrealistically high estimates (Pereira, 2017). Second, sources of financing should be specifically identified and developed. Third, BI should be framed as an investment in population health, educational attainment and the capacity to work.

A fourth lesson is that in a federated state advocates must attend to the difficult questions of funding and jurisdiction between the national and sub-national levels. In Canada, a cooperative federal-provincial BI scheme may be more fiscally sustainable, but it may be more difficult to develop, given the fact that ten provinces, three territories and the federal government must agree. Recent experience with failure to agree on carbon taxation is illustrative (Carter, 2018). On the other hand, if either the federal or provincial/territorial governments implement BI on their own a perverse incentive is provided to the other order of government to decrease or, at least restrain, its expenditures on income support (Frankel & Mulvale, 2014).

Fifth, in order to broaden the base of support for BI it is important deploy the arguments that go beyond just reducing poverty among people who are currently poor. This might include a poverty prevention logic related to precarious work (Lewchuk, 2017). An additional argument for BI is improvement in population health through raising income as a powerful determinant of health (Young, 2005), which should result in significant health care savings (Forget, 2011). Another argument for BI is the increased control over time and freedom that it would provide. Individuals would have opportunities to do non-remunerative artistic, service or caring work, or to pursue further education or different careers.

Implementation

Canada's experience with BI experiments and quasi-experiments suggests the following lessons. Given the history described above, a first lesson from Canada's experience with experiments is the political risk of cancellation as governments change and political priorities evolve. Attempting to mitigate this risk by developing support across all parties and among all voters is important. This may involve more than communicating about the experimental scheme. It may necessitate finding elements of BI that align with the values of each relevant political party as the experiment proceeds. It may also involve garnering support for an experiment among a broad range of civil society organizations, as well as reaching out to the general population through a variety of media to tell authentic and evocative stories of how basic income can change the lives of individuals and families for the better.

A second lesson related to implementation flows from the Mincome experiences of not presenting preliminary results, and not distinguishing between experimental and operational costs. During the Mincome experiment, gross operational costs were made public without netting out savings in other income support programmes (Simpson et al., 2017). This resulted in a perceived absence of political payoff in the short term and an exaggerated view of the cost of the experiment, which made continuation unpalatable to governments. It also limited the opportunity to develop broad public support, even among those who favoured poverty reduction. Therefore, emergent findings should be presented to attract support, and should be tailored so as to be accurate but to also limit experimental reactivity and negative reactions among BI critics. In addition, research costs should be separated from operational costs and presented as exceptional and related to the experiment rather than as inherent to BI delivery. Benefit costs should be presented after netting out savings in other income support programmes to present a more realistic picture of the cost of fully implementing BI.

A third lesson relates to the design of a quasi-experimental implementation, and the need to produce evidence of the health and educational effects of BI. A unique feature of the Mincome project was inclusion of a saturation site, in which all residents of the Town of Dauphin (approximately 10,000) and the surrounding rural municipality (approximately 2500) were eligible for inclusion (Forget, 2011). About a third of residents were enrolled. This allowed the study of community-wide and local labour market effects. Forget (2011) found a decrease of 8.5% in hospital admissions, and a decline in rates for accidents, and injuries, and mental health hospital admissions in Dauphin during the experimental period. She (Forget, 2011) also compared aggregate data for Dauphin and the rest of the province on the proportion of high school students continuing to the next grade. The Dauphin rates were significantly higher during the experimental period.

A fourth lesson for BI advocates relates to the guarantee level studied in Dauphin, which was only 60% of the Low-Income Cut-Offs, a semi-relative poverty threshold often used to calculate poverty statistics in Canada (Forget, 2011). Statistics Canada describes the Low-income Cut-Offs as an "income thresholds below which a family will likely devote a larger share of its income on the necessities of food, shelter and clothing than the average family" (Statistics Canada, 2013). The maximum benefit level under Mincome was $3800 (1974 dollars) for a family of four composed of two adults and two children younger than 15 (Simpson, Mason, & Godwin, 2017). This was approximately 38% of median family income (Calnitsky, 2016). Therefore, a guarantee level well below the poverty line can produce significant health and educational benefits. As advocates, policy analysts and policymakers attempt to balance cost with impact they should not dismiss the pragmatic option of implementing a low guarantee to get BI's foot in the policy innovation door, so to speak. Once implemented, attention can then be turned to increasing the benefit level and the resultant positive effects.

A fifth lesson follows from Calnitsky's (2016) analysis of 407 community experience surveys completed by Mincome beneficiaries in the Dauphin saturation site (approximately 65% of adults enrolled). As outlined in the previous section, Calnitsky found that Mincome participants did not report subjective feelings of being stigmatized, and their levels of community involvement indicated that they did not occupy a stigmatized social role. Mincome recipients saw their benefits as an acceptable and pragmatic programme for everyday people "who were short of money." A key factor within the group receiving Mincome in avoiding the subjective and social effects of stigma was found to be the absence of surveillance and regulation which is inherent in last-resort social assistance payments. Beyond impairing the dignity of recipients, stigma demonstrates significant negative health effects (Link & Phelan, 2006; Reutter et al., 2009), which in turn significantly increase health care costs (Sharac, Mccrone, Clement, & Thornicroft, 2010).

These Canadian lessons cannot be applied in a facile or automatic fashion to the Australian context. In particular, lessons from the Mincome project of the 1970s may be instructive, but analyses must also take into account the passage of time and changes in labour markets and social contexts (Forget, Marando, Surman, & Urban, 2016). Nonetheless, experience counts for something in both life and social policy development.

Conclusion

Our purpose in this chapter has been twofold: first, to describe developments among Canadian politicians, parties and constituencies in their support for the adoption of a BI; and second, to describe Canadian experience regarding design and implementation of a BI. In both cases, we have derived lessons. It is up to those situated in the Australian context to determine the extent to which these lessons are applicable, and how they might be applied. But based on our analysis of Canadian experience with BI advocacy and implementation, it seems important to develop broad coalitions promoting expanded rationales for BI. It also seems important to do the hard work of costing and developing real-world implementation strategies. In these ways, we could move from BI as a general concept to BI as a detailed proposal with broad public support and acceptance among key political decision-makers.

References

Basic Income Canada Network. (2016). *The basic income we want*. https://www.basicincomecanada.org/the_basic_income_we_want. Accessed 9 Nov 2018.

BC Gov News. (2017, July 3). *Researchers explore the potential of basic income in B.C.* https://news.gov.bc.ca/releases/2018SDPR0048-001317. Accessed 9 Nov 2018.

BC Green Caucus and BC New Democrat Caucus. (2017). *2017 Confidence and Supply Agreement between the BC Green Caucus and the BC New Democrat Caucus.* http://bcndpcaucus.ca/wp-content/uploads/sites/5/2017/05/BC-Green-BC-NDP-Agreement_vf-May-29th-2017.pdf. Accessed 9 Nov 2018.

Bird, R. M., & Zolt, E. M. (2015). Taxation and inequality in Canada and the United States: Two stories or one? *Osgoode Hall Law Journal, 52*(2), 401–426.

Calnitsky, D. (2016). “More normal than welfare”: The mincome experiment, stigma, and community experience. *Canadian Review of Sociology/Revue canadienne de sociologie, 53*(1), 26–71.

Campaign 2000. (2017). *A poverty-free Canada requires Federal leadership.* Toronto, ON: Campaign 2000. https://campaign2000.ca/wp-content/uploads/2017/11/EnglishNationalC2000ReportNov212017.pdf Accessed 9 Nov 2018.

Canada. (2018a). *Opportunity for all – Canada's first poverty reduction strategy.* Ottawa, ON: Government of Canada. https://www.canada.ca/en/employment-social-development/programs/poverty-reduction/reports/strategy.html. Accessed 12 Nov 2018.

Canada. (2018b). *Introducing the Canada workers benefit.* Ottawa, ON: Government of Canada. http://publications.gc.ca/collections/collection_2018/fin/F2-263-18-008-5-eng.pdf. Accessed 9 Nov 2018.

Caputo, R. (2014). *Policy analysis for social workers.* Thousand Oaks, CA: Sage.

Carrick, R. (2016, July 21). New Canada Child Benefit is a win for most families. *The Globe and Mail* [Toronto, ON], p. A4.

Carter, A. V. (2018). Policy pathways to carbon entrenchment: Responses to the climate crisis in Canada's petro-provinces. *Studies in Political Economy, 99*(2), 1–24.

Cook, T. D., Campbell, D. T., & Shadish, W. (2001). *Experimental and quasi-experimental designs for generalized causal inference.* Boston: Houghton Mifflin.

Cooke, J., & De Wispelaere, J. (2018, September 4). Basic income movement strong despite Ontario's actions. *Toronto Star*. https://www.thestar.com/opinion/contributors/2018/09/04/basic-income-movement-strong-despite-ontarios-actions.html. Accessed 9 Nov 2018.

Curry, B. (2016, February 5). Minister eyes guaranteed minimum income to tackle poverty. *The Globe and Mail*, p. Al. https://www.theglobeandmail.com/news/politics/guaranteed-income-has-merit-as-a-national-policy-minister-says/article28588670/. Accessed 9 Nov 2018.

De Wispelaere, J., & Stirton, L. (2012). A disarmingly simple idea? Practical bottlenecks in the implementation of a universal basic income. *International Social Security Review, 65*, 103–121. https://doi.org/10.1111/j.1468-246X.2012.01430.x.

De Wispelaere, J., & Stirton, L. (2013). The politics of unconditional basic income: Bringing bureaucracy back in. *Political Studies, 61*(4), 915–932.

Department of Finance. (2018). *Backgrounder: Strengthening the Canada child benefit*. Government of Canada. https://www.fin.gc.ca/n18/data/18-008_4-eng.asp. Accessed 9 Nov 2018.

Finkel, A. (2006). *Social policy and practice in Canada: A history*. Waterloo, ON: Wilfred Laurier University Press.

Forget, E. (2011). The town with no poverty: The health effects of a Canadian guaranteed annual income field experiment. *Canadian Public Policy, 37*(3), 283–305.

Forget, E., Marando, D., Surman, T., & Urban, M. C. (2016). *Pilot lessons: How to design a basic income pilot project for Ontario* (Research paper #126). Toronto, ON: Mowat Centre. https://mowatcentre.ca/pilot-lessons/. Accessed 9 Nov 2018.

Forget, E. L. [and 23 other signatories]. (2018). *An open letter to premier Ford and Minister MacLeod on basic income*. Winnipeg, MB: EvidenceNetwork.ca. https://evidencenetwork.ca/an-open-letter-to-premier-ford-and-minister-macleod-on-basic-income/. Accessed 9 Nov 2018.

Frankel, S., & Mulvale, J. (2014). Support and inclusion for all Manitobans: Steps toward a basic income scheme. *Manitoba Law Journal, 37*(2), 425–464.

Fraser, M. W., & Galinsky, M. J. (2010). Steps in intervention research: Designing and developing social programs. *Research on Social Work Practice, 20*(5), 459–466.

Globe and Mail. (2018, August 1). Cancellation of Ontario's basic-income project is callous and wasteful [Editorial]. *The Globe and Mail*. Toronto, ON. https://www.theglobeandmail.com/opinion/editorials/article-globe-editorial-cancellation-of-ontarios-basic-income-project-is/. Accessed 9 Nov 2018.

Haddow, R. (1994). Canadian organized labour and the guaranteed annual income. In A. E. Johnson, S. McBride, & P. J. Smith (Eds.), *Continuities and discontinuities: The political economy of social welfare and labour market policy in Canada* (pp. 350–366). Toronto, ON: University of Toronto Press.

House of Commons. (2010, November). *Federal poverty reduction plan: Working in partnership towards reducing poverty in Canada*. Report of the Standing Committee on Human Resources, Skills and Social Development and the Status of Persons with Disabilities. Ottawa, ON: 40th Parliament, 3rd Session.

Khanna, A. (2016). Six principles to guide a basic income program. In A. Himelfarb & T. Hennessy (Eds.), *Basic income: Rethinking social policy* (pp. 54–57). Toronto, ON: Canadian Centre on Policy Alternatives, Ontario Office.

Lewchuk, W. (2017). Precarious jobs: Where are they, and how do they affect well-being? *The Economic and Labour Relations Review, 28*(3), 402–419. https://doi.org/10.1177/1035304617722943. Accessed 10 Nov 2018.

Liberal Party of Canada. (2014). Adopted resolutions: Biennial Convention. Montreal 2014. *#100: Creating a basic annual income to be designed and implemented for a fair economy* (p. 17). https://www.liberal.ca/wp-content/uploads/2010/05/Priority-Resolutions-EN-FINAL.pdf. Accessed 10 Nov 2018.

Liberal Party of Canada. (2016). *Adopted priority resolutions, Biennial Convention, Winnipeg 2016*. Poverty reduction: Minimum income. Retrieved from https://www.liberal.ca/wp-content/uploads/2017/07/Adopted-PRIORITY-Resolutions-Biennial-2016-EN.pdf. Accessed 10 Nov 2018.

Liberal Party of Canada. (2018). *Implementation of a guaranteed minimum income model*. Policy resolution 11. Retrieved from https://2018.liberal.ca/policy/implementation-of-a-guaranteed-minimum-income-model/. Accessed 10 Nov 2018.

Link, B. G., & Phelan, J. C. (2006). Stigma and its public health implications. *The Lancet, 367*(9509), 528–529.

Macdonald, D. (2016). *A policymaker's guide to basic income*. Ottawa, ON: Canadian Centre for Policy Alternatives, National Office. https://www.policyalternatives.ca/publications/reports/policymakers-guide-basic-income. Accessed 10 Nov 2018.

Monsebraaten, L. (2018, September 18). Cancellation of Ontario's basic income project sparks global outrage. *Toronto Star*. https://www.thestar.com/news/queenspark/2018/09/14/cancellation-of-ontarios-basic-income-project-sparks-global-outrage.html. Accessed 14 Nov 2018.

Mulvale, J., & Frankel, S. (2016). Next steps on the road to Basic Income in Canada. *Journal of Sociology and Social Welfare, 43*(1), 27–50.

New Democratic Party. (2016). *Resolutions passed at Convention 2016*. Ottawa, ON: New Democratic Party.

OECD [Organisation for Economic Co-operation and Development]. (2018). *Poverty rate (indicator)*. https://doi.org/10.1787/0fe1315d-en. Accessed 6 Nov 2018.

Offe, C. (2001). Pathways from here. In P. Van Parijs (Ed.), *What's wrong with a free lunch?* (pp. 111–118). Boston: Beacon Press.

Office of the Taxpayers Ombudsman. (2018). *Benefits unsheltered: An examination into the Canada Revenue Agency's communication and outreach efforts to shelters and other support organizations about benefits and credits administered by the Canada Revenue Agency*, December 2017. (Cat. Rv10-16/2018E-PDF, 978-0-660-24428-0). Ottawa, ON: Minister of Public Services and Procurement Canada.

Ontario. (2017). *Ontario basic income pilot*. Toronto, ON: Government of Ontario. https://www.ontario.ca/page/ontario-basic-income-pilot. Accessed 10 Nov 2018.

Pereira, R. (2017). Cost of universal basic income: Public savings and program redundancy exceed cost. In R. Pereira (Ed.), *Financing basic income: Addressing the cost objection* (pp. 9–45). New York/London: Palgrave Macmillan.

Porter, A. (2015). Austerity, social program restructuring, and the erosion of democracy: Examining the 2012 employment insurance reforms. *Canadian Review of Social Policy, 71*, 21–52.

Presse Canadienne. (2018, September 12). Québec solidaire vows to establish a guaranteed minimum income. *Montreal Gazette*. https://montrealgazette.com/news/quebec/quebec-solidaire-vows-to-establish-a-guaranteed-minimum-income. Accessed 10 Nov 2018.

Raphael, D., Bryant, T., & Mendly-Zambo, Z. (2018). Canada considers a basic income guarantee: can it achieve health for all? *Health Promotion International, 2018*, 1–7. https://doi.org/10.1093/heapro/day058

Reutter, L. I., Stewart, M. J., Veenstra, G., Love, R., Raphael, D., & Makwarimba, E. (2009). "Who do they think we are, anyway?": Perceptions of and responses to poverty stigma. *Qualitative Health Research, 19*(3), 297–311.

Revenue Canada. (undated). *Canada Child Benefit and related provincial and territorial programs for the period from July 2017 to June 2018*. Ottawa, ON: Revenue Canada.

Robson, L. (2016, May 30). The problem of child benefits in shared custody: What the planned changes to the federal child benefits really mean for divorced or separated parents. *Macleans* [magazine].

Royal Commission on the Economic Union and Development Prospects for Canada. (1985). *Report* (Vol. 2). Ottawa, ON: Supply and Services Canada.

Segal, H. (2012, December). Scrapping welfare. *Literary Review of Canada, 20*(10), 8. http://reviewcanada.ca/magazine/2012/12/scrapping-welfare/. Accessed 10 Nov 2018.

Senate of Canada. (1971). *Report of the special senate committee on poverty* (Croll report). Ottawa, ON: Information Canada.

Senate of Canada. (2009). *In from the margins: A call to action on poverty, housing and homelessness*. Standing Senate Committee on Social Affairs, Science and Technology (Sub-Committee on Cities). Ottawa, ON: Senate of Canada.

Seth, L. S. (2017). *Case study. Oxford county: Leveraging a community sustainability plan to tackle poverty*. Waterloo, ON: Tamarack Institute. http://www.tamarackcommunity.ca/library/case-study-oxford-county-leveraging-a-community-sustainability-plan-to-tackle-poverty. Accessed 10 Nov 2018.

Sharac, J., Mccrone, P., Clement, S., & Thornicroft, G. (2010). The economic impact of mental health stigma and discrimination: A systematic review. *Epidemiology and Psychiatric Sciences, 19*(3), 223–232.

Shingler, B. (2017, December 12). *Quebec's new basic income plan has proponents dreaming big, others skeptical*. Montreal, PQ: CBC News. https://www.cbc.ca/news/canada/montreal/quebec-basic-income-plan-francois-blais-1.4442902. Accessed 10 Nov 2018.

Simpson, W., Mason, G., & Godwin, R. (2017). The Manitoba basic annual income experiment: Lessons learned 40 years later. *Canadian Public Policy, 43*(1), 85–104.

Statistics Canada. (2013). *Low income lines 2010, 2011* (Income research series, catalogue number 75F0002MWE2012002). Ottawa, ON: Statistics Canada.

Stone, L. (2016, May 16). Federal budget to restore Old Age Security eligibility to 65. *Globe and Mail* [Toronto, ON]. https://www.theglobeandmail.com/news/politics/liberals-to-return-oas-eligibility-to-65/article29271018/. Accessed 10 Nov 2018.

Tollstam, G. (2016). New Canada child benefit. *Canadian Tax Highlights, 24*(8), 7.

Toronto Star. (2018, August 11). Save basic income pilot: Social assistance [Editorial], *Toronto Star*, p. IN 10.

Widerquist, K. (2005). A failure to communicate: What (if anything) can we learn from the negative income tax experiments? *The Journal of Socio-Economics, 34*(1), 49–81.

Young, T. K. (2005). *Population health: Concepts and methods* (2nd ed.). New York: Oxford University Press.

Young, M. (2007). Introduction. In M. Young, S. Boyd, G. Brodsky, & S. Day (Eds.), *Poverty: Rights, social citizenship, and legal activism*. Vancouver, BC: UBC Press.

Young, M., & Mulvale, J. (2009). *Possibilities and prospects: The debate over a guaranteed income*. Vancouver, BC: Canadian Centre on Policy Alternative. https://www.policyalternatives.ca/publications/reports/possibilities-and-prospects. Accessed 10 Nov 2018.

14

Concluding Remarks and an Invitation

Elise Klein, Tim Dunlop, and Jennifer Mays

Sometimes it is forgotten how radical universal health care was considered when Prime Minister Gough Whitlam introduced it in 1975. Now taken as a crucial pillar of Australian social security, Medibank, as it was then called, suffered prolonged and passionate opposition (which continues today in some segments of society). In fact, even after it was legislated in parliament, universal health care suffered rollbacks during the Fraser years, only to be reinstated again under Hawke in the 1980s. Most of us now know that our lives have been improved profoundly by having such a universal scheme, to the extent that any perceived efforts to undermine

E. Klein (✉)
John Medley Building, University of Melbourne, Parkville, VIC, Australia
e-mail: elise.klein@unimelb.edu.au

T. Dunlop
University of Melbourne, Parkville, VIC, Australia

J. Mays
Queensland University of Technology, Brisbane, QLD, Australia
e-mail: j.mays@qut.edu.au

E. Klein et al. (eds.), *Implementing a Basic Income in Australia*, Exploring the Basic Income Guarantee, https://doi.org/10.1007/978-3-030-14378-7_14

it almost instantly generate a community pushback (as happened during the 2016 federal election and the so-called Mediscare campaign).

In justifying why universal health care was essential for Australia, Whitlam said in a 1972 speech, "I personally find quite unacceptable a system whereby the man who drives my Commonwealth car in Sydney pays twice as much for the same family cover as I have, not despite the fact that my income is four or five-times higher than his, but precisely because of my higher income". His words are interesting to reflect on here because similar arguments are made today about a universal basic income. Indeed, as universal health care was deemed too expensive, so too is basic income (BI).

These are important aspects of the story of Australian social progress that we must remember when considering a basic income. Issues of implementation are important and, as we have seen in the pages of this book, can be quite complex. Yet, this must not overwhelm our ongoing desire to seek a better society, economy and life.

Nonetheless, the progress we seek today faces different challenges. Unlike the Whitlam era, we are now faced with climate change, exposing more than any other problem the ultimate failure of neoliberalism's economic rationality. Other "inconvenient truths" loom too, including the global rise in inequality that continues at pace, especially within countries, while racism, patriarchy and coloniality endure. Furthermore, financialisation, neoliberalism and the failure of full and dignified employment for all are bringing about social unease, emboldening racism, and helping fuel right wing populism. Processes of settler colonialism in Australia continue to dispossess First Nations of land and language whilst aiming to assimilate people into Western ways of being. Some may aspire to this, but what is telling is how options to live beyond this are actively foreclosed on by the settler state—particularly through conditional welfare programmes, imprisonment, cuts to funding and continued denial of sovereignty. We are also on the cusp of a technological revolution which will either further exploit these inequalities, or help restore democratic power. All of this means that bold initiatives are needed, supported by well thought-through implementation pathways.

The authors in the pages of this book take basic income seriously. They have outlined various possibilities to advance the implementation of an Australian BI. There is still a lot of work to do and more questions to be answered, and let us briefly consider some of them: should young people be given the basic income first, or is another group preferable? What specific measures within the tax system need to be enhanced in order for redistribution to work more effectively? Do we need to establish a sovereign wealth fund that allows us to better share the common resources of the nation, including the data extracted from us via our smartphones and other technologies? How does a basic income challenge existing primary and secondary education? How can policy makers optimise non-conditional employment creation initiatives alongside basic income? Should all people be eligible to the same amount? This is a matter that is especially important within a settler colonial context such as in Australia where First Nations people have and continue to suffer attempts of elimination through violent means or through processes of assimilation. Interestingly in the US, Black Lives Matter places their policy on basic income within a reparations framework, and see basic income as a way to address past and continuing harm. They argue that, "The government, responsible corporations and other institutions that have profited off of the harm they have inflicted on Black people—from colonialism to slavery through food and housing redlining, mass incarceration, and surveillance—must repair the harm done[1]". The reparations policy platform includes not only full and free access to education for all Black people as well as mandated public-school curriculums that critically examine the political, economic and social impacts of colonisation and slavery, funding to support the restoration of cultural assets and sacred sites but also a basic income. This proposal for the basic income is U PLUS BI—a payment to all Americans, but black Americans would receive extra as a form of reparation. To Black Lives Matter, this "PLUS" aspect is framed as a grand bargain with white America: all would benefit, but those who suffered through slavery and continuing racism would benefit slightly more. Given Australia's past and present dispossession, perhaps this is something that needs to be placed in the implementation proposal.

[1] See https://policy.m4bl.org/reparations/

There will be more questions, and in some ways, it feels we are just getting started. We cannot cover all issues of implementing a basic income in Australia in one book, but we hope the chapters here provide a way forward. It is no surprise that this book coincides with the 50-year commemoration of Professor Ronald Henderson and his pivotal work in shaping basic income debates today. This book extends much of the work that has occurred to date, and views the time right for actioning basic income. It is time for mobilising greater support and political will to progress basic income design and implementation initiatives.

Some will want to wait for "leadership" on the issue of basic income in the hope there will be another Whitlam to walk the halls of Parliament. But given recent events that leave many of us feeling that leadership in Canberra is wanting, perhaps it is up to us, the people, to demand basic income. Coalitions of academics, activists, trade unions, think tanks and other members of the public can do so much together. Ultimately, it will take what many are doing already, asking for more information, demanding the idea is taken seriously, refusing to be dismayed by the naysayers, and then being willing to ask the question at the heart of all social progress: what if…?

And so we invite you, the reader, to continue the conversations, the inquiries and the activism to make possible what others say is impossible: to implement the basic income.

Index[1]

A
AASW, *see* Australian Association of Social Workers
ABS, *see* Australian Bureau of Statistics
ACTU, *see* Australian Council of Trade Unions
Adequacy, 6, 10, 57, 58, 113, 114, 118
Affluence tested payment, 170, 172, 173, 176
Affluence testing, 167, 170, 175, 176
Affordability, 30, 32, 54, 104, 113, 114, 118, 119, 121, 189, 246
Age pension/aged pension, 55, 148–150, 175, 176, 184
  old, 155, 156
  universal, 164, 166–170, 207
Alaska Permanent Fund Dividend, 2, 73, 150, 153, 154, 219
ALP, *see* Australian Labor Party
Altman, J. C., 4, 16, 92, 94n5, 132
Anglican Church of Australia, 9
Anglicare, 9–10, 139
Anglicare Rental Affordability Snapshot, 189
Anglophone welfare state, 223
Anti-oppressive practice, 216, 226
Antipodean social model, 166, 167
Atkinson, A. B., 113–114, 156
Australian Association of Social Workers (AASW), 223, 225
  educational standards of, 226, 227
Australian Bureau of Statistics (ABS), 88n2, 94, 97

[1] Note: Page numbers followed by 'n' refer to notes.

E. Klein et al. (eds.), *Implementing a Basic Income in Australia*, Exploring the Basic Income Guarantee, https://doi.org/10.1007/978-3-030-14378-7

Australian Census (2016), 70
Australian Constitution/Constitution of Australia, 238
Australian Council of Trade Unions (ACTU), 222
  Congress, 10
Australian Human Rights Commission, 77–78
Australian Industrial Relations Commission, 77
Australian Labor Party (ALP), 8, 33, 34, 77, 133–137, 139, 157, 158, 158n1, 167, 169, 211, 225
Australian Senate's Standing Committee on Community Affairs, 225
Australian social assistance sector, 216, 219–221
Australian social assistance system, 217
Australian social progress, 260
Authoritarianism, 47
Automation, 3, 8, 11, 25, 26, 28, 29, 32, 34, 35, 46, 58, 136, 141, 200, 217, 244

B

Baby boomers, 207
Bandt, A., 136
Basic first approach, 148, 154–155, 158, 161
Basic income (BI), 50–53
  in Australia, 6–11
  benefit for, 170
  in Canada (*see* Basic income, in Canada)
  challenges for considerations, 1–17, 180
  cost of basic income, 13, 173, 250
  critics of, 164, 211
  definition of, 149, 164
  framing of, 11–12
  implementation of, 11–13
  importance of, 185
  initiatives, 117–119
  level of payment, 247
  making sense of, 113–121
  need for, 2–5, 23–24, 45–50, 69–72, 87–90, 111–112, 131–143, 148–153, 163–164, 189, 192, 199–200, 215–217, 237–238
  radical models of, 166
  stepping stones approach, 164–166
  SWHS and, 221–228
  trials of, 12–13
  universal age pension, 166–170
  varieties of, 148–153
  Youth Basic Income, 170–175
Basic Income Canada Network (BICN), 243–245
Basic Income Earth Network (BIEN), 112–114, 164, 223, 243
Basic Income/Flat Tax (BI/FT) model, 165
Basic Income Guarantee Australia (BIGA), 223
Basic income, in Canada, 237–252
  adoption of, 248–249
  implementation of, 246–252
  political history of, 238–245
  provincial government initiatives of, 244–245
Basic Income Pilot project, 244, 245
Bauman, Z., 35

BCA, *see* Business Council of Australia
Belgium, 142
Benn, C., 222, 223
BI, *see* Basic income
BICN, *see* Basic Income Canada Network
Biddle, N., 93, 94n5
BIEN, *see* Basic Income Earth Network
BI/FT, *see* Basic Income/Flat Tax model
BIGA, *see* Basic Income Guarantee Australia
Birnbaum, S., 52–53, 55
Black Lives Matter, 261
Blind Pension, 16, 45, 55–64
  dimensions of, 57–58
Blue collar workers, 167, 210
Boettke, P. J., 53–54
Bowen, C., 8, 133, 134, 139, 141
Brady, D., 56
Bregman, R., 79
Brotherhood of St Laurence (BSL), 117, 118, 184, 187, 222, 223
Burke, T., 24
Business Council of Australia (BCA), 10

C

Calnitsky, D., 240, 251
Cameron, D., 135
Canada, 30, 47, 217, 223, 226
  basic income in (*see* Basic income, in Canada)
  Constitution Act (1982), 238
  provincial advocacy group, 244
  trials of basic income, 115, 116, 118–120, 180
Canada Child Benefit (CCB), 242, 247
Canada Workers Benefit, 242
Canadian Association of Social Workers (CASW), 224, 225
Canadian Centre on Policy Alternatives, 243
Canadian Charter, 238
Canadian labour movement, 240, 243
Canadian labour unions, 242
Canadian Medical Association, 224
Canadian Public Health Association, 224
Canadian Social Work Association, 223
Capital, 28, 37, 54, 73, 159, 168
  accumulation, 33, 90, 116
  distribution, 46
  human, 182, 183
  social, 183, 193
  symbolic, 36
Capitalism, 5, 11, 63, 70, 71, 159, 181, 216
  colonial, 88
  global, 184, 185, 190, 227
  inequality-generating dynamics of, 227
  late, 33, 158
CAQ, *see* Coalition Avenir Québec
Carnegie, M., 140
Caron, G., 243
Cashless Debit Card, 225
Cash payments, 1, 112, 116, 118, 119, 121, 163, 164, 171
CASW, *see* Canadian Association of Social Workers
CCB, *see* Canada Child Benefit

CDEP, *see* Community Development Employment Projects
Centre Alliance, 137
Centre for Independent Studies (CIS), 8, 35
Centrelink, 49, 179n1, 180
Charter of Rights and Freedoms, 238
Child protection system, 220
CIS, *see* Centre for Independent Studies
Coalition Avenir Québec (CAQ), 244
Coalition National Party, 131
Colonial capitalism, 88
Commission of Inquiry into Poverty, 117
  Henderson Poverty Report, 6
Commonwealth Conciliation and Arbitration Commission, *see* Australian Industrial Relations Commission
Commonwealth Invalid and Old-Age Pension, 46
Community development, 91, 222, 223
Community Development Employment Projects (CDEP), 4, 16, 90–103, 132
Conditionality, 31, 47, 48, 52, 55, 57, 61, 65, 113–114, 118, 121, 164, 167, 211
  conditional welfare programmes, 260
Conservative Party, 239–242, 245
Constitution of Canada, 238
Constructive scepticism, 200–202
Consumer Price Index (CPI), 55
Contemporary neoliberal discourses, 216
Corbyn, J., 135, 142
Councils of Social Services, 139
Cox, E., 16, 139
CPI, *see* Consumer Price Index
Craik, C., 225
Critical awareness, 227
Critical social analysis, 227
Critical social work
  education, 226, 227
  educators, 227
  renewal of, 216, 228
Croll, D., 239
Cultural participation for remote-living indigenous Australians, basic income and, 87–105
  Community Development Employment Projects, 90–93
  methods, 94–97
  results, 97–101
  settler colonialism, vi, 16, 87–90
  surplus populations, 87–90

D

Dauphin, Mincome payments in, 223–224, 239, 240, 250, 251
De Wispelaere, J., 56, 57, 63, 64, 113, 114
Decommodification, 31, 33, 199
Demogrant, 112, 147, 149, 224, 248
Denmark, 142, 199, 201, 204–206
Denniss, R., 169, 220
Detractors, 74, 190, 246
Di Natale, R., 9, 33, 135
Dignity, 8, 36, 48, 60, 62, 63, 82, 193, 251
  of participation, 136, 137, 143
  of work, 131, 133, 136

Disability, 193
Disability Allowance, 59, 245
Disability pension, 51, 55–57
Disability Support Pension, 59, 156
Distinct political dynamics, 167
Distributive inequity, 49, 60
Distributive justice, 218
'Dual earner' policy nations, 203–204
Dualistic pension system, 167–169
Duclos, J.-Y., 242
Dunlop, T., 8, 34

E

Ecological justice, 4
Economic equality, 204
Economic inequality, 6, 14, 215–219, 223, 225–228
Economic justice, 216, 226, 228
Economic security, 1, 4, 5, 11, 15, 31, 64, 112, 121, 206, 237, 242–244
Education, SWHS, 226–228
Egalitarian, 51–53, 55, 57, 61, 63, 64, 193, 218
  democracy and social policy, 50
  distribution of income and wealth, 46
  social transformation, 216
Egalitarianism, 46, 50, 51, 132
  design features inclusive of, 54–55
Employee-Driven Innovation, 205–206
Employment future, 209
Employment insecurity, 185
Employment services, deficiencies in, 208
Equality, 52, 56, 72, 193
  gender, 1, 203
  marriage, 130, 132
  political, 26
  social, 26
Equitable BI, 180, 181, 185, 189, 192–194
Equitable payment, 188
Equity, 55–59, 69, 113, 115, 168, 169, 180, 224
  financial, 79, 83
  gender, 70, 71
  social, 79
Equivalence, 148, 151–153, 171, 175
Equivalent BI, 179
Erikson, E. H., 181, 193
Escobar, A., 89
Esping-Anderson, G., 199, 200
Europe, 2, 61, 217

F

Family Action Centre project (1972–1975), 118
Family Centre Project (FCP), 118, 222, 223
Fast Food Industry Award, 187
FCP, *see* Family Centre Project
Feminist perspectives on basic income, 69–83, 140
  background of, 69–72
  current scenario, 72
  flexible and shorter paid working hours, creation of, 79–80
  gender pay gap for work of equal value, fixing, 77
  long full-time working hours, valorisation of, 77–78
  options for universal social dividend, designing, 81–82

Feminist perspectives on basic income (*cont.*)
seriously flawed malfunctioning social security payment system, fixing, 80–81
universal basic income and unpaid social contributions, 72
unpaid work contributions, recognition of, 78–79
Ferguson, J., 5
Fetishisation of paid work, 131, 134, 137, 143
Financialisation, 260
Financial stress, 92, 119, 191
Finland, 34, 113, 199
basic income experiment, 203
trials of basic income, 12, 120–121, 205
First Nations, 13, 71, 72, 119, 140, 260, 261
Fisher Commonwealth Government, 56
Flexicurity, 206, 208
Forget, E., 239, 240, 250
Foucault, M., 228
Foundation for Young Australians (FYA), 189
Framing, 5, 11–12, 16, 24, 25, 147
France, 142
Fraser Liberal government, guaranteed minimum income in, 7
Frequency/duration, 114
Friedman, M., 4, 136, 149
Functionalist constructions, young people, 181
Furlong, A., 183, 184
FYA, *see* Foundation for Young Australians

G
GDP, *see* Gross domestic product
Gender
equality, 1, 203
equity, 71
inequity, 81
male dominated biases, need for feminist policy leadership to counter, 74–76
pay gaps, 70, 77, 79, 82
politics, 139
Germany, 204
GetUp!, 142
GFC, *see* Great Financial Crisis
Gig economy, 3, 30, 81, 185
Gillard, J., 133
Giroux, H., 183, 184, 193
Global capitalism, 227
effects of, 190
Global Financial Crisis (GFC), 71, 76, 96, 157
GMB, 138
GMI, *see* Guaranteed minimum income
Gorz, A., 36
Government of Quebec, 244
Great Depression, 238
Green Institute, 35, 130, 135, 135n2, 136, 142
Greens Party, 9, 33, 130, 133, 135, 136, 142, 203, 211, 244
Gross domestic product (GDP), 75, 76, 78, 167, 174
Guaranteed Adequate Income, 135, 142
Guaranteed Income Supplement, 222, 239
Guaranteed minimum income, *see* Basic income (BI)

H

Hall, S., 181, 193
Hanson, P., 136
Harper, S., 241
Harvester Judgement, 70, 204
Henderson, R., 6, 7, 13, 117, 262
Henderson, T., 159, 193
Henderson Inquiry, 222
Henderson Poverty Line, 6, 7, 63, 114, 117, 118, 150, 222
Henderson Poverty Report, 6
HILDA, *see* Household, Income and Labour Dynamics in Australia
Home ownership, democratisation of, 168
Homo economicus, 74
House of Commons Committee, 241
Household, Income and Labour Dynamics in Australia (HILDA), 208
Housing tax concessions, 168, 174
Howard, J., 58, 130
Hum, D., 114–116
Human capital, 182, 183

I

Income distribution, 46, 49, 55, 61
Income entitlements, 81, 82
Income inequality, 16, 25, 28, 35, 224
Income security programmes, 248
Income tax, negative, *see* Negative income tax (NIT)
Incrementalism, 31, 175
Indebtedness, 185
India, 2, 30, 61
Indigenous Australians, 31, 209
  basic income and cultural participation for, 87–105
Individualism, 184
Industrial arbitration tribunals, 204
Industrial capitalism, 216
Industrial Revolution, 70, 184
Industry superannuation funds, 210
Inequality, 46, 48, 50, 52, 63, 79, 117, 134, 135, 157, 192, 201, 220, 221, 244, 260
  economic, 6, 14, 215–219, 223, 225–228
  income, 16, 25, 28, 35, 224
  intergenerational, 164, 171, 174, 185
  intra-generational, 185
  material, 227
  structural, 49, 60, 216, 220, 228
  wealth, 45, 47, 226, 227
Insecurity of work, 185
Institute for Public Affairs (IPA), 8, 35, 132
Institutional racism, 49
Intergenerational inequalities, 164, 171, 174, 185
Intergenerational justice, 4
Internships, 138, 185, 186, 192
Interprofessional advocacy, 223–226
Intra-generational inequality, 185
Invalid Pension, 56, 57
IPA, *see* Institute for Public Affairs

J

Job creation, 30, 200, 211
Job Guarantee, 14, 15, 61, 91, 135, 142, 159

Jobs Allowance, *see* Newstart Allowance
Jobs Availability Snapshot 2018, 9
Junior wages, 179, 180, 185
Justice, 51, 53, 59, 60
  distributive, 218
  ecological, 4
  economic, 216, 226, 228
  intergenerational, 4
  redistributive, 61
  social, 30, 39, 47, 52, 53, 55, 64, 74, 215, 219, 221, 223, 226–228
  temporal, 37
  wage, 188, 190, 193

K

Katter Party, 136
Keynes, J. M., 29, 79
Keynesian policies, 201
Klein, E., 132

L

Labour force, 3, 27, 92, 97, 98, 103, 119, 120, 167, 173
Labour markets, 3, 4, 6, 11, 25, 26, 28–31, 33, 37, 46, 55, 61, 90–92, 103–105, 111, 118, 120, 158–159, 167, 169–171, 174, 183, 184, 187, 200, 201, 203, 218, 240, 250, 251
Labour movement, 133, 138, 166, 240, 243
Lakoff, G., 26
Late capitalism, 33, 158
Leigh, A., 8, 134, 139, 141
'Less eligibility' principle, 27
Leyonhjelm, D., 136
Liberal-corporatist regimes, 46
Liberal government, 7, 119, 242
Liberalism, 216
Liberal Party, 131, 131n1, 132, 207, 242
Long full-time working hours, valorisation of, 77–78
Low-Income Cut-Offs, 251

M

Male 'breadwinner,' 70
Male Total Average Weekly Earnings (MTAWE), 150, 155, 156
Managerialism, 157–160
Manitoba, 115, 116
  federal government and provincial government of, 239
  Mincome trial in, 82, 223–224, 241
  urban and rural communities, 239
Marginal tax rates, 3, 116, 117, 152, 157, 160, 165, 168, 170–175
Market liberalisation, 218
Marriage equality, 130, 132
Martin, A. G., 53–54
Marx, K., 227
Mason, P., 135, 142
Mature-age workers, 207–209
Means-tested payment, 57, 58, 62, 120, 152, 157, 160, 167, 170, 175
Medibank, 259
Medicare, 53, 130, 134, 221
Mediscare campaign, 260

Meritocratic extremism, wealth and, 46
Mincome project, 82, 116, 180, 223, 239–241, 250, 251
Moase, G., 134, 138
Moral adulthood, 36
Moreton-Robinson, A., 87n1
MTAWE, *see* Male Total Average Weekly Earnings
'Muddling through,' 23

N

National Aboriginal and Torres Strait Islander Social Survey (NATSISS), 93–101
National Disability Insurance Scheme (NDIS), 53, 59–61, 64, 80–81
National Tertiary Education Union, 138
NATSISS, *see* National Aboriginal and Torres Strait Islander Social Survey
NDIS, *see* National Disability Insurance Scheme
NDP, *see* New Democratic Party
Negative income tax (NIT), 2, 3, 13, 112, 119, 147–149, 151, 152, 160, 239, 241, 243, 247
  definition of, 149
  models, 165, 248
Neoliberalism, 46–48, 50, 55, 157, 159, 185
  economic rationality, failure of, 260
Netherlands, the, 204, 205
New Democratic Party (NDP), 239, 242–245
New Democrats, 242, 245
Newspeak, 151, 156
Newstart Allowance, 10, 58, 59, 151, 156, 164, 172, 188, 188n3
New Zealand, 172
  flat-rate pension, 169
Nilan, P., 181, 182, 188
NIT, *see* Negative income tax
Non-government organisations (NGOs), 118, 142, 220
Non-governmental social policy advocacy organizations, 243
Nordic nations, 200, 201, 203, 205, 206
  positive work design and industrial democracy, 205
  trials of BI in, 201
Norway, 199, 204, 205

O

O'Dwyer, K., 132
OECD, *see* Organisation for Economic Cooperation and Development
Office of Economic Opportunity, 115
Old Age Security programme, 239, 242
Ontario, 244
  pilot, cancellation of, 245
  provincial government of, 245
  trial, 119–120
  See also Canada
Ontario Basic Income Network, 245
Organisation for Economic Cooperation and Development (OECD), 27, 29, 49, 73, 112, 204, 220
Ottawa trial, 12

P
Paid employment, 8, 26, 90, 121, 131, 204, 207–210
  income from, 201
  See also Paid work
Paid work, 2, 8, 27–30, 36, 38, 39, 70–72, 74–77, 79–83, 90, 133, 134, 137, 143, 159, 172, 184, 186, 188, 192, 199–211, 239, 245
  limitations of, 200
  mature-age workers, 207–209
  opportunities of, 201
  pressure to work longer, 207
  proposals and policy trials, 202–203
  quality of working life, 205–206
  support unemployed to find jobs, 206
  training, jobs and transitions to retirement, 209–210
  work/life balance, 203–205
  See also Paid employment
Paid working hours
  flexible and shorter, creation of, 79–80
Paine, T., 51
Participation income, 36, 113, 114, 156
Paternalism, 26, 31, 36, 46–47, 64
Pension age, 113, 167, 207
Pension asset test, 169
Pessimism, 39, 201
Piketty, T., 46, 50
Pilot programme, 31, 180, 223
"PLUS" aspect, 261
Policies of basic income, 32–38
Policy incrementalism, 31
Policy landscape, in Australia, 55, 61, 210
Policy options, 30–32
Political obstacles, 159–160, 166
Political strategy, for basic income, 129–143
Post-Reformation Weberian Protestant ethics, 70
Poverty, 25, 32–33, 45–52, 56, 59, 61, 63, 64, 88, 112, 114, 115, 117–120, 164, 217, 225, 226, 228
  Henderson Inquiry, 222
  relief, 27, 219
  social-structural analysis of, 226
  social-structural causes of, 220
  structural issues of, 220
Poverty Reduction Strategy, 242
Practitioner activism, 16, 217, 221–223, 228
Precarious employment, 47, 187
Precarious labour market, 163, 174, 183
Precarious nature of work, 185
Precarious work, 184–187, 190, 191
PricewaterhouseCoopers, (PWC)
  Understanding the Unpaid Economy report, 79
Private pension savings, 168
Privatisation/privatization, 47, 225
Productivity Commission, 208
Professional advocacy, 223–226
Provincial government initiatives, 244–245
Public pensions, 166, 167, 169
Public/private partnerships, 220

Q

QS, *see* Québec solidaire
Quality of working life, 200, 205–206, 211
Quasi-experimental implementation, 250
Quasi-experiments, 247, 249, 250
Québec solidaire (QS), 244
Quiggin, J., 159

R

Radical social-work activists, 221
Ravallion, M., 113
Raventós, D., 51
Reciprocity, lack of, 190
Redistributive effects, 165, 170, 171, 219
Regressive housing tax concessions, 174
Retirement income, 114, 148, 150–151
Retrospective analysis, 222
Royal Commission on the Status of Women, 239
Royal Commission on the Economic Union and Development Prospects for Canada, 240, 243
Rudd, R., 207
Rundle, G., 136

S

Sanders, B., 142
Scutella, R., 165, 166
Second Wave feminists, 75
Segal, H., 119, 241
Self-determination, 91, 139, 218
Self-reliance, 27, 48
Self-sufficiency, 27, 89, 201
Senate Inquiry into the Adequacy of the Allowance Payment System for Jobseekers and Others, 10
Settler colonialism, 87–90, 260
Siewert, R., 136
Simpson, W., 115, 116
Skills training, 8, 209–210
Social capital, 183, 193
Social citizenship, 30, 39, 51, 54–55, 57, 61, 62
Social Credit Party, 238
Social democratic Nordic welfare states, 199
Social democratic party, 242
Social democratic welfare states, 199
Social dividend, 2, 5, 13, 25, 78
  definition of, 73
  universal, designing, 81–82
Socialisation of young people, 182
Socialism, 216
Social justice, 30, 39, 47, 51–53, 55, 64, 74, 215, 218, 219, 221, 223, 226–228
Social policy, 30, 33, 39, 50, 51, 56, 112, 115, 166, 207, 220, 222, 226, 228, 240, 243, 245, 252
Social protection model, 166
Social rights, 163, 180
Social scientists, 35, 93, 175, 226
Social security, 6, 16, 25–27, 29–31, 46–49, 52, 58, 64, 91, 112, 115–117, 120, 121, 166, 203, 206, 259
  benefits, 151, 165
  pensions, 39
  policy, 26
  reclaiming, 121–122

Social security payment system, fixing seriously flawed malfunctioning, 80–81
Social spending, 166, 169, 171, 175
Social welfare programmes, 238
Social work and human services (SWHS), 215–217, 220
  critical approaches to, 221–228
  education, 226–228
  exploration of, 216
  practitioner activism, 221–223
  professional and interprofessional advocacy, 223–226
  social issues, 218
  working environments, 220
Socio-economic analysis, 227
Soft paternalism, 36
Solidarity, 31, 39, 51, 57, 61, 135, 240
South Africa, 30
South America, 61
Southern Africa, 61
Spies-Butcher, B., 193
Standing, G., 55, 74
Stepping stones approach, 16, 31, 32, 138, 163, 176
  to basic income, 164–166
  universal age pension, 166–170
  youth basic income, 170–175
Stewart, M., 115, 122
Stilwell, F., 46
Stirton, L., 56, 57, 113, 114
Structural inequalities, 49, 60, 216, 220, 228
Structural social work, 224, 226
Structural unemployment, 10, 201
St Vincent de Paul Society, 139
Superannuation concessions, 149, 150, 168, 169, 208, 210
Sustainability, 3, 28, 38, 45, 63, 73, 88, 103, 132, 160, 242, 249
Sweden, 199, 204, 205
Switzerland, 204, 205
Symbolic capital, 36

T

Targeted cash payments, 164
Targeted payments system, 164
Targeting, 46–48, 50, 52, 55, 59, 65, 105, 115, 160, 164, 167
Tax and transfer system, 122, 163, 165, 173
Tax system, 5, 12, 13, 32, 53, 54, 115, 157, 165, 168, 170, 171, 175, 219, 261
  concessions, 154, 168, 169, 174
    converting to social spending, 169
    elimination of, 170
    for private health insurance, 169
  marginal rates of, 165
  regressive system of expenditures, 176
  revenue, 6, 152, 168, 169
Tax-welfare system, 148, 153
  fully integrated, 157
Techno-utopians, 29
Thatcher, M., 71
Titmuss, R., 134
Tomlinson, J., 222, 223
Top Opportunities Party (TOP), 172
Trade-offs, 113–115, 122
Transformative leadership, 38
Transformative politics, 176
Transition, 153, 160, 182–183
Transitioning to basic income, 53–54
Transitions to retirement (TTR)
  training, jobs and, 209–210

Trials, limitations of, 115–119
Trudeau, J., 242

U

UBI, *see* Univeral Basic Income
UISP, *see* Universal Income Security Program
Unconditionality, 1–3, 16, 26, 31, 45, 51, 52, 55–58, 60, 61, 63, 72, 73, 78, 112, 113, 118, 119, 129, 148, 149, 156, 164, 165, 203, 218, 242, 245
Underemployment, 9–11, 29, 60, 112, 136, 218
Unemployment, 26, 27, 32, 58, 60, 87, 97, 103, 112, 119, 120, 132, 151, 153, 155, 158, 171, 173, 183, 186, 191n4, 201
  benefits, increasing, 155–156
  benefits to young people, 188–189
  insurance, 206, 211
  long-term, 34
  rates, 204
  structural, 10
  support to find jobs, 206
  technological, 3, 8, 11, 25, 28, 33–35
  youth, 187, 188
Uniformity, 56, 58, 113–114
Unions, 3, 35, 36, 135, 137–139, 143, 208, 210, 242, 243, 262
United Kingdom, 49, 71
United States (US), 49, 117, 134, 217
  social payments models in, 166
  trials of basic income, 115, 118, 119
Universal age pension, 164, 166–170, 207
Universal basic income (UBI), 2, 8, 13, 34, 45, 50, 56, 60, 63, 105, 112, 115, 119, 130, 137, 138, 142, 224, 244, 260
  definition of, 149
  models, 165, 166, 174, 175
  pathways of, 147–161
  and unpaid social contributions, 72–74
Universal Credit, 121
Universal demogrant model, 224, 248
Universal first approach, 148, 153–154, 158, 161
Universal grant, 149–150
  See also Demogrant
Universal health care, 243, 259, 260
Universal Income Security Program (UISP), 240
  critics of, 240
Universalism, 46, 47, 53, 55–62, 164, 167, 170, 173, 176
Universality, 51, 57, 113
Universal payment, 13, 56, 57, 72, 74, 79, 147, 151–154, 160, 161, 164, 170, 175
Universal pension, 165, 168, 169, 176
Universal social dividend (USD), 73
  options for, designing, 81–82
Universal strike fund, 138
Universal welfare, 199
Unpaid work contributions, recognition of, 78–79
U PLUS BI, 261
US, *see* United States
USD, *see* Universal social dividend
Utopianism, 157–160

V

Van Parijs, P., 193
Vanderborght, Y., 193
Voucher system, 4

W

"Wage earner" model of welfare, 166
Wage justice, 188, 190, 193
Wealth, 2, 9, 28, 37, 47, 73, 104
  accumulation, 70, 74
  distribution, 1, 4, 10, 46, 216
  extremism, 50, 60
  inequality, 45, 47, 217, 218, 226, 227
  and meritocratic extremism, 46
  redistribution, 5, 13, 51, 55, 61, 135
  tax, 50
Weber, M, 70
Weeks, K., 37, 140
Welfare programmes, 164, 238, 260
Welfare state, 2, 4, 26, 36, 38, 47, 49, 51, 71, 134, 140, 199, 200, 223, 238, 243
Welfare-state regime models, 46
Welfare system, 9, 10, 55, 80, 114, 119, 132, 134, 148, 153, 155, 171, 211, 224
  fully integrated tax, 157
Well-being, 36, 38, 52, 62, 64, 71, 72, 78, 94, 116, 180
  human, 70
  intergenerational, 70
  material, 69
  social, 74, 76, 81
Western European Industrial Revolution, 70
Western societies, 218
Westminster parliamentary model, 237
White, R., 184, 185, 187, 191, 192
Whiteford, P., 115
Whitlam, G., 259, 260, 262
Whitlam Labour government, guaranteed minimum income in, 7
Why The Future is Workless (Tim Dunlop), 34
Widerquist, K., 12, 116, 117
Wilkie, A., 137
Woolf, V., 75
Work ethic, 37, 38, 163, 180, 190, 191, 219
  protestant, 70, 134
Work/life balance, 184, 200, 201, 203–205, 211
Workforce participation rates, 169, 201
Wright, E. O., 219

Y

YBI, *see* Youth Basic Income
Young Homeless Allowance, 190
Young people
  as active participants in society, 181
  in America laments, 183
  and BI, 190, 191
  BI for, 192
  conservative constructions of, 182
  frustration for, 185
  functionalist constructions of, 181
  as 'human capital,' 183
  junior wages, 185
  mainstream constructions of, 183
  negative constructions of, 190–193
  payments to, 179
  precarious work, 185–187
  precarity traps for, 185

rate for, 180
rates of conflict, 181
skill levels and experience, 180
social contexts of, 184
socialisation of, 182
societal constructions of, 179
transition approaches, 182–183
unemployment, 183
unemployment benefit of, 188–189
work of, 184
Youth Allowance, 170, 172, 173, 188, 188n3, 189
Youth Basic Income (YBI), 138, 164, 168, 170–175
Youth incomes, 180, 184, 192
Youth wages, 187–189
  lower rates of, 192

Z
Zuckerberg, M., 140

FSC
www.fsc.org
MIX
Papier | Fördert
gute Waldnutzung
FSC® C083411

Kolibri 360 GmbH
Ferdinand-Jühlke-Straße 7
99095 Erfurt, Deutschland
produktsicherheit@kolibri360.de